Advance Praise

"Heal attachment trauma at its roots with *EMDR and Family Therapy*, the latest book from Debra Wesselmann. This updated guide empowers clinicians to integrate EMDR with family therapy, transforming the lives of children suffering from loss, neglect, or early trauma. With the Integrative Attachment Protocol for Children (IATP-C), therapists can strengthen parent–child bonds, improve emotional regulation, and foster lasting healing. A must-read for EMDR-trained professionals seeking to create deep, lasting change."

—**Teresa Brown, LPC-S, NCC, RPT,** director, Attachment & Trauma Center of Houston

"Another outstanding and comprehensive book by Debra Wesselmann! Clinicians so often struggle to treat developmental trauma in children. Fortunately, Wesselmann's IATP-C model has redefined the way clinicians heal developmental trauma in children, and do so with greater ease. In this latest publication, Wesselmann offers invaluable insights, tools, and information to assist clinicians working in this complex arena. What a wonderful contribution to the field of counseling and psychology!"

—**Tamra Hughes, MA, LPC,** EMDRIA-approved trainer and consultant and founder of EMDR Center of the Rockies and Greenwood Counseling Center, PLLC

"As clinical director at a faith-based children's home, I rely on the IATP-C framework to assist children affected by attachment trauma. Over a third of our children face brain-based conditions, including effects of *in utero* substance exposure. I'm thrilled Wesselmann's new book includes specialized methods for helping these children and provides invaluable guidance for explaining their conditions to parents—a resource we've been seeking to enhance our care."

—**Scott Herman, MA,** clinical director of Mustard Seed Ranch, a faith-based child care facility

"Debra Wesselmann offers an invaluable resource to therapists working with families affected by attachment disruptions and childhood trauma. *EMDR and Family Therapy* is a comprehensive guide to effective, evidence-informed techniques with practical tools and real-life scenarios for incorporating Integrative Attachment Trauma Protocol into family therapy.

More than a companion to Wesselmann's previous work, this book provides innovative strategies to deepen and enhance therapeutic approaches, making it an essential read for professionals in the field."

—**Krista Reichert, LCSW RPT-S,** director of postadoption services at The Baby Fold, and private child and family therapist

"Wesselmann's latest edition weaves together family therapy and attachment theory with an understanding of trauma and dissociation in ways that magnify the potency of EMDR. The chapter about increasing the reflective function capacity of parents alone is a vital resource for any therapist. Although the book is brimming with practical tools including therapeutic stories, therapy scripts, and checklists, the model is never mechanical. The Integrative Attachment Trauma Protocol for Children is innovative, individualized, and comprehensive. I would recommend this book to anyone working with children and families."

—**Karen Doyle Buckwalter, LCSW,** Carolina Attachment and Trauma Services

EMDR and Family Therapy

EMDR and Family Therapy

Integrative Treatment for Attachment Trauma in Children

Second Edition

Debra Wesselmann

Norton Professional Books

*An Imprint of W. W. Norton & Company
Independent Publishers Since 1923*

Note to Readers: This book is intended as a general information resource for professionals practicing in the field of psychotherapy and mental health. It is not a substitute for appropriate training or clinical supervision. Standards of clinical practice and protocol vary in different practice settings and change over time. No technique or recommendation is guaranteed to be safe or effective in all circumstances, and neither the publisher nor the author can guarantee the complete accuracy, efficacy, or appropriateness of any particular recommendation in every respect or in all settings or circumstances.

Names and identifying details of patients described in this book have been changed. Some patients described, and the session vignettes are composites. Any URLs displayed in this book link or refer to websites that existed as of press time. The publisher is not responsible for, and should not be deemed to endorse or recommend, any website other than its own or any content that it did not create. The author, also, is not responsible for any third-party material.

Foreword copyright © 2025 by Robbie Dunton
Copyright © 2025, 2014 by Debra Wesselmann, Cathy Schweitzer, and Stefanie Armstrong

Illustrations by Julia Deese

All rights reserved
Printed in the United States of America
Second Edition

For information about permission to reproduce selections from
this book, write to Permissions, W. W. Norton & Company, Inc.,
500 Fifth Avenue, New York, NY 10110

For information about special discounts for bulk purchases, please contact
W. W. Norton Special Sales at specialsales@wwnorton.com or 800-233-4830

Manufacturing by Versa Press
Production manager: Gwen Cullen

ISBN: 978-1-324-05335-4

W. W. Norton & Company, Inc., 500 Fifth Avenue, New York, NY 10110
www.wwnorton.com
W. W. Norton & Company Ltd., 15 Carlisle Street, London W1D 3BS

1 2 3 4 5 6 7 8 9 0

To the late Francine Shapiro, EMDR pioneer, in honor of her dedication to helping others.

Contents

Foreword — xi
Acknowledgments — xv
Introduction — xvii

PART I. IATP-C Stage 1: Parent Psychoeducation and Case Conceptualization — 3

   CHAPTER 1. Afraid to Love — 5

   CHAPTER 2. The Integrative Attachment Trauma Protocol for Children (IATP-C): Overview — 17

   CHAPTER 3. IATP-C Parent Psychoeducation Sessions — 28

   CHAPTER 4. IATP-C History Taking and EMDR Treatment Planning — 41

PART II. IATP-C Stage 2: Building Good Feelings and the Capacity for Trust — 53

   CHAPTER 5. IATP-C Foundational Family Therapy Activities — 55

   CHAPTER 6. IATP-C Foundational EMDR Therapy Activities — 93

PART III. IATP-C Stage 3: Healing Triggers and Traumas — 131

   CHAPTER 7. Addressing Present and Future Through Integrative Family and EMDR Therapy — 133

   CHAPTER 8. Entering the Past Gently Through Timeline and the EMDR Therapeutic Story — 164

CHAPTER 9. Addressing the Hardest Parts With
    EMDR Trauma Work   182

PART IV. Addressing Additional Challenges With Kids
    and Parents   209

CHAPTER 10. Strategies for Problematic Dissociation   211

CHAPTER 11. Adaptations for Fetal Alcohol Exposure,
    Autism, and Other Brain-Based Conditions   228

CHAPTER 12. Enhancing Reflective Functioning (RF) for
    Parents Through EMDR Therapy   245

Appendices
  A. IATP-C Checklist   259
  B. History-Taking Checklist   261
  C. Transmission of Attachment Patterns, Parent to Child   267
  D. Useful Child Assessments   270
  E. The Tale of the Hamster and the Porcupine Coat   273
  F. A Quick Review of the EMDR Phases With Tips
    for Working With Kids   276
  G. The EMD to EMDR Continuum   282
  H. Suggested Books for Young Children   284

References   285
Index   297

Foreword

I am deeply honored to be invited to write the foreword for this important book. Debra Wesselmann is one of the most humble, endearing, and talented individuals I have had the privilege of knowing. Her depth of understanding of children, parents, and families is remarkable.

EMDR and Family Therapy: Integrative Treatment for Attachment Trauma in Children discusses various forms of attachment trauma, adaptations of the Integrative Attachment Trauma Protocol for Children (IATP-C) of different ages, and the integration of parent psychoeducation, family therapy, EMDR therapy, and peer consultation. Debra skillfully engages the reader through a systematic organization of chapters and creative interventions that guide families toward healthier relationships and the repair of attachment issues. In my own early work, I developed a passion for helping children, and I've found this book brings a state-of-the-art EMDR approach to helping children with the most difficult early lives.

I became close friends with Dr. Francine Shapiro in 1984, when I was an associate director and educational therapist with an institute dedicated to children and adolescents facing dysregulated behavior and learning challenges. In 1987, Francine came to me with her groundbreaking discovery of EMD, which later became EMDR therapy. Francine was eager to explore whether it could be as effective with children as it was with adults. After extensive instructional sessions with her to understand the nuances of EMD, I became the first person to introduce EMD(R) to children and adolescents as part of a treatment plan to help them succeed in school. I only wish I had access to the knowledge and works of Debra Wesselmann at that time!

In 1990, Francine and I set up the EMDR Institute to provide EMDR trainings to mental health practitioners globally. I had the fortune of meeting Debra Wesselmann in 1995, during an EMDR training in Denver, Colorado. I quickly became aware of her groundbreaking work in attachment and family therapy when Francine asked me to review Debra's chapter, "Treating Attachment Issues through EMDR and a Family Systems Approach," for the *Handbook of EMDR and Family Therapy Processes* (Shapiro, Kaslow, & Maxfield, 2007). In this chapter, Debra effectively integrates attachment, Adaptive Information Processing, and family systems to enhance treatment for attachment issues. Since this chapter, she has contributed immensely to the EMDR community through her articles, books, workshops, and the phenomenally successful EMDR Institute basic training focused on treating children and adolescents.

My introduction to family therapy stemmed from the pioneering work of the esteemed Virginia Satir, who emphasized the importance of interactional interventions in fostering positive family communication and nurturing relationships. What makes this second edition of *EMDR and Family Therapy* particularly impressive is its attention to and integration of Satir's experiential family therapy concepts with attachment theories and current neurobiological research. The content is grounded in scientific principles and the author's extensive clinical experience with attachment-disordered individuals and families. The eloquent and poignant case studies illustrate effective interventions and strategies for collaborating with both parents and caregivers and children and adolescents. Regardless of the challenges presented, the author consistently uses encouraging and supportive language to build trust and foster healthy relationships. The result is a book that is inviting, engaging, and inspiring. Another significant addition is this edition's focus on applying the IATP-C model to adolescents. A 2013–2023 survey from the Centers for Disease Control and Prevention among U.S. high school students reported alarming statistics about mental health, including:

- 40% experienced persistent feelings of sadness or hopelessness in the past year
- 20% seriously considered attempting suicide in the past year
- 16% made a suicide plan
- 9% attempted suicide
- 22% consumed alcohol in the past 30 days
- 17% used marijuana in the past 30 days
- 4% misused prescription pain medication in the past 30 days
- 10% reported using illicit drugs

Furthermore, a national survey indicated that mental health conditions can begin in early childhood, with prevalence increasing with age (Child and Adolescent Health Measurement Initiative, 2021–2022). The guidance provided in Debra's book equips therapists with effective self-esteem–building interventions to bring hope and healing to their teenage clients.

Debra's inclusion of adaptations to the IATP-C model for special populations is also particularly encouraging, highlighting the importance of tailoring treatment approaches to the unique needs of each client. Within these chapters lies a wealth of information that empowers EMDR practitioners to adjust the model to fit clients' cognitive abilities and levels of understanding.

In conclusion, Debra Wesselmann has expertly woven together the threads of parent–child interactions, providing a comprehensive resource for fostering healthier relationships and emotional healing. As I read, I found myself inspired to share various segments by reading them to family, friends, and colleagues. I passionately believe that sections of this book should be essential reading for all parents, caregivers, teachers, doctors, and anyone who interacts with children or adolescents and seeks to foster positive, successful experiences.

—Robbie Dunton
executive director of the EMDR Institute of Francine Shapiro

REFERENCES

Centers for Disease Control and Prevention. (2024). *Youth Risk Behavior Survey Data Summary & Trends Report: 2013–2023*. Retrieved from https://www.cdc.gov/yrbs/dstr/.

Child and Adolescent Health Measurement Initiative. (2021–2022). National Survey of Children's Health. Data Resource Center for Child and Adolescent Health supported by the U.S. Department of Health and Human Services, Health Resources and Services Administration (HRSA), Maternal and Child Health Bureau (MCHB). Retrieved August 8, 2024 from https://nschdata.org/browse/survey?s=2&y=51&r=1&#home

Shapiro, F., Kaslow, W., & Maxfield, L. (Eds.). (2007). *Handbook of EMDR and family therapy processes.* John Wiley & Sons, Inc.

Acknowledgments

First and foremost, I'd like to express my deepest appreciation to Cathy Schweitzer and Stefanie Armstrong for their contributions to the development of the model and for their assistance with writing the first edition of this book. Our work together was critical in bringing this model to fruition. I'll be forever grateful to the late Francine Shapiro for dedicating her life to bringing EMDR therapy to the world and for encouraging me and teaching me so much through our collaborative projects. A heartful thank you also to Robbie Dunton of the EMDR Institute for her tireless commitment to continuing Francine's work and for supporting the development of the basic EMDR training with a child focus. I also wish to thank my colleague, Carolyn Settle, for initiating the child-focused basic training project and inviting me to be a part of it. It's been a joy, and I've learned so much from Carolyn.

I'd like to acknowledge the important work of Irma Hein, Nathalie Schlattmann, and Mara van der Hoeven, along with their colleagues in the Netherlands. Their excellent research on our integrative EMDR and family therapy model with maltreated children residing in foster care in the Netherlands was invaluable. Through our collaborative efforts over the past several years and through their work on the Dutch translation of the first edition of this book, they have influenced the model in important ways that are reflected within the content of this book.

I wish to express deep appreciation to my friend Joan Lovett for her pioneering work in developing the EMDR therapeutic story method, an important component of the integrative model. I'm extremely fortunate for the generous input and assistance of Erica Wollin regarding prenatal substance exposure and for the help I received from Scott Herman regarding assessment tools. Thank you to Teresa Brown for her help, and another special thank you to my friend and colleague Ann Potter for her contributions in the development of the protocol, and to the whole team at the Attachment Center of Nebraska for the pool of ideas generated during our brainstorming sessions in peer consultation. I'd like to acknowledge Julia Deese for her lovely illustrations and say thank you to all my consultees through the years for challenging me with questions and ideas. Thank you to our Attachment Trauma Child listserv colleagues for their ongoing comradery and inspiration.

Thank you, also, to my editor Deborah Malmud of W. W. Norton for her support through both editions of this book and to Irene Vartanoff, and McKenna Tanner and the rest of the staff at W. W. Norton who assisted me with this second edition.

Finally, my heart goes out to all the children, adolescents, and parents who have trusted us and let us be a part of their lives over these past years.

—Debra Wesselmann

Introduction

If you're reading this book, you most likely have a passion for helping adolescents and children who exhibit severe behaviors subsequent to early neglect; verbal, emotional, physical, or sexual abuse; attachment losses and separations; and early medical traumas. You may be new to the field or new to EMDR or family therapy and contemplating working with this special population, in which case I encourage you to read on, as the field desperately needs more clinicians who are willing and able to impact the lives of hurt children and teens. If you're naturally compassionate and patient, enjoy a challenge, and have a love for kids, this book may be your first step into the most rewarding (albeit challenging) work you could ever do. You may already be a seasoned therapist in either EMDR or family therapy or both, with many tools already in your toolkit. One of the beautiful characteristics of EMDR and the integrative model you'll find here is the way in which additional modalities can be seamlessly integrated into the work. You don't have to set aside anything that you already do.

I am excited to present this second edition with revisions and updates that are a culmination of new advances in the fields of attachment and trauma and new ideas and enhanced old ideas gained in our work and research with kids and families through this past decade. I've also gained inspiration and ideas through many discussions with our Netherlands colleagues and regarding their application of the Integrative Attachment Trauma Protocol for Children (IATP-C), their research with the model, and their translation of the book and parent guide into Dutch (Schlattmann et al., 2023; van der Hoeven et al., 2023; Wesselmann et al., 2021). For example, within this new edition you'll find a new organization of the IATP-C into three stages, with an initial focus on parent psychoeducation, all of which inspired by our Dutch colleagues.

This edition includes more guidance in using the model with adolescents throughout all of the family therapy and EMDR therapy activities. Because attachment-injured kids, especially teenagers, are frequently stuck in compulsive, unhealthy behaviors, the section on addressing addictions and compulsions has been expanded.

This revision devotes an entire chapter to therapeutic stories, with many more examples of language that can help kids make sense of the most difficult early situations. The book includes an expansion of the cognitive interweaves sections and offers the option of shifting between full EMDR reprocessing and some version of EMD for kids who are easily overwhelmed.

A new chapter for assisting kids with problematic dissociation offers up-to-date information and nuanced strategies to create internal safety and strengthen the *biggest kid* self. Another chapter offers information to help kids and parents challenged by prenatal substance exposure, autism, or other forms of neurodivergence. The chapter includes modifications to the IATP-C for increased effectiveness when working with kids with brain-based challenges. The book closes with a new chapter on treating parents with poor reflective capacity through EMDR therapy.

If you read the first edition of our book, you'll also note the change in the title, eliminating the word "team." Although we're still believers in the advantages of working as a two-person EMDR and family therapist team, we've discovered that many therapists don't have the luxury of applying the model in this way. At our center, we've applied the model solo at times for reasons of logistics, even though it's not my first choice when it comes to the more difficult cases. This edition provides more support for solo therapists applying the model.

Note about references to parents in this book: To keep things simple, the text refers simply to *parents*, even though parents may be foster parents, biological parents, adoptive parents, guardians, and/or biological relatives. Parents may be a couple who self-identifies as part of the LGBTQIA community or a heterosexual couple. The child may have a single parent. Parents may reside together or apart. If there are two parents, we encourage involvement of both, but for logistical reasons, one parent may attend with more frequency than the other. In our scripts we often say *Mom* or *Dad*, as these are the titles most often used by kids to address their parents.

The accompanying parent guide, *Attachment Trauma in Kids: Integrative Strat-*

egies for Parents, Second Edition (Wesselmann, 2025), provides parents with more skills to help their children or teens overcome problems related to early attachment trauma. The revised and updated parent guide provides methods for building trust, calming traumatic stress symptoms, addressing developmental deficits, and assisting children and teens with brain-based conditions. I wish the best to all of you in your work with struggling children, teens, and families.

EMDR and Family Therapy

Part I

IATP-C Stage 1: Parent Psychoeducation and Case Conceptualization

CHAPTER 1

Afraid to Love

> Through reading this chapter, you'll come to understand:
>
> – The behaviors and symptoms through the attachment lens
> – The behaviors and symptoms through the developmental trauma lens
> – The ultimate dilemma and what we can do

The Beatles' 1967 song "All You Need is Love" says it all. Love really is foundational to our lives. So where does that leave kids who are afraid to love or be loved? Most likely, it means they can't get what they need in life. Chances are they will suffer feelings of loneliness, anxiety, and insignificance, with no way to feel better.

Kids who are afraid of love enter the therapy office with self-protective defenses well in place. They may express anger or fear, or they may mask. They may have many challenging behaviors such as aggression, stealing, or lying, or symptoms that are more internalized. Their parents may feel mystified, frustrated, and hurt, and the parent–child relationship may be full of turmoil.

Kids who trust that it's okay to love and be loved will frequently enter the therapy office eager to share, and they're receptive to our ideas. They may have some ups and downs in their relationship with parents, but overall, there's connection and communication. As EMDR therapists, we can see a clear path to successful treatment.

This book is designed to help you effectively treat the kids who lack trust and who struggle with their attachment relationships. The EMDR and family therapy integrative approach is designed to overcome the obstacles they bring to therapy, including mistrust of parents and other adults, quick dysregulation or dissociation, difficult behaviors, and self-protective defense mechanisms. Before we dive into the integrative treatment approach, let's make sense of their symptoms and behaviors.

THE ATTACHMENT LENS

This section summarizes the seminal work of early pioneers in the field of attachment. The attachment lens is a good start to understanding the self-protective behaviors observed in children with attachment trauma.

Secure Attachment Patterns in Children

The infant's drive to engage parents is critical to human survival. In an optimal situation, a parent who grew up in a secure environment responds with sensitivity and affection to their infant's feelings and needs, and the infant feels soothed and trusting of the parent's continued care. As the child grows and the parent continues to attune to the child's emotions, the growing child develops comfort with emotions and the capacity to recognize their internal state. This capacity eventually expands into the capacity to recognize the internal state of others. The securely attached child naturally trusts and enjoys closeness with the secure parent but also develops positive expectations of others and a desire to explore the world, trusting the secure base will always be there. In adulthood, attachment *security* leads to a strong capacity to self-reflect, to reflect upon the feelings of others, and to respond with sensitivity to their children (Ainsworth, 1967; Bowlby, 1973, 1989).

Nonsecure and Disorganized Attachment Patterns in Children

Infants whose needs are met only intermittently, however, remain anxious about the possibility of getting their needs met and about their safety in the world generally. Therefore, they learn to increase the intensity of their demands to get their needs met more often. Control and angry outbursts are largely successful and feel critical to survival. This *ambivalent/resistant attachment pattern* therefore reduces feelings of vulnerability and anxiety. The pattern will likely be carried into other relationships due to the biological drive to survive. This will likely impact interactions with any other adults who may care for them and with their partners and their offspring in adulthood.

In other infant–parent dyads, the parent moves away when the infant cries or seeks closeness. The infant learns that by repressing their feelings and needs, they can keep their parent from withdrawing. This *avoidant attachment pattern* is nature's clever way of keeping the parent in proximity when a parent is uncomfortable with closeness. Because the child's suppression of emotional needs is associated with safety and survival, the pattern will likely affect their behaviors in other significant relationships as the child matures (Ainsworth, 1967, 1982).

When children become fearful of their parent, they experience a classic double-bind. They want to run for comfort to the very person who is causing their fear. In this situation, there is no adaptation that works. Survival feels threatened. There is a breakdown in defenses, leading to mental disorganization. The disorganization can actually be observed, as infants and toddlers who are disorganized will often exhibit very strange behaviors in the presence of the parent, such as twirling, covering their face or head, or crawling backward toward the parent. Disorganization can be associated with maltreatment, but it can be related to more subtle triggers such as facial expressions in which the parent looks frightening or frightened (which is also frightening). The parent's reactions are triggered by the child and related to the parent's own unresolved losses or abuse history (Ainsworth, 1982; Lyons-Ruth & Jacobvitz, 1999; Main & Hesse, 1990; Main & Solomon, 1990).

Disorganization is associated with extreme distress and inadequate defenses. Research indicates that children with a pattern of attachment disorganization are predisposed to dissociative disorders by adolescence (Liotti, 1999). Researchers have also found that by school age, children with attachment disorganization may become punishing and controlling or caretaking toward their parent (Lyons-Ruth et al., 1993). As they get older, they may be easily triggered with mental disorganization by other relationships, including relationships with future caregivers or adoptive parents and relationships with their own kids.

Attachment disorganization is apparent only when there is a trigger of some sort. Since it's not observed all of the time, the disorganized classification does not stand on its own. There is always an accompanying designation of ambivalent resistance or avoidance.

Children with early attachment injuries, untreated, likely have a nonsecure attachment pattern in addition to attachment disorganization. Some kids may have a mixed classification, exhibiting both avoidance and ambivalence. These attachment disturbances are not formal diagnoses, but children with nonsecure and disorganized attachment patterns are at higher risk for mental disorders than secure children (Hesse, 1999; Lyons-Ruth et al., 1993). For clinical purposes a general hypothesis about the observed patterns of attachment-injured children and teens can assist in understanding the behaviors in terms of defensive adaptations or disorganization due to a breakdown of defensive mechanisms. See Appendix C, "Transmission of Attachment Patterns, Parent to Child," for more information.

It's important to understand that all attachment pattern designations are on a continuum from severe to moderate to mild. There can be a mix of nonsecure patterns, and folks with secure attachment can have underlying tendencies toward disorganization or nonsecure patterns but still develop healthy relationships with others. Secondly, although attachment patterns tend to stay consistent, research also shows that attachment patterns do change through significant emotionally corrective experiences. This provides hope for kids who struggle with trust and closeness, as the emotionally corrective experiences provided through therapy and through improved relationships with parents have the potential for moving them down the continuum toward greater attachment security.

Attachment Loss and Attachment Disorders

Whether temporary or permanent, the placement of children in orphanage, foster, adoptive, or guardianship care means loss and separation from their biological parents. During the late 1940s and early 1950s, Bowlby studied children who were separated from attachment figures due to the war or lengthy hospitalizations. He observed that children separated from their attachment figures were devastated by the loss and moved through stages of grief; protest, despair, and resignation. He noted that even if they became reunited after a lengthy separation, they continued to have superficial attachments and were at risk for behavioral problems later on (Bowlby, 1973). This description of postwar children is consistent with the protest behaviors, despair, and resignation frequently observed in children living in out-of-home care.

Some children who've suffered severe neglect or perhaps frequent changes in caregivers appear to have missed a window of opportunity for developing the capacity to experience deep connectedness to others. They appear emotionally detached and uninterested in relationships, a condition described by Zeanah and Boris (2000) as a disorder of "nonattachment." This condition may be equivalent to the *DSM-5* (American Psychological Association, 2013) diagnosis of reactive attachment disorder (RAD) listed now under the category of trauma- and stressor-related disorders, in which the child appears detached and uninterested in genuine relationships. The child with RAD, shut down to relationships for self-protection, could be viewed as an extreme version of the avoidant attachment pattern. The diagnosis of RAD is associated with extremes of insufficient care, failure to seek comfort or respond to comfort, keeping social and emotional distance, having limited positive affect, and having episodes of sadness, fear, and irritability.

The *DSM-5* (APA, 2013) diagnosis for disinhibited social engagement disorder involves a pattern of actively seeking attention and affection from any adult in proximity. The criteria for this disorder include extremes of insufficient care and overly familiar and affectionate behavior with strangers. The child attempting to self-protect by getting unmet needs met in this way is clearly at high risk for further maltreatment. This diagnosis could be viewed as an extreme version of the ambivalent-resistant attachment pattern in which the child takes control of getting what they need from the parent.

THE DEVELOPMENTAL TRAUMA LENS

Chronic attachment trauma keeps the child or teen vigilant to danger, unable to trust, and easily triggered and dysregulated by sympathetic nervous system activation. The perpetual feelings of distress interfere with learning and create delays in social, emotional, and cognitive development. Subsequently, an older child or teen with a history of extensive attachment trauma may function like a younger child. Their internal resources for expressing emotions, seeking help, reflecting, and communicating remain undeveloped, and they lack the trust they need to utilize support from parents or others.

Developmental Trauma and Brain Development

Childhood emotional or physical neglect or verbal, physical, or sexual abuse have significant and direct impact on the child's developing brain structure and functioning. Numerous studies involving scans of the brain have proven that stress hormones caused by emotional neglect, physical neglect, verbal abuse, sexual abuse, and physical abuse destroy neural connections and alter important structures of the brain responsible for social and emotional development (Teicher et al., 2016). For example, the corpus collosum, the brain region that allows communication between the emotional right hemisphere and logical left hemisphere is underdeveloped, limiting capacity to make sense of and manage emotional states and experiences. Neural connections in the prefrontal brain are reduced, decreasing capacity to problem solve, think, plan, focus, delay gratification, and learn. The hippocampus is impacted, reducing memory, and the amygdala is underdeveloped, reducing capacity to discern threat from nonthreat.

Changes in brain functioning associated with childhood maltreatment appear to ready the brain for detecting and responding to threat and minimize activity in the processing and problem-solving cortical areas that might slow down reactions to threats in a dangerous environment. Unfortunately, when children's circumstances change and the environment becomes safe, the built-in survival strategies interfere with self-regulating, tolerating stress, reasoning, and learning. EEG studies with individuals who experienced childhood abuse have shown that the repeated exposure to developmental trauma kindles the developing limbic system into ongoing limbic irritability (Teicher & Parigger, 2015). The EEG readings are similar to those observed in individuals with temporal lobe epilepsy.

Studies in epigenetics have demonstrated that childhood trauma can even change the way genes are expressed by changing DNA myelination and the way the body reads the DNA. These epigenetic effects can negatively impact both mental and physical health. The changes in the expression of genes can be passed down from parents to children.

On top of brain changes caused by trauma, many kids with a history of maltreatment related to parental substance abuse have brain problems caused by prenatal exposure to the substances. Alcohol has the most deleterious effects and is the most common form of exposure. (See Chapter 11 for more about applying the EMDR and family therapy integrative approach with kids with trauma and prenatal substance exposure.)

Developmental Trauma and Health

Many kids with a history of attachment trauma are already engaging in high-risk behaviors such as overeating, drinking alcohol, smoking, and drug use. An enormous 10-year project called the Adverse Childhood Experiences (ACE) study showed clear evidence that childhood trauma impacts health-related behaviors into adulthood and raises the risk of early death (Felitti et al., 1998). Over 9000 adults completed a questionnaire and responded to questions about early experiences, mental and physical health, and habits of behavior. Participants received up to 7 points, scoring 1 point for each category of abuse experienced. As the score went up, so did the likelihood for obesity, mental illness, promiscuity, alcoholism, drug use, and death. The study concluded that adverse childhood experiences affect neurodevelopment, and that unhealthy, high-risk behaviors are attempts to alleviate emotional pain.

More recent research added additional questions to the Adverse Childhood Experiences questionnaire about adverse experiences related to social and cultural adverse experiences. The research demonstrated that social and cultural trauma has serious and lasting consequences to children's health functioning (Cronholm et al., 2015). Many children and adolescents in foster and adoptive homes suffer from trauma related to rejection, bullying, or discrimination due to ethnicity, cultural background, physical disabilities or learning problems, gender identification, or romantic preferences.

Developmental Trauma Disorder

Van der Kolk (2005) has proposed developmental trauma disorder (DTD) as a formal diagnosis that identifies the pervasive impact of chronic early trauma on children's development and functioning. The diagnosis identifies their pervasive symptoms and behaviors as caused by traumatic stress; inability to process or tolerate emotions or think logically, learn, or socialize due to interrupted cognitive, emotional, and social development. The proposed diagnosis would clearly replace many commonly used diagnoses such as oppositional defiant disorder, reactive attachment disorder, and intermittent explosive disorder. Although the proposed diagnosis was not included in the *DSM-5* (APA, 2013), the debate on inclusion has continued and further studies have supported the appropriateness of this diagnosis (e.g., Spinazzola et al., 2021).

Adaptive Information Processing (AIP) Model

Francine Shapiro's adaptive information processing (AIP) model (2018) brings more depth to understanding how events when we're very young can continue to affect our thoughts, feelings, and behaviors as we get older. The AIP model explains that our thoughts, feelings, perceptions, and reactions in day-to-day life are a product of our past experiences because all of those experiences are stored either adaptively or maladaptively within our memory networks. Ordinary daily life events are easily integrated and stored adaptively through the natural processes of the AIP system. What is needed from each experience is filed away where it can be accessed as needed, and what is not needed is discarded.

In the face of highly disturbing events, however, the AIP shuts down. The inadequately processed event is stored in a raw form, encapsulated along with the emotions, sensations, and perceptions present at the time of the event. Within maladaptive memory networks, there is essentially no passage of time. These raw memory components are easily activated by conscious or subconscious reminders of the event, hijacking our perceptions, thoughts, and feelings at any future time, no matter how far away from the original event. This is nature's primitive way of getting us to stay on guard and self-protective when early life has taught us that relationships are dangerous. When our unprocessed memory components are activated, we're immediately geared up to fight or flee.

Consider kids who've experienced multiple disturbing events that left them feeling unsafe over a long period of time. Their large storage of inadequately processed memories activates their fight-or-flight system on a regular basis, readying them for more unsafe situations—helpful from the standpoint of surviving danger, but not helpful when the danger is over but the reactivity is not.

When traumatic memories related to parents are maladaptively stored, parents represent danger. There is no secure base; there's nowhere to go to find safety or receive comfort. Due to maladaptive storage, the raw emotions and sensations related to mistrust, fear, anxiety, and hurt don't lessen over time.

Attachment trauma comes in many forms. Early medical procedures that are no one's fault can constitute attachment trauma because the pain and separations related to the procedures leave the child with the belief that their parents must not care enough to help. Attachment trauma may come in the form of separation from or loss of parents; witnessing of parents' frightening behaviors, facial expressions, or voice tones caused by their own history of trauma, substance abuse, mental illness; or domestic violence. Attachment trauma may come in the form of physical or emotional neglect or rejection or overt physical or sexual abuse. The U.S. Centers for Disease Control (Centers for Disease Control, 2023) estimates one in seven children in the United States experience some form of abuse and neglect. In addition to trauma in the home, a common adverse situation experienced by children and teens involves some type of marginalization, discrimination, or bullying within their school or community due to race, culture, gender identity, affectional preferences, sexual orientation, physical features, or disabilities. The child or teen may perceive rejection from family members for any of these reasons as well.

EMDR Therapy

The research evidence is clear. EMDR therapy is an effective treatment for symptoms and problems related to early trauma and adversity. EMDR therapy is recommended as an evidence-based treatment for symptoms of posttraumatic stress for adults and children by the California Evidence-Based Clearinghouse for Child Welfare (CEBC, 2010), the International Society for the Study of Trauma and Dissociation (Forbes et al., 2020), the World Health Organization (WHO, 2013), and the United Kingdom's National Institute for Health and Clinical Excellence (NICE, 2018). EMDR therapy is recommended as a first-line treatment by the Department of Veterans Affairs and Department of Defense (Veterans Affairs/Department of Defense, 2023). Over 60 randomized controlled studies with adults and over 14 randomized controlled studies with children point to EMDR's efficacy with trauma-related symptoms. (See emdr.com for a full list of randomized controlled trials (RCTs) as well as other important studies.) Meta-analyses support EMDR's effectiveness in reducing many types of internalizing and externalizing symptoms in children for a variety of types of adverse and traumatic experiences (e.g., Adler-Tapia & Settle, 2009; Beer, 2018; Civilotti et al., 2021; Manzoni et al., 2021).

The Integrative Attachment Trauma Protocol for Children (IATP-C)

EMDR therapy is an evidence-based treatment for symptoms of trauma in children and adults. However, due to resistance, dysregulation, mistrust, and self-protective defenses commonly observed in children or teens affected by early attachment trauma, it is difficult to gain full cooperation with any treatment method.

The Integrative Attachment Trauma Protocol for Children (IATP-C) improves trust, cooperation, self-awareness, and regulation. The protocol provides gentle methods for approaching the difficult events of their past. The model integrates parent work, family therapy activities, EMDR resource activities, and the EMDR reprocessing phases (Wesselmann, 2013; Wesselmann & Shapiro, 2013; Wesselmann et al., 2015; Wesselmann et al., 2017a; 2017b; Wesselmann et al.,

2018; Wesselmann et al., 2012; Wesselmann et al., 2025a; 2025b). The strategies outlined for clinicians in this book have been nuanced and improved since the first edition of the book through experiences with numerous clinical cases over the past decade as well as influences and ideas gleaned from collaborations with colleagues and advances in the fields of EMDR and traumatic stress.

Specifically, the IATP-C integrates four components: parent psychoeducation, family therapy, EMDR therapy, and peer consultation to help attachment-injured children and teens through three stages. This new three stage organization for the treatment model was influenced by the work of our Dutch colleagues (Schlattmann et al., 2023; van der Hoeven et al., 2023; Wesselmann et al., 2025a).

Stage 1

- Parent psychoeducation and case conceptualization

Stage 2

- Integrative family therapy and EMDR therapy for building good feelings and capacity for trust

Stage 3

- An integrative, gentle approach for healing triggers and traumas with EMDR

IATP-C Research

In a single case study with an adopted 12-year-old with a history of abuse and neglect and problems of attachment, dysregulation, behavior, and traumatic stress, weekly family and EMDR therapy with the IATP-C was applied for 6 months. Measures of target symptoms indicated improvement and follow-up measures at 3 and 6 months indicated gains were maintained (Wesselmann et al., 2012). In another single case study, a simplified IATP-C improved behaviors and attachment security with a 17-month-old who experienced a life-threatening medical trauma (Swimm, 2018). In a case series study, 23 adopted children, ages 7 to 12, were treated with the IATP-C due to a history of abuse and neglect and problems of attachment, dysregulation, behavior, and traumatic stress. Treatment length averaged 12.7 months (ranging from 6 to 24 months), during which the protocol activities were applied through weekly family therapy and EMDR therapy sessions with significantly improved symptoms at group level (Wesselmann et al., 2018). In the 15 cases where 3-month follow-up measures were completed and returned, gains were maintained. In a case series study in the Netherlands with 8 children ages 6 to 12 with similar history and symptoms living with foster parents, measures indicated improved target symptoms at group level following 9 months of weekly family therapy and EMDR therapy utilizing the IATP-C protocol (van der Hoeven et al., 2023). An IATP-C case study in New Zealand also showed promising results (Dreckmeier-Meiring, 2024).

CONCLUSION

Think about children and adolescents whose development, brain functioning, and attachment patterns have been impacted by early family neglect and abuse. They are unable to trust or utilize coregulation from others. They live largely in a state of hyper- or hypo-arousal, and they perceive a threatening world. If they are removed from their family of origin by the authorities, they are physically safe but grief-stricken over the loss of their parents, to whom they had an attachment—albeit a disorganized one. If they enter foster care or care by relatives, they remain in survival mode, reacting with aggression to their present caregivers' attempts to parent them. At other times, they may become shut down and unreachable. Their caregivers often become punitive as they attempt to control alarming behaviors. The child's behaviors escalate in response.

Children and teens with stored, unprocessed trauma and a brain structured to be reactive are commonly delayed in their emotional, social, and cognitive development. Due to their neurological and psychological injuries and their poor ability to manage stress, they may receive multiple diagnoses over the years. They may also have a genetic predisposition to mental health disorders.

Many kids with a history of attachment trauma have been removed from abusive or neglectful biological families and placed with new caregivers. Others are reunited with their rehabilitated biological parents. Despite an end to the mistreatment, the children are left with inadequately processed attachment memories and their associated emotions, sensations, thoughts, and images. They continue to function with a brain structured to be emotionally reactive and self-protective within their most important attachment relationships, and they continue to self-regulate through maladaptive behaviors. When their current parents or caregivers become frustrated and punitive, the children's negative beliefs about themselves and others are reinforced.

When attachment injured kids reach the therapy office, their mistrust and fight-or-flight reactions lead to resistance and avoidance for any type of therapeutic intervention. Challenging behaviors show up in the therapy office as well as at home and school. The IATP-C is designed to overcome the special challenges to treating this special population. The parent education improves emotional support in the home, and the family therapy and EMDR foundational activities improve trust, cooperation, and emotion regulation prior to EMDR processing of triggers and traumas.

There is an enormous population of children who are suffering from attachment injuries. Traumatized children require compassionate and effective help from the society that has failed to provide them with an appropriate, nurturing environment during the first months or years of life. They deserve treatment that will reduce reactivity and fear, facilitate neurological integration, and allow them to discover the joy of human connection, trust, and love.

CHAPTER 2

The Integrative Attachment Trauma Protocol for Children (IATP-C): Overview

> In this chapter, you will come to understand:
>
> – The difference between a team approach and a solo application of the IATP-C
> – An overview of the three stages of the IATP-C
> – Effective therapist demeanor
> – Rationale and tips for peer consultation

The four components of the IATP-C include: (1) parent psychoeducation, (2) family therapy, (3) EMDR therapy, and (4) peer consultation. Integrating those four components, the IATP-C sequence involves Stage 1, parent psychoeducation and case conceptualization; Stage 2, a family and EMDR therapy approach for building good feelings and capacity for trust; and Stage 3, an integrative, gentle approach for healing triggers and traumas.

Figure 2.1 illustrates the sequence of the IATP-C. (See Appendix A, "IATP-C Checklist," for a general sequencing guideline for all the IATP-C activities.)

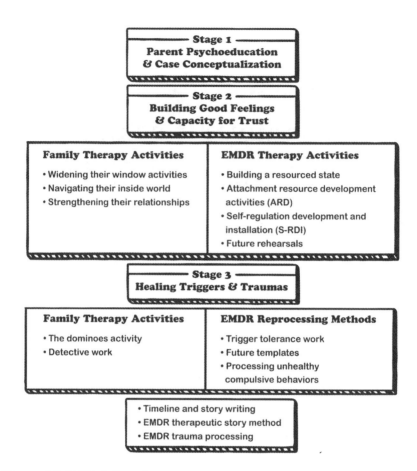

Figure 2.1: IATP-C Overview

THE IATP-C WITH VARIOUS AGES AND CHILD POPULATIONS

The language and procedures of the IATP-C can be easily adapted to match the developmental age of the child or teenager. Throughout this book, scripts are provided designed for school-age children and teens. However, further simplification of language and procedures can allow application to much younger children. In the case described by Swimm (2018), the IATP-C methods were simplified for application with a 17-month-old who had become fearful and rejecting of his mother with frequent episodes of dysregulation following an incident in which food became lodged in his throat. To allow him to breathe until the emergency surgery could be performed, his mother had to hold him upside-down for two hours. The therapist provided education to the parents (IATP-C Stage 1) followed by family therapy playful activities and the EMDR foundational activities with very simple language and little songs to build trust and emotion regulation (IATP-C Stage 2). A short, simple therapeutic story was created and a baby doll and doctor toys were utilized to activate the boy's memory networks for reprocessing with bilateral stimulation (IATP-C Stage 3). Parents also repeated attachment-related activities at home. The boy's symptoms were eliminated within five sessions.

The IATP-C can be applied to children of various ages residing in biological or adoptive homes or in out-of-home placements. The method is equally appropriate for children and teens who identify with their birth gender as for those who identify as nonbinary or transgender. It is equally applicable to children and teens with differing romantic preferences and to children and/or their families in diverse ethnic, cultural, or religious groups. (In keeping with our patient confidentiality obligations, we typically leave out these types of details in case examples unless such details are pertinent to a particular case example, in which case, we substitute analogous details for the actual ones.) If children or teens have experienced discrimination or rejection based on gender, social, or cultural differences, those adverse experiences are included in the list of traumas for reprocessing. The IATP-C therapist also looks for positive resources to highlight related to the child's gender, social, and cultural identity.

When the child or parent identifies with a different cultural, social, or ethnic group than the therapist, it's important to recognize the potential impact on therapeutic trust. The IATP-C therapist should demonstrate an open and humble attitude toward discussions of their different life experiences and take steps to explore and repair any misunderstandings and missteps that might happen in the course of therapy.

As mentioned earlier, the IATP-C is applicable to children and teens impacted by prenatal substance exposure or some form of neurodivergence. It's important to adjust therapeutic expectations to match the challenges and characteristics with respect to any of these brain-based conditions. Chapter 11 guides the therapist in adapting IATP-C procedures to children's learning, social, and emotional challenges, while highlighting their talents and strengths.

TEAM VS. SOLO APPLICATION OF THE IATP-C

Serious attachment injuries in early childhood impact the capacity of the child to tolerate distress, trust and receive support, and address traumatic memories. Either family therapy or EMDR therapy alone cannot adequately address the problematic symptoms and behaviors. The IATP-C addresses attachment and trauma in tandem through an integration of the two therapies.

If You Have a Team

There are great advantages to application of the IATP-C by a two-therapist team:

1. Each therapist has a specific role, and the child and the parents know what type of therapy to expect going into each session, reducing the tendency for the client, the parents, and the therapist to get off track.
2. The two therapists can check in with each other and brainstorm how to overcome treatment challenges. The mutual support improves the morale of the therapists.
3. The parents and the child hear the same messages from both therapists, increasing the likelihood the parents and the child will trust and integrate the educational information.

In the case of a two-therapist team, the roles of family therapist and EMDR therapist are divided. Depending upon the tolerance of the child or teen and the willingness of the insurance company, family therapy followed by EMDR therapy may take place on the same day. Back-to-back therapy isn't required, but it assists with continuity between the family and EMDR therapy.

If You Are a Solo Therapist

The IATP-C can be provided by a solo therapist if a two-therapist team is unavailable or if the child's symptoms allow for a less intense approach. To provide the IATP-C as a solo therapist with a challenging case, the therapist meets with the child and parents twice per week until symptoms are reduced, designating the first meeting as a family therapy session and the second meeting as an EMDR therapy session. With a less challenging case, the therapist may meet with the child and parents once per week, alternating the family therapy and

EMDR therapy sessions or conducting family therapy activities during the first half hour and EMDR therapy activities the last half hour.

Integrating the IATP-C With Other Modalities

One of the advantages of EMDR therapy is the ease with which EMDR can be integrated with other modalities (Shapiro, 2018, p. 19). The IATP-C is an integration of family therapy with EMDR therapy strategies to improve coregulation, attachment relationships, and emotional support for the child prior to assisting them with addressing their difficult past. However, if you routinely provide other therapies like play therapy (Beckley-Forest & Monaco, 2020), equine therapy (Schultz, 2007), trauma-focused cognitive behavioral therapy (TF-CBT; de Arellano et al., 2014), child parent psychotherapy (CPP; Guild et al., 2021), or dyadic developmental psychotherapy (DDP; Hughes, 2017), to name a few, you can use your clinical judgement and supplement the IATP-C with other methods you find useful.

STAGE 1: PARENT PSYCHOEDUCATION AND CASE CONCEPTUALIZATION

Parent psychoeducation and case conceptualization begin with the first phone call as well as the intake and history taking sessions. During intake, spending one-on-one time with the parents so that traumatic past experiences and challenging behaviors can be discussed without triggering the child is critical. During the earliest contact with the family, the therapist is considering the parents' capacity for attunement and sensitive responsiveness, the stability of the home environment, and the parents' understanding of trauma and attachment.

One-on-one time with the child is also important during the intake to attune to the child's feelings and complaints and gain an early view of the child's belief system and capacity for trust and regulation. One-on-one time also allows the therapist to plant the seeds for therapeutic trust.

Following the intake and information-gathering session, the therapist schedules the parents for one-on-one parent psychoeducation sessions. Optionally, the therapist may offer formal classes for a group of parents. This format can be an efficient method of presenting and discussing the material and allows parents to receive support from one another. The number and length of class sessions depend upon your goals and whether you wish to allow time for sharing and discussion.

Beginning the child's treatment with parent psychoeducation sessions, whether individual or in a class, can help parents make internal changes that enable them to respond differently to their child and set the stage for the family and EMDR work to come. Parents are often stressed, frustrated, hurt, and angry, and their parenting decisions are often emotion driven and therefore punitive, worsening their child's symptoms and behaviors. The first important goal of the parent sessions is to help parents gain a thorough understanding of how their child's behaviors are directly linked to the traumatic events in their child's early life and to understand any additional brain-based disorders, such as prenatal substance exposure or neurodivergence. The second important goal is increasing parents' capacity for strategies that develop the child's sense of connection and trust and provide coregulation, safety, and improved mentalization as a prerequisite to IATP-C Stage 2 and Stage 3.

When working as a therapist team, the family therapist typically conducts the parent education sessions, although technically either therapist could conduct individual or class sessions. Clinical judgment regarding parent needs determines the number of parent sessions, but at least two to six parent sessions can help most parents establish important initial changes.

STAGE 2: THE FAMILY THERAPY FOUNDATIONAL COMPONENT

The family therapy Stage 2 foundational activities provide the child or teen and their parent with important skills for tolerating stress and distress without sympathetic nervous system activation or dorsal vagal shutdown. The activities help the child understand their inner world and gain adaptive information about their outside world. Skills-based activities improve parent and child communication and help make up for the child's developmental deficits related to social skills or basic life skills.

The family therapist meets for 10 to 15 minutes with the parent one-on-one at the beginning of each family therapy session to reinforce the attuned, integrative parenting methods and allow parents to express any frustrations about the challenges of that week out of earshot of their child. The rest of the session usually involves the child or teen and the parent together, but clinical judgment determines when or if there is a need for one-on-one time with the child.

STAGE 2: THE EMDR FAMILY THERAPY FOUNDATIONAL COMPONENT

The EMDR therapist, like the family therapist, checks in with the parent one-on-one for approximately 10 minutes to prepare parents for the EMDR foundational activities that are planned. The parent is an essential part of the activities for development of attachment security and trust. The EMDR activities create positive emotional experiences in tandem with soothing, slow bilateral stimulation (BLS) to deepen positive affect for the child or teen. For example, slow BLS is applied to deepen feelings of safety accessed through a guided visualization of a safe place. Later, a mature state is accessed through a role-play of a situation in which the child or teen showed mature behavior and deepened with slow BLS. The child or teen is encouraged to view this positive state as their "biggest kid" self. The Attachment Resource Development (ARD) activities access feelings of closeness and trust with the parent and then deepen the child's positive feelings with slow BLS. Self-Regulation Development and Installation (S-RDI) calms the child through coaching and then deepens the positive feelings associated with the coregulation through slow BLS.

Following EMDR resource work, EMDR future rehearsals are conducted with playful role-plays and mental movies. Art, sand tray, and play therapy materials are incorporated into the activities to keep children engaged.

STAGE 3: ADDRESSING TRIGGERS AND TRAUMAS WITHIN THE FAMILY THERAPY COMPONENT

Within family therapy sessions, parents and their children or teens identify triggers, emotions, sensations, thoughts, and reactions through the Dominoes Activity, identifying where they might pull a domino next time with new skills for a better outcome. Further *Detective Work* around their triggers and negative beliefs involves connecting the dots to the past (without delving into the past memories just yet).

To assist with transitioning to past trauma work, the solo therapist—or either therapist from the team—then helps the child or teen and parent create a coherent story and make sense of the difficult things that happened in the child's life. They create a Timeline showing where the child lived throughout the early years, showing times when the child experienced positive events, and marking points on the Timeline at which the child experienced difficult events. Negative and positive beliefs associated with events may also be added to the Timeline. With younger children, the therapist can draw pictures on the Timeline instead of writing words.

Once the Timeline is created, the therapist and parents collaborate (sometimes with help from the child or teen) to write a therapeutic story. The story follows a specific outline developed by Lovett (1999). The story incorporates adaptive information and helps the child make sense of the things they've experienced.

STAGE 3: ADDRESSING TRIGGERS AND TRAUMAS WITHIN THE EMDR THERAPY COMPONENT

The EMDR therapist begins by targeting and reprocessing present triggers and developing future templates to give children and teens a first experience with reprocessing that is easy to manage. The EMDR therapist draws upon the work completed in family therapy with the Dominoes Activity and Detective Work to identify relevant triggers and negative beliefs. EMDR reprocessing of present triggers helps stabilize the child and helps the child become comfortable with EMDR reprocessing, lowering the child's resistance to reprocessing traumatic memories.

To safely address memories, the EMDR therapist utilizes bilateral stimulation with the child or teen throughout the reading of the therapeutic story, repeating as needed during follow-up sessions until the child is less reactive to their story as a whole and has integrated important adaptive information. When the child is ready, the EMDR therapist targets and reprocesses individual events that still hold an emotional charge with EMDR Phases 3 through 7.

The EMDR therapist utilizes various strategies that help bring the memory safely to adaptive resolution. For example, the therapist may utilize cognitive interweaves (brief statements, questions, or suggestions) offered as needed during reprocessing to facilitate an emotional shift, access missing information, or release disturbing sensations in the body. Parents may be invited to provide extra support during reprocessing and loving statements as interweaves.

As the child or teen exhibits improved functioning and symptoms are reduced to the satisfaction of the parent and child, the frequency of sessions overall is reduced and discharge is planned. Final activities that celebrate the family's progress are planned. However, due to the complexity of families overall and new challenges that can arise as children move through developmental stages, we let families know that tune-ups are often needed by children and families and that they are not a sign of a setback. Returning for a tune-up is a healthy response to the new challenges that can arise as children move toward adulthood.

PEER CONSULTATION

We consider peer consultation a vital component of the IATP-C, whether the therapists are from the same practice and meeting together as a team or whether IATP-C therapists from separate practices are meeting regularly to exchange ideas online. Peer consultation improves therapist morale and helps therapists keep fidelity to the model. It's a way to share strategies and ideas for overcoming obstacles with parents, kids, and teens. Although cases are shared without identifying details, it's important to obtain written permission from parents or guardians during intake to discuss cases in peer consultation. Gathering weekly is optimal.

A helpful way to proceed is to create an agenda at the start of the meeting, prioritizing the cases appropriately. Cases in which there are serious safety issues occurring in the home or in which the child's placement is at risk of disruption are prioritized followed by cases in which there is resistance or a stuck point. The therapist outlines a brief history of the child's life and traumatic events and summarizes therapeutic gains or challenges. Following the summary, a brainstorming session begins with thoughts, suggestions, or insights offering possible solutions or ideas.

For example, suggestions might include revisiting a part of the protocol, adding outside services such as occupational therapy, or inviting a parent to participate in individual therapy. The team might roleplay a way to initiate a difficult discussion with parents who are overly punitive, or the team may hypothesize negative cognitions and emotions underlying a child's stuck behaviors. Peer consultation can ignite the fortitude and creative energy needed to meet the challenges presented by the families in treatment. Many exciting and sometimes unique approaches to a problem are discovered during group brainstorming.

The peer consultation time provides an opportunity to ask for and provide helpful feedback from one another and discuss personal feelings related to difficult cases. It's normal for therapists to experience a variety of emotions when working with complex and challenging cases, such as disappointment in a parent's decision to place a child outside the home, self-doubt about providing a certain intervention, or countertransference issues with a parent. Peer consultation reduces therapist stress through mutual support and encouragement. Part of the recipe for treatment success is the therapists' positive morale and enthusiasm for the work.

THE IATP-C THERAPIST DEMEANOR

Children and teens often start therapy feeling angry, hurt, and defensive. They may have been involved in previous therapies and be resistant to starting over once again. They may be mistrustful of parents and all adults.

Parents often come into a session feeling battered and at a loss as to how to handle their child. They may be angry and resentful toward their child due to many overwhelming problems and behaviors, and they may be hoping to temporarily place them outside their home or disrupt the placement or the adoption. They may fear being judged by the therapist and enter the treatment with strong defenses. The philosophy of the treatment may be completely new and feel quite foreign to them.

With children or teens and their parents, the IATP-C therapist maintains an attitude of playfulness, flexibility, humility, openness, curiosity, and genuine interest. This provides appropriate modeling and reduces anxiety for parents and children. A nonjudgmental, accepting, and warm demeanor provides a safe space where every member of the family feels respected and heard. Inviting parents and their child to work together with the therapist to solve problems and come up with ideas helps establish a sense that everyone is part of the therapeutic team, and that everyone on the team matters. During the family therapy and EMDR activities, the IATP-C therapist remembers to keep it simple, keep it playful, stay attuned to tolerance and mood, and be flexible and supportive.

ADDRESSING ADDITIONAL TREATMENT COMPLICATIONS

Kids who carry psychological injuries related to attachment trauma and loss are naturally complicated to treat due to their difficulty trusting adults, fears related to memories and emotions, poor reflective capacity, and emotional dysregulation. Challenges related to dissociation, prenatal substance exposure, autism, or other forms of neurodivergence add further complexity to the treatment. Chapter 10 provides strategies specific to highly dissociative children, and Chapter 11 provides modifications for kids exposed to substances prenatally or challenged by autism or other forms of neurodivergence.

Additional complications arise when parents lack the capacity for sensitive, attuned parenting due to mental health conditions or their own childhood history of adversity. Chapter 12 assists therapists with applying EMDR individually with parents to address relevant memories and triggers.

CONCLUSION

This model combines family therapy and EMDR therapy, two approaches working in sync with one another to strengthen closeness and connection within struggling families. As children and teens grow in their capacity to trust and utilize the support of the adults who care for them, they become willing and able to utilize the integrative approach for developing new skills and addressing their painful past. Moving hurt children toward healthier functioning is exciting and meaningful work. One mom said, "You gave our family our life back."

CHAPTER 3

IATP-C Parent Psychoeducation Sessions

> Through reading this chapter, you'll gain skills for:
>
> – Providing psychoeducation regarding child behaviors
> – Introducing the IATP-C
> – Modeling and encouraging a mentalizing state
> – Promoting home accommodations for brain-based problems
> – Attuning to parents' attachment struggles
> – Inviting parents to participate in their own therapy when appropriate

When a child exhibits severe behavioral challenges related to attachment trauma and struggles to accept affection or enjoy closeness, it's normal for their parent to experience disappointment, frustration, and self-doubt. Whether they are guardians, foster, adoptive, or biological parents, parents need hope, and they need a safe space to speak honestly about what they're feeling.

The companion parent guide, *Attachment Trauma in Kids: Integrative Strategies for Parents,* serves as a basic curriculum for parent psychoeducation sessions. Reading the parent guide helps parents know they are not alone and reinforces the teaching points from the psychoeducation sessions.

"WHAT'S WRONG WITH MY CHILD?"

This is the most common question parents ask. The behaviors of their child or adolescent overwhelm them, confuse them, and frustrate them. Their stress level is through the ceiling. Their parenting responses are driven by anger and frustration, which worsens their child's behaviors.

The following are four critical points to help parents make sense of their child's behaviors. The points highlight the interrupted development, the neurobiological deficits, and the maladaptively stored trauma as responsible for their child's extreme symptoms and problems.

However, there's a difference between understanding the information intellectually and holding onto the information in the middle of a highly challenging moment with their child. The attachment trauma lens may be a full 180 degrees from the way the parents have conceptualized their child's behaviors for several years. It likely contradicts views shared by extended family, neighbors, or friends. Be prepared to return to these points again and again when the parents get frustrated. Encourage parents to ask questions regarding the following four teaching points.

Speaking to Parents: Stuck Traumatic Memories Script

Say to the parent, "Traumatic memories are stored in a raw form that is easily activated within our memory networks. Even if your child's memories are preverbal or not in conscious memory, the feelings and beliefs associated with old traumatic events light up again and again. Furthermore, the disturbing feelings and thoughts are connected to traumas within their attachment relationships. Therefore, present-day interactions with you trigger the stuck negative feelings and thoughts."

Speaking to Parents: Stuck Negative Beliefs About Self and Others Script

Say to the parent, "The stuck negative beliefs related to early experiences may be completely irrational, but they feel completely real and true because of the stored trauma. These negative beliefs are affecting your child's thoughts and perceptions during interactions with you and others every single day. Common stuck negative beliefs that can feel very, very true even if they're not true include 'I can't trust my parents,' 'My parents don't care about me,' 'My parents are against me,' 'I don't belong,' 'I have to protect myself,' 'I can't rely on others to meet my needs,' 'I'm bad,' and 'I'm not worthy of love.' These stuck beliefs have left your child with a felt sense that they don't belong, they will never belong, and it's not safe to trust. These kids live with constant fear of rejection, and often it's easier for them to shut down their needs for closeness and connection and pretend they don't care."

Speaking to Parents: Downstairs Brain Script

(Consider using a drawing or model of the brain as a visual aid.) Say to the parent, "Trauma in early life led to overdevelopment of the lower, more primitive regions of your child's brain, often referred to as the *downstairs brain*. Your child's overdeveloped downstairs brain was a design of mother nature to assist your child with vigilance and quick reactions in an unsafe world (Siegel, 2001, 2007, 2010; Siegel & Bryson, 2011). The overdeveloped downstairs brain still activates fight-or-flight responses and shutdown responses. These responses are no longer needed, but your child can't turn them off."

Speaking to Parents: Prefrontal Brain Script

Say to the parent, "Children require enriching and supportive early attachment experiences for optimal social, emotional, and cognitive development. Trauma in your child's early life interrupted development of trust and connection for feeling safe and for age-appropriate gains. Scientists can even see the consequences of the developmental deficits in the prefrontal brain, often referred to as the *upstairs brain* of traumatized children. They find fewer neural connections in this front part of the brain due to the traumas and deficiencies in the early attachment environment. This causes problems in reasoning, problem solving, managing emotions, and communicating. The deficits left your child with no way to manage their survival brain responses, causing the downstairs brain to have even more control."

An article available online by Bruce Perry (2002) includes pictures of brain scans showing the serious effects of neglect on the developing brain, which can be helpful as a visual aid during the above scripts. When parents view the behaviors of their child or teen as driven by stuck traumas and its impact on the developing brain, they become more understanding of the child's struggles and more willing to adopt integrative parenting methods. However, psychoeducation can be easily forgotten during times of stress. Parents typically need reminders throughout treatment of the trauma driving their child's behaviors.

Talking to Parents About Their Child's Grief

Often, in the case of adoption, foster care, or guardianship, parents have a difficult time understanding children's loyalty to their first parents. They may have argued with their child about the first parents in an attempt to help change their feelings, or they may have denigrated the biological parents in front of their child, causing a strong reaction. It can be helpful for parents to understand how children's attachment to their first parents is wired into the survival system. If children weren't driven to seek proximity to the parents to whom they were born, they would be more likely to end up in a dangerous situation.

Speaking to Parents: Grief and Loyalty Script

Say to the parent, "Even though it's unlikely your child had a secure attachment with their biological parents, the attachment system is part of our survival system, whether or not there's security or trust. We're wired to stay connected and in proximity with our biological attachment figures to help us stay alive. We're biologically programmed to be loyal. Separation naturally leads to overwhelming feelings of loss, despair, and fear. Kids can't be talked out of those feelings because they're part of their makeup, and if they sense you don't approve, it can create a breach in your relationship. However, if your child believes you understand their feelings, it will strengthen their sense of connection with you."

Addressing Social and Cultural Trauma

Many parents who adopt or foster children are not fully aware of the ways in which their child may be experiencing trauma caused by discrimination or marginalization within their school, community, or extended family. Kids in adoptive or foster homes may be experiencing alienation or sensing judgments from others due to their ethnicity or cultural background. Kids with developmental deficits or physical disabilities may be left out of social activities. Teens beginning to recognize differences in sexual identity or romantic preferences may experience negative reactions from family members, peers, or others. These are just a few examples of social and cultural trauma. The IATP-C therapist emphasizes the impact of this type of trauma on the developing brain, self-concept, and capacity for trust and closeness with others and promotes sensitive, attuned responses from parents.

INTRODUCING INTEGRATIVE PARENTING STRATEGIES

Parents need hope and motivation to practice new parenting approaches. The following is a sample script that helps parents understand how integrative parenting strategies help mitigate the challenges outlined above.

Speaking to Parents: Integrative Parenting Strategies Introductory Script

Say to the parent, "The integrative parenting strategies we teach are informed by the science of attachment and trauma. We have brought together methods that can help rewire your child's brain and nervous system over time. Obviously, this is a tall order, so this doesn't happen overnight. We want to keep three primary goals in mind. The first is calming your child's self-protective downstairs brain by strengthening your child's feelings of trust and connection with you. This goal might be hard on your end, because kids self-protect by pushing others away, but we'll help you navigate this. The second goal is strengthening your child's prefrontal brain. We can do that by helping your child express thoughts and feelings. The third goal will be helping your child feel safe enough and supported enough to participate in EMDR work to heal traumatic memories and triggers. It's a lot, but we'll take it step by step and support you along the way."

The therapist explains to parents that when the parents respond with anger, as natural as that may be, the downstairs brain of the traumatized child or teen is triggered and the fight-or-flight reaction is reinforced. Show the parents the window of tolerance diagram in the parent guide and discuss how connection widens the window of tolerance for all of us and disconnection narrows our window of tolerance. Ask the parents to reflect on the clues that their child or teen is feeling disconnected and moving into fight-or-flight or shutting down. Ask the parents to reflect on their own internal state when they are moving into fight-or-flight or shutting down. Next, develop a plan for expanding their own support system and for improving trust and connection with their child in the home.

Some parents are not able to engage in a discussion about connection and closeness early on, due to a hyperfocus on their child's most upsetting behaviors. In that case, start by identifying strategies for addressing specific behaviors as described in the parent guide, and later circle back to strategies for closeness and connection.

Vignette With the Father of 14-Year-Old Lania
The following is an example of a parent psychoeducation session conversation with the parents of 14-year-old Lania, adopted from an orphanage in Colombia at 3 years of age.

> **Lania's father (looking skeptical):** The trauma stuff is all well and good, but what about accountability? It sounds like you want us to let Lania off the hook for her behaviors. If we don't hold her accountable for her bad choices, she'll become a selfish, irresponsible grownup. I've told her again and again that if she doesn't change, she's going to end up being a disappointment to her family, to herself, and to society.
>
> **Therapist:** I can understand how worried you are. Her behavior has been really concerning. You care about her and want her to have a decent life. That's why you feel frustrated and scold her, but no matter how often you do, she doesn't change. (*The father nods.*) Lots of parents of attachment-injured kids feel as you do, and lots of people grew up with the idea that an authoritarian approach is the way to get children to change. But practically speaking, even though you're trying to get her to change, scolding doesn't work because it doesn't change her brain and nervous system. Scolding doesn't add neural connections to her underdeveloped prefrontal brain to help her think better, and it doesn't calm the fight-or-flight response in her downstairs brain. Quite the opposite—the scoldings activate her fight-or-flight system. I want to help you help Lania's brain and nervous system, so she'll have the capacity to function differently. If you're okay with it, I'd like us to look at some of the ideas in the parent guide and see what strategies you think might be doable for you. I know these methods are not easy to implement when you've been under so much stress for such a long time. What are your thoughts?

MODELING AND ENCOURAGING A MENTALIZING STATE

A mentalizing state is a state in which we are able to reflect upon our own and others' inner thoughts, feelings, desires, and motivations. When we're in a mentalizing state, we're nonjudgmental, empathizing, validating, genuine, and collaborative. We don't make assumptions about the internal state of others, but instead we stay curious, open to learning, and humble regarding what we don't really know. A mentalizing state enhances others' capacity to feel trust and connection with us (Allen & Fonagy, 2006; Fonagy et al., 1997). None of us stays in a mentalizing state 100% of the time, but we can increase our capacity for mentalizing with mindful practice.

The IATP-C therapist attempts to interact with parents from a mentalizing state and simultaneously teaches parents to maintain a mentalizing state as much as possible with their child as a way to build trust and connection and improve coregulation. The following is a script for motivating parents to practice mentalization during interactions with their child.

Speaking to Parents: Mentalization Script

Say to the parent, "It will be important for both of us to stay in a mentalizing state throughout the therapy sessions as much as possible. Mentalization with children is coregulating, and approaching kids from a mentalizing state teaches them to think, reason, and reflect. As much as possible, you'll want to practice staying in a mentalizing state at home, too. It's not easy to do all of the time, but with practice, it becomes easier. It will definitely pay off in terms of your child's brain development. Let's look together at the description of the mentalizing state provided in the parent book."

HELPING PARENTS WITH HIGHLY DISSOCIATIVE KIDS

During case conceptualization and EMDR treatment planning, stay alert to clues the child or teen may be affected by high levels of dissociation. Liotti (1999) explains that dissociation is not a coping mechanism, but a breakdown of coping mechanisms, rooted in early attachment disorganization. They may have a pattern of staring off into space or retreating into fantasies. Children who are dissociative may be highly avoidant of feelings and difficult memories. They may become quickly overwhelmed when triggered and lose orientation to time and place so that the past feels present. Chapter 10 of this book and the accompanying parent guide provide strategies to help parents raising children or teens with patterns of dissociation.

PROMOTING ACCOMMODATIONS IN THE HOME FOR ADDITIONAL BRAIN-BASED PROBLEMS

During Stage 1 parent psychoeducation and case conceptualization, look for clues that some of the concerning behaviors may be related to prenatal substance use exposure, autism, or some other form of neurodivergence. If there is concern, refer the parent for a good psychological or neuropsychological assessment by a clinician with expertise in brain-based conditions as well as assessment by an occupational therapist. If the child is affected by one or more brain-based difficulties, it is critical they have the appropriate accommodations at school and also in the home. Accommodations in the home may include consistent routines and assistance with doing things the child or teen cannot do on their own. Parents need assistance with separating "can't" from "won't" (Malbin, 2017). Chapter 11 of this book provides more parent psychoeducation information and adaptations to the IATP-C for therapists. The accompanying parent guide, *Attachment Trauma in Kids: Integrative Strategies for Parents,* provides additional guidance for parents raising traumatized children or teens impacted by prenatal substance exposure, autism, or another form of neurodivergence.

ATTUNING TO PARENTS' ATTACHMENT STRUGGLES

Parents who grew up with fairly secure attachments or who had a rough start but found healing through the help of others can reflect upon their own internal state and accurately imagine the internal state of others. They're comfortable with closeness and connection and tend to be pretty accepting of the mistakes of others and of themselves. Parents who are on the positive end of the attachment-security continuum can listen to the point of view of others and can repair breaches in their relationships. Parents with a secure attachment are intuitively able to understand their child's behaviors through the lens of attachment trauma, and integrative parenting strategies naturally make sense to them.

Many parents attending IATP-C with their children grew up with unhealthy patterns in their families of origin and struggle with their own ability to feel connected and worthy of connection. Their own stuck mistrust and fear may be driving reactivity and interfering with building trust with their child. Their capacity for reflecting upon their own and others' internal states is likely underdeveloped, which means they have difficulty recognizing the ways in which their own reactions are making their child's problems bigger, not eliminating them. (See Appendix C, "Transmission of Attachment Patterns, Parent to Child," for more information regarding specific patterns of attachment and how they are transmitted generationally.)

Dismissive Attachment Pattern

Parents with a dismissive pattern likely grew up with dismissive parents who frowned upon the expression of feelings or needs. Therefore, they learned to suppress their emotions and needs and built a self-image around independence and strength.

There are two subtypes: The parent with a dismissive derogatory subtype avoids vulnerability by making negative judgments about others. The parent with a dismissive idealizing subtype stays in pretend mode, in which problems or negative emotions are denied. Both subtypes are defense mechanisms developed in childhood.

Parents with a strongly dismissive attachment style typically have difficulty recognizing or acknowledging their kids' needs for connection. Bringing their child to therapy may be quite anxiety provoking. They may struggle with willingness to participate in the therapy and balk at the suggestion of individual therapy for themselves.

To build rapport and lower the parent's defenses, the therapist should lower their own emotional intensity and use a very laid back, matter-of-fact approach and stay open, curious, and nonjudgmental. Strongly dismissive parents may always have blind spots related to their child's internal states. The therapist should emphasize to dismissive parents the very practical rationale for integrative parenting methods.

Speaking to the Dismissive Parent Script

Say to the parent, "Through research with kids with developmental issues and stuck trauma, we know that parent strategies you can do at home are a necessary supplement to what we'll be doing in the office. The overall goal, remember, is calming the overactive fight-or-flight part of your child's brain and strengthening reasoning and coping skills with a stronger upstairs brain. The at-home methods begin with calming the fight-or-flight system through connection and coregulation. Are you willing to try some of the methods? The methods may feel a bit unnatural, but I think you'll find them to be worth the effort."

Parents With a Preoccupied Pattern

Parents with a preoccupied attachment pattern grew up struggling to feel seen and heard. As children, they learned to be demanding, intense, and proactive in their search to get their needs met. Unfortunately, in adulthood, their anxiety about getting their needs met can overshadow attunement to their kids' feelings and needs. If their child is affected by attachment injuries, their child's extreme behaviors and needs can intensify the parent's anxiety and lead to overwhelming feelings and dysregulated responses.

In the case of the parent with strong characteristics of the preoccupied pattern, the therapist should attune to the parent's emotions and attend to the parent's needs prior to directing the parent to attune to the child's internal state. The therapist should be expressive and observant of the parent's cues and engage in active listening, so the parent feels seen and heard.

Speaking to the Preoccupied Parent Script

Say to the parent, "From everything you've said, it sounds as if your child's behaviors have been extremely overwhelming and your stress is to the ceiling right now. Do I have that right? Before we work on understanding your child's behaviors through the attachment trauma lens, I want to attend to your stress. I'd like to work with you on developing a plan for self-care that will help you manage this stress. Then I'd like to help you with the integrative parenting strategies as described in the parent guide, because improving your child's behaviors will also lower your stress."

Parents With an Unresolved/Disorganized Pattern

Parents with an unresolved/disorganized pattern hold stored, unprocessed trauma of their own that gets triggered easily by their child. The dysregulation in the parent further triggers their child, leading to an endless negative feedback loop. For example, for the parent who was mistreated as a child, the cries of their young child may trigger stored fear and activate the fight-or-flight centers of their brain. Instead of responding to their child with comfort, the parent may shut down or become irritated, causing more distress for the child.

Parents operating from their own stored trauma cannot mentalize and self-reflect when they're in a triggered state. If the therapist hears the parent describe strong, sudden reactions to certain child behaviors, the therapist should stay nonjudgmental and express curiosity about the parent's early experiences as a way to open the door to the idea of doing their own therapeutic work. Individual EMDR therapy may be a game changer related to their capacity to respond calmly to their child.

INVITING PARENTS TO PARTICIPATE IN THEIR OWN THERAPY

When the parent appears unable to shift from a stuck place, the therapist can help the parent look at the possibility of seeking individual help from a nonjudgmental point of view.

Speaking to Parents: Invitation to Do Their Own Therapy Script

Say to the parent, "How can we help you find more support for yourself? We're not doing our job if we don't address your needs as well as your child's needs. Raising kids with attachment trauma can be incredibly stressful and will naturally activate any trauma we carry within our own neural networks. This is no one's fault; it's just the situation. Sometimes when we live in a highly stressful situation, our own window of tolerance shrinks, and we find ourselves triggered again and again. I think getting involved in your own therapy would help you feel supported."

Parents can be referred to community supportive sources as well, such as respite care (temporary care for the child often offered through local nonprofit family service organizations), community treatment aids (paraprofessionals trained to work with the child in the home or school setting), and support groups for adoptive parents, adult children of alcoholics, or adult survivors of abuse.

Unfortunately, some parents who bring children or adolescents in for therapy have behaviors themselves that constitute abuse or neglect of the child. If it appears this could be the case, the IATP-C therapist must contact Child Protective Services.

Vignette With James's Mother, Marcia:
Invitation to Think Back to Childhood

Marcia, a single mother, had adopted her 6-year-old son James 3 years earlier. She and James had been meeting regularly with the family therapist and EMDR therapist team for approximately 2 months. At the beginning of the family therapy session, while James was still playing in the waiting room, Marcia had stated one of her worst struggles was at bath time.

Family Therapist: Would you be willing to try a little exercise with me? (*Marcia nods.*) See if you can bring up the memory of bath time last night—before you lost your cool. Take your time and notice what you feel.

Marcia: I get really anxious just thinking about it.

Family Therapist: Okay, and now I wonder if you could think back on your own childhood for a moment. Just be open to whatever comes up for you.

Marcia: Hmm, what pops up in my head is something that happened when I was about 8 years old. My dad asked me to fill the bathtub for my little brother. I didn't know what I was doing. My brother hopped into the water and started screaming because it was too hot. I got a really bad spanking that night.

Family Therapist: No wonder you have a tough time at bath time! Subconsciously, you probably believe something bad is going to happen.

Marcia: Yes, my dad was really harsh, and something bad usually did happen—because it seemed like I was always getting punished for something.

Family Therapist: I wonder if your experiences growing up have created anxiety for you in other areas related to parenting. Of course, James is also anxious and reactive, which is challenging in itself. So you and James are stuck in a negative feedback loop.

Marcia: Yes, my anxiety and reactivity trigger him, and his anxiety and reactivity trigger me.

Family Therapist: You know, Marcia, these kinds of reactions rooted in early life experiences are really hard to get a handle on without some assistance. I would really like you to consider working with one of the therapists on our adult team. Remember how we have talked about the family as a system? I would be doing you and James a disservice if I didn't give you the same opportunity for healing as we have given James. We have some wonderful therapists here who could really help you feel better.

Marcia: Maybe . . .

Marcia needed time to digest what was discussed, but a couple of weeks later, she asked the therapist for the name of a therapist she could work with individually. EMDR was able to help Marcia reprocess trauma from childhood that was directly related to anxiety and overreactions to James. Marcia was able to calm her anxiety and become more attuned and nurturing with James—the kind of mother she really wanted to be.

Couples in Crisis

Marital conflict can be traumatic to children, and the stress of raising a traumatized child can intensify partner conflict. The therapist should normalize the stress the couple is experiencing but encourage relationship counseling to help them get on the same page and feel more mutual connection and support. In addition to relationship therapy, partners should be encouraged to take care of their relationship by finding reliable respite care and engage in some pleasurable activities for the two of them.

Unwilling Parents

Occasionally, parents want their child in therapy but are unwilling to change a punitive approach or engage in their own therapeutic work. Working one on one in the case of an older adolescent may be possible, utilizing adult protocols (Potter & Wesselmann, 2023). In the case of either children or adolescents with resistant parents or parents with little capacity for empathy, it may be helpful to make a referral to a behavioral therapist, as appropriate use of behavioral strategies can reduce parents' excessive use of shame and punishments and bring greater stability to the home environment.

CONCLUSION

Two to six parent psychoeducation sessions is the estimated number of sessions you'll need, but use your clinical judgment regarding frequency and duration. Following parent psychoeducation sessions, you'll ideally meet with the child or adolescent one to two times per week, hopefully, with parent involvement most of the time. Children's relationship with their parents is central to their emotional well-being throughout their growing-up years. Parent psychoeducation is fundamental to their growth and healing.

CHAPTER 4

IATP-C History Taking and EMDR Treatment Planning

> Through reading this chapter, you'll gain skills for:
>
> – Initial information gathering and use of the IATP-C History-Taking Checklist
> – Conceptualizing the symptoms and problems of the child or teen through the History-Taking Checklist
> – Creating a general IATP-C treatment plan

Stage 1 of the IATP-C includes history taking and treatment planning informed by the adaptive information processing (AIP) model. Ideally, treatment planning prior to application of EMDR involves the client in reflecting upon the their most concerning issue, their negative feelings and beliefs, and tracing them back to relevant early events. Because children and teens with attachment injuries are easily triggered and dysregulated by references to their painful past early in treatment, the initial history taking and treatment planning at the start of the IATP-C is conducted with the parent, without the child or teen in the room.

GATHERING INITIAL INFORMATION

Initial contact is typically a phone call from a parent struggling with the symptoms and behaviors of their child or adolescent. During the phone call, the

IATP-C therapist (or intake professional) asks briefly about the struggles the child and family are facing and briefly inquires about the child's history. If the child or teen appears to have serious behaviors and symptoms related to a history of attachment trauma, the therapist can explain over the phone that the child may be appropriate for a family therapy and EMDR therapy integrative approach. The parents should be informed that the approach involves one to two sessions per week depending upon severity of the problems of the child or teen, and that at least one parent attends most sessions along with their child. The professional also explains that the therapy begins with two to six parent sessions without the child present to provide the parent with special methods for addressing their child's needs. If the parent agrees to the treatment methods, the therapist proceeds to scheduling the intake session.

The professional goes on to explain that the first session will begin with some information gathering, first with the parent(s) while the child or teen stays in the waiting room, and then with the child or adolescent one-on-one. If the child is too young to stay in the waiting room, the therapist asks the parent to bring along another family member to wait with the child until it's time to bring the child into the room. By meeting first one on one with the parent, the IATP-C therapist avoids exposing the child or teen to the parent's behavioral complaints or descriptions of traumatic events, either of which may be triggering and dysregulating for the child.

Beginning Case Conceptualization for the Child or Teen

Formal assessments can be mailed ahead of time or provided later during the in-office visit to help gather information. It's important to gather a general psychosocial history, including medical history, academic functioning, sleeping, and nutritional habits. Look for possible symptoms of traumatic stress, dissociation, attentional problems, impulsivity, and attachment problems.

Children with a history of attachment trauma may have a disorganized attachment pattern along with an ambivalent-resistant or avoidant pattern. These patterns are not diagnoses. Observing clues to attachment patterns, however, assists with understanding children's responses to interactions with their parents. Furthermore, the therapist can adjust therapeutic demeanor based on the observed attachment pattern. For example, children who are outwardly seeking of attention/connection may respond positively to intense, empathic responses from the therapist, while children who avoid closeness or vulnerability are more cooperative with casual, superficial interactions in the beginning of therapy. (See Appendix C, "Transmission of Attachment Patterns, Parent to Child.")

Children and teens with attachment injuries may or may not meet the *DSM-5* criteria for reactive attachment disorder diagnosis or its counterpart, indiscriminate social engagement disorder. They may or may not meet criteria for posttraumatic stress disorder. They commonly suffer from comorbid behavioral disorders, mood disorders, and/or dissociative disorders. Through the lens of attachment trauma and Shapiro's AIP model (2018), the diagnoses and problematic attachment patterns identified in affected children are driven by inadequately processed stored trauma and related developmental deficits.

In addition to history taking and assessments, it is often necessary to refer children and teens to an occupational therapist to evaluate sensory issues. The therapist should also be alert to indications of prenatal substance exposure, autism, or other brain-based issues. A full psychological exam or neuropsychological exam may be important for understanding complex child or teen cases. (See Appendix D, "Useful Child Assessments," for a list of screening tools that may be helpful for making appropriate diagnoses.)

The History-Taking Checklist

During the first session, prior to inclusion of the child or teen, the IATP-C therapist and parents discuss the History-Taking Checklist (see Appendix B). The History-Taking Checklist helps parents gain insight regarding the impact of trauma on their child's present beliefs, feelings, and behaviors. Parents may feel overwhelmed as they make checkmarks next to behavior after behavior on the History-Taking Checklist, but at the same time, parents learn that their child's behaviors are common for kids with a history of attachment trauma. The checklist helps parents think about possible abuse, neglect, frightening parental behaviors, separations, losses, criticism, or ridicule. It helps them recognize painful illnesses or medical interventions as trauma that may have led to core mistrust. The checklist helps parents think about possible bullying, discrimination experiences, or other frightening experiences outside of the family as well.

The parents also reflect on the list of negative beliefs and hypothesize which ones might be associated with which behaviors and how those beliefs naturally developed through the child's early experiences. As parents look over the list of desired positive beliefs, the therapist explains that processing stuck memories with EMDR therapy can help change beliefs, feelings, and behaviors.

At times there is little known information about the child's experiences as an infant or toddler. Sometimes it's possible to contact current or previous caseworkers or social workers who may be able to provide additional information. Parents may be surprised by the idea that preverbal events can be impacting their child's functioning in present day. The therapist should explain to parents that even in the case of very early trauma that can't be recalled consciously by the child or teen, associated fear can remain stuck in an unprocessed form that is easily triggered by subconscious reminders.

As the information gathering progresses, therapists are directly and indirectly assessing the parents' level of understanding regarding attachment issues, their parenting skills, their support system, their relationships with others, and their emotional wellbeing. Questions regarding the parents' extended family support and the style of parenting in which they were raised can help determine whether the parents may suffer from trauma in their own past.

Vignette With Aubre

Therapist: Aubre, as I look over this checklist, your granddaughter's behaviors make sense to me.

Aubre: Make sense? They make no sense whatsoever. My granddaughter is in self-destruct mode. She's always flying off the handle, and she's always in trouble for mouthing off—and don't get me started on her stealing and lying behaviors.

Therapist: You're exactly right. Her behaviors are not making sense for her life. But the behaviors do make sense when I look at her early history and her probable negative beliefs. Let's take a closer look at these negative beliefs you checked.

Aubre: Yeah, those look about right. She pushes people away like she can't trust them, and she definitely acts like she has to be in control, which I forgave when she was little because I understood it was the abuse. But she's been with me 11 years now. I always keep her safe. I always give her the things she needs. I've spent a fortune on her. It's time she shows some respect to me and to her teachers and she starts treating people right.

Therapist: That is definitely what we want for her. But here's the thing. These bad things that happened—the things you checked off—they're all stored in her brain, in this part of her brain here (points to lower brain) and her feelings from the past are stuck in there. The feelings keep lighting up as if it was yesterday. She can't control what her brain is doing, unfortunately. She's operating out of these stuck memories, beliefs, and feelings.

Aubre: Her brain is definitely stuck all right.

Therapist: Yes, it is. But that's why you're here. We have some methods that help kids' brains when they have stuck traumatic memories. Let me explain how we do the therapy here, and you can see if you think it's something you'd like to participate in.

During the information gathering, the therapist explains that IATP-C begins with one-on-one parent sessions. The therapist may suggest the parents begin reading the companion parent guide, *Attachment Trauma in Kids: Integrative Strategies for Parents,* Second Edition (Wesselmann, 2025).

The therapist schedules the parent psychoeducation sessions. If it is a two-parent home, it will be critical to involve both parents, either together or one at a time.

Before the information-gathering session is over, the therapist meets one on one with the child or teen. The goal for the first meeting with the child is to help them feel comfortable with the therapist and the idea of therapy. When the child or teen enters the office, the therapist shows them what they can hold onto or play around with during the session, such as fidget toys, clay, or drawing tools. Some younger children need to be told what items in the office they can touch and what areas are off limits. Alternatively, the therapist can engage the child or teen in a brief game or art activity. The therapist keeps the discussion to light, easy questions designed to get to know them and establish some rapport. Using clinical judgment, the therapist may ask the child about their "worries or bothers" (Adler-Tapia & Settle, 2023, p. 47) and explain the goal is to help them in any way they can.

After meeting with the parent(s) and child or teen, the therapist takes time to examine their notes, the History-Taking Checklist, and any formal assessments, and then consider priority issues, parent resources and needs, and the child's resources, negative beliefs (hypothesized), triggers, and trauma history. This is only a start to EMDR history taking and treatment planning. There is likely much to learn about the child or adolescent. As the therapist assists the child and parents with developing greater connection and trust, the goal is to provide the child with a sense of safety and support to help the child explore their feelings, beliefs, triggers, and memories prior to processing present triggers and past events with EMDR.

CASE CONCEPTUALIZATION EXAMPLES

Consider how this therapist utilized the History-Taking Checklist with parents to begin case conceptualization and initial parent psychoeducation.

Mark, 8 Years Old

Mark was an 8-year-old boy removed from his biological mother at age 3 due to neglect and abuse related to the mother's drug and alcohol use. He spent a year in foster care and then came to live with his adoptive family at age 4. Mark's parents explained that his behavioral problems began about 6 months after he came to live with their family. During the history-taking session, the therapist and the parents examined the History-Taking Checklist and identified the most concerning symptoms/behaviors:

- Arguing
- Meltdowns
- Aggression
- Clingy with parents
- Lying
- Stealing

The IATP-C therapist assisted Mark's parents with identifying important traumas from his past by jointly examining the list of traumas on the History-Taking Checklist and discussing what the parents knew from things Mark had said as well as information they had received from his caseworker. Traumatic incidents included:

- Being ignored when his birth mother was drinking
- Being locked in his bedroom by his birth mother's boyfriend
- Witnessing a violent episode involving his birth mother's boyfriend
- Two foster placements prior to present placement

- The goodbye visit with his birth mother and subsequent feelings of loss
- Being called names related to his skin color by schoolmates at recess

With the help of the checklist, the therapist and parents worked together to identify the present-day situations or triggers associated with Mark's concerning behaviors. The therapist explained that the IATP-C procedures assist with reducing the emotional charge associated with the triggers and developing coping and interpersonal skills.

Mark's triggers included:

- Being sent to his room
- Being told "No"
- Waiting for dinner to be prepared
- Bedtime
- Being left with a sitter
- Getting up for school
- Going to the playground

The therapist invited the parents to look at the History-Taking Checklist while considering Mark's trauma history and current behaviors to hypothesize the negative beliefs fueling his actions. The therapist encouraged Mark's parents to consider the overwhelming feelings of abandonment, rejection, disappointment, and isolation he must have felt in his biological home. The therapist asked Mark's parents to consider how the bullying related to his skin color might have intensified his feelings of alienation and unworthiness and made him feel unsafe in school. The therapist pointed out that Mark also may have feelings he hasn't shared related to being of a different ethnicity than his adoptive family. The therapist explained that it was possible Mark may be interpreting being left with a sitter or being told "no" as evidence that he didn't belong in his family and he wasn't good enough.

Mark's parents gained insight into Mark's struggles and hypothesized the following negative beliefs:

- "My parents don't want me."
- "I'm unlovable. I'm bad."

- "I don't belong in my family."
- "I can't trust anyone."
- "I won't get enough."
- "I don't fit in at school."
- "I'm not safe anywhere."

During the history taking, the therapist and parents examined the list of possible positive beliefs. The parents grew thoughtful when the therapist suggested that they consider how Mark might respond to redirection or inattention if he truly believed that he belonged, that he was loved, and that he was good. The parents and therapist collaborated to identify the following desired positive beliefs and made sure each belief identified was reasonable and factual:

- "My parents love me."
- "I'm lovable and good."
- "I belong in my family."
- "I can trust my mom and dad. I can trust some other adults. I can trust some kids."
- "I'll have enough."
- "I fit in with the kids who are friendly."
- "I have places where I can feel safe."

Working through the History-Taking Checklist was a beginning step to helping Mark's parents develop greater insight and a more compassionate perspective regarding his behaviors. Mark's parents acknowledged that they hadn't considered the real significance of his trauma history, nor had they recognized how Mark might be impacted by belonging to a minority ethnic group in an all-white family and school. They acknowledged that helping him with his traumatic experiences, his beliefs, and his emotions would be critical and that they must use a more attachment- and trauma-informed approach to assist Mark.

The therapist discovered that the mother's parents lived in the area and assisted the parents with Mark's care. The parents reported that the grandparents also struggled to understand Mark's behaviors and were irritable with Mark at times. The therapist scheduled the parents to return for one-on-one psychoeducation sessions and suggested that the grandparents participate so that the whole family could be on the same page. The therapist also developed a beginning treatment plan for Stage 2 foundational activities and Stage 3 activities to address the present, future, and past.

Taylor, 15 Years Old

Fifteen-year-old Taylor was living with their biological father and stepmother. Their biological mother was diagnosed with schizoaffective disorder when Taylor was 2 years old. The mother left the family, and Taylor has not had contact since. Taylor's father remarried when Taylor was 3 years old. Taylor's parents avoid discussing their biological mother with Taylor.

Taylor was born female, but throughout elementary school, Taylor wanted to dress in boys' clothes and wear short hair, for which they were teased and bullied. At age 14, they told their parents and friends they did not want to be a boy or a girl. They wanted to use a new name and wanted to be referred to as "they" or "them." Their parents and older sister argued about their decision for several weeks and then begrudgingly accepted their nonbinary status. Their closest friends support them, but they've experienced insults from some classmates regarding their attire and their chosen name and pronouns. Taylor also occasionally experienced negative comments from cousins and aunts.

Both parents attended the initial sessions. They explained that Taylor exhibited these behaviors for years, but in the past year, the behaviors escalated. Taylor's parents identified the following symptoms/behaviors:

- Arguing and shouting
- Meltdowns over homework, chores, and other stressors
- Refusal to eat dinner with the family
- Repeated school absences with complaints that they are sick
- Refusal to attend school events
- The parents and therapist made a list of traumas/adverse events:
- Early rejection/abandonment/loss related to their biological mother
- Feeling different from female peers while growing up
- Recent judgments from parents and sister related to nonbinary identity
- Continuing feelings of rejection from some of their relatives
- Experiences of rejection from some peers

Taylor's parents stated they have difficulty understanding Taylor's trauma around loss because Taylor was very young when their biological mother left. The therapist explained that the early feelings of loss are stored in a very raw form within Taylor's memory networks, and the more recent experiences of rejection related to gender identity tap into the early life experiences.

The parents next identified the present-day situations that seemed to trigger behaviors:

- Being given a correction or direction, especially by their stepmother
- Family dinner time
- Family gatherings
- Stress related to schoolwork or peer relationships
- School events

The parents hypothesized Taylor's negative beliefs with the help of the therapist:

- "I can't trust my parent."
- "I'm not loved."
- "I'm unlovable."
- "I don't fit in."
- "I'm different."
- "I can't cope."
- "I'm not safe anywhere."

Taylor's parents identified what they would like Taylor to believe:

- "I can trust both my parents."
- "My parents both love me and want the best for me."
- "I'm lovable as I am."
- "I fit in with friends and family who are safe."
- "Everyone has differences. I'm different and the same as others."
- "I can ask for help. I can learn things to help me cope."
- "I have places where I can feel safe."

The IATP-C therapist pointed out that Taylor suffers from significant trauma; in addition to the in-office work, it will be crucial for Taylor's parents to begin utilizing the attachment- and trauma-informed integrative strategies to strengthen trust, connection, and safety for Taylor. Parents agreed to begin reading the parent guide and attending one-on-one psychoeducation sessions.

GENERAL IATP-C TREATMENT PLAN
Goals
1. Improve parents' attunement and trauma-informed parenting methods (Stage 1)
2. Improve child's self-awareness, self-reflection, and self-regulation through family therapy foundational activities (Stage 2)
3. Increase positive interactions between child and parent through family therapy foundational activities (Stage 2)
4. Enhance child's sense of connection and trust with parent as well as positive sense of self through EMDR resource activities (Stage 2)
5. Improve child's awareness of triggers and develop new responses through family therapy activities (Stage 3)
6. Expand trigger tolerance through EMDR reprocessing (Stage 3)
7. Make sense of the past through a therapeutic story (Stage 3)
8. Move traumatic memories to adaptive resolution through EMDR reprocessing (Stage 3)

CONCLUSION

Identification of the negative cognitions, memories, and triggers driving the behaviors of kids impacted by early attachment injuries assists with case conceptualization and parent psychoeducation and guides implementation of the IATP-C. As parents gain increased understanding, attunement, and compassion through psychoeducation, they gain the capacity to provide their child with greater attachment security and emotional support throughout the activities of the IATP-C.

Part II

IATP-C Stage 2: Building Good Feelings and the Capacity for Trust

CHAPTER 5

IATP-C Foundational Family Therapy Activities

> Through reading this chapter, you'll gain skills for the following foundational family therapy activities:
>
> **WIDENING THEIR WINDOW**
> – The Language of the Window
> – The Pause
> – Breathwork and Bodywork
> – Brainwork Activities
> – High-Alert/Low-Alert Language
> – Facts About Feelings
> – Recognizing Their Biggest Kid Self
>
> **NAVIGATING THEIR INSIDE WORLD**
> – What Babies Need
> – Recognizing and Appreciating the Smaller Child on the Inside
>
> **STRENGTHENING THEIR RELATIONSHPS**
> – Relational Games
> – The Jobs of Moms and Dads
> – Who Has the Floor? Communication Game
> – Skills Practice

As previously described, attachment trauma is stored maladaptively in memory networks, keeping kids stuck in fear and vigilance. Furthermore, chronic trauma interrupts emotional and social development and negatively impacts the development of frontal brain executive functions. Parents may struggle with reactivity and overactive defensive mechanisms due to adverse events in their own early lives. IATP-C Stage 1 parent psychoeducation helps parents provide a more attuned, supportive environment to support their children's healing. The Stage 2 activities begin the therapeutic work with kids and their parents.

The Stage 2 family therapy activities described in this chapter take place in tandem with the Stage 2 EMDR activities described in Chapter 6. Typically, family therapy sessions precede EMDR therapy sessions each week. The Stage 2 family therapy activities are designed to provide information and skills to build the capacity of kids and their parents for tolerating distress, for reasoning, for coregulating, for understanding their outside and inside world, for communicating, and for building trust. The Stage 2 EMDR therapy activities center around providing the child or teen with a positive sense of self and creating experiences of safety and closeness with the parent along with application of slow, relaxing bilateral stimulation to reinforce the associated positive affect.

INITIATING THE STAGE 2 FAMILY THERAPY ACTIVITIES

At the onset of the family therapy work, the IATP-C therapist uses a nonjudgmental and warm demeanor that enables the child or teen and the parents to feel safe and accepted so the healing work can begin. The IATP-C treats the child or teen, the parent, and the parent–child relationship. The integrative model views healing of the family system as crucial to healing of the child.

Involving Parents

Sessions may be attended by only one parent due to logistical reasons. When this is the case, the IATP-C therapist tries to involve the second parent in at least some of the sessions or part of some sessions, even if it means including them via an online video platform such as Zoom, so that both parents have a chance to develop the shared language and connection with the child.

In the case of children or teens in foster care or residential care with no permanent placement, the IATP-C therapist attempts to find an adult who is willing to be an ongoing support or ongoing mentor in the child's life to be present in place of a parent in as many sessions as they reasonably can attend. Alternatively, a temporary foster parent or temporary staff member who has established a supportive relationship can perform the role of a caring adult to support and mentor the child between sessions. If the sessions must be conducted without a supportive adult, the therapist provides the supportive role individually.

All family sessions usually begin with the parent one-on-one with the therapist for 10 to 15 minutes. The therapist should take time to explain to the child that "Mom and Dad come in first because there are things they need to learn, too. Everyone is here to get help."

The therapist does need to attune to the child's capacity to wait. There are cases in which the child is unable to tolerate waiting or can only sit out for 5 or 10 minutes. Sometimes families are able to bring along a friend or extended family member to stay with the child in the waiting room.

For some adolescents or older children, staying in the waiting room can trigger mistrust or old feelings of abandonment. In this case, the family therapist may want to communicate initially with the parents through phone or email prior to each session.

At the beginning of the parent's check-in time, the parent is invited to share their observations and honest reactions to the events of the previous week. This provides an opportunity to reinforce the parent's understanding of their child's behaviors through the attachment and trauma lens and problem solve the parent's approach at home. Compassion for the parent's stress is critical before reframing the child's behaviors to maintain therapeutic trust. Toward the end of the parent's check-in time, the therapist explains the plan for the session and reminds the parent, "It can take time to gain kids' trust and cooperation for the therapy. If your child is resistant, don't worry. If we attune and connect through a mentalizing approach, we'll get there, little by little."

Optional Introductory Kintsugi Activity

I credit colleague Amy Fry for the idea of offering this Kintsugi activity in the beginning of treatment as a beautiful way to talk about the process of therapy to a child. The therapist can choose whether to involve the parent in the introductory activity. Kintsugi is a Japanese art in which broken pottery is reassembled with gold filigree along the breaks, resulting in a piece of pottery that is now more beautiful than it was before it was ever broken. Kintsugi kits can be purchased in craft stores or online, and old cups, plates, or other types of pottery can be purchased at thrift stores to use for the activity. To introduce the activity, the therapist asks, "Do you ever feel broken?" The child or teen will usually say yes. (If the answer is no, suggest that everyone feels broken at some point in their lives.) Then say, "In Japan, the art of kintsugi uses broken cups and dishes to create beautiful art by repairing them with gold glue. The result is a piece of pottery that is more beautiful than before it was broken." The therapist invites the child or teen to use the hammer to break the pottery and reflects upon the hammer, and how it might represent the hard things that happen in life. They therapist asks what the child or teen thinks the gold glue might represent. (Friends and family members who love us? God? Therapy? Kids will have their own ideas.) Assembling the pieces requires some effort and patience, and as the therapist engages the child or teen in the process, they might say, "This requires a lot of patience, doesn't it? It takes time and effort to put the pieces together and create the artwork. But look, this is going to be so beautiful—even more beautiful than before. You know, it takes time, but if we're gentle and patient with ourselves, we can heal our broken parts the same way so that our specialness and goodness can really shine through."

WIDENING THEIR WINDOW

The first set of activities for children, adolescents, and their parents is designed to widen the window of tolerance for distress by improving their capacity for being self-aware, calming their body, reasoning, and problem solving.

The Language of the Window

When kids develop trust and experience parents as a source of safety due to positive family experiences early on, turning to others for support becomes natural, leading to enhanced tolerance for the ups and down of life. When children and teens hold a large store of disturbing attachment memories within their neural networks, along with brain changes caused by trauma, they are left unable to utilize parents or anyone else for comfort and support. Tolerance for distress becomes minimal. Much of life is spent in sympathetic nervous system activation or a shutdown or dissociated state, where they are unable to access the executive functions in their frontal brain for communicating, problem solving, and coping with emotion. The Language of the Window activity provides language kids and parents can use to begin understanding their struggles. Figures 5.1 and 5.2 provide visual aids that may be used during the Language of the Window activity.

The Language of the Window Script

Say to the child or teen and parents, "This picture shows what can happen in our body and our brain when we have a problem that causes big feelings (*pointing to Figure 5.1*). This middle window is the *calm window* (*pointing to the middle circle*). Even when something happens that makes us feel sad or mad or scared, when we stay in our calm window, we can think about the best way to handle the hard thing. That always works the best, right? But when things get really hard and we're super sad or mad or scared, our brain and body can get so worked up that we leave the calm window. We start moving into high alert like this dog up here is doing (*pointing*). When this happens, the fight-or-flight part of our brain is lighting up. If our brain and body feel overloaded by the fight-or-flight part of our brain, our brain and body can shut down. It looks like that's what's happening to this dog on the bottom (*pointing*). Now let's look at this other picture (*pointing to Figure 5.2*). Do you notice how this calm window is a lot bigger? I want to help you have a bigger calm window so it's easier for you to stay calm in your body and brain and think about the best way to manage the hard thing, even when your feelings get super big. We'll be practicing some breathwork and bodywork skills that can help the whole family with staying in the calm window. Now, what do you notice about the dog in the bigger calm window?" _____ "That's right! The dog in the bigger calm window is not alone! There's a cat with him there, helping him. Animals, kids, and adults all do better together. When we can talk to someone, it almost always helps our window get bigger. When our window is bigger, we can handle more things."

Following the explanation of the window of tolerance pictures, the therapist facilitates a discussion, asking the child or teen and parent to talk about what they notice in their body or in their brain when they're inside their calm window and outside their calm window. Next the child or teen and parent are invited to talk about how the parent might be able to recognize their child is struggling to stay in the calm window, how the child might communicate that they are struggling, and how the parent might be able to help.

Vignette With 12-Year-Old Jacob and His Dad

Jacob was adopted at age 4, and he claims that he has been "mad ever since." When triggered by a directive from either parent, Jacob usually yelled and argued, resulting in lengthy timeouts in his room.

Figure 5.1: "When my window is small, it's hard to handle things."
Source: Based on the concept as described by Ogden et al. (2006), Porges (2009), and Siegel (1999).

> **Therapist:** Remember this past week, when your dad asked you to empty all the bathroom trash cans and take the garbage out to the curb for pickup?
>
> **Jacob:** Yeah, I remember. I got really mad and told him that I hated him, and that it wasn't fair. I said no one else in the family has to take out the trash except me.
>
> **Therapist:** Yes, that did happen, and that wasn't very much fun for you or Dad, was it?
>
> **Jacob:** No. I wasn't allowed to play because of that.
>
> **Therapist:** Remember this window picture (*pointing to the window of*

IATP-C Foundational Family Therapy Activities   61

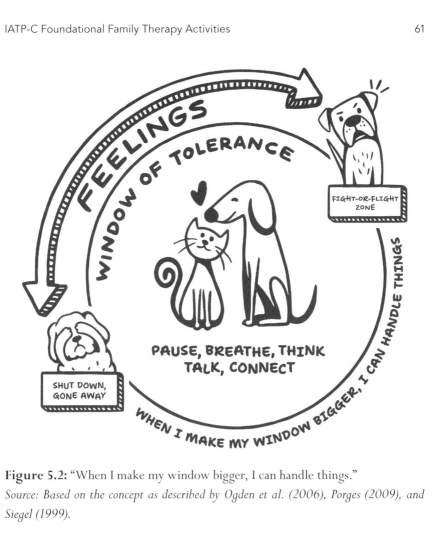

Figure 5.2: "When I make my window bigger, I can handle things."
Source: Based on the concept as described by Ogden et al. (2006), Porges (2009), and Siegel (1999).

    tolerance picture)? Would you say your brain and body got all worked up like this dog on top (*pointing*)? (*Jacob nods.*) I know that's a pretty miserable feeling. Sometimes it's so miserable that our brain and body get worn out and shut down like this dog down here (*pointing*). Dad, have you ever noticed that happening to Jacob?

Dad: Yes, in fact after his meltdown was over, he just wanted to go in his room by himself.

Therapist: Is that right, Jacob? (*Jacob nods.*) You know, everyone has this happen, sometimes. But we can learn and practice ways to help our window stay open. I try to practice keeping my window open, and it really helps me stay calm. Would you like to learn some ways to help you keep your window open? (*Jacob nods*.) Dad, does your window ever close? Would you like to learn how to keep it open?

Dad: Yes, I would. Sometimes I get impatient with Jacob when he's worked up. I guess you would say that when Jacob's window closes, my window sometimes closes, too. I'm not happy with myself when that happens.

The Pause

The pause is critical for self-awareness, self-regulation, and interruption of automatic reactions to triggers. None of us can mentalize or self-regulate without the capacity to pause. The pause gives us the opportunity to step back and rethink things or engage in some self-regulating breaths. The difficulty, of course, is that when our nervous system becomes activated, we become less able to reason and consider taking a pause, and for kids it's even more difficult. Kids often require a regulated parent to manage the situation until their nervous system calms. It's important to help parents have reasonable expectations regarding their child's capacity to utilize the pause. Parents need to understand that their own use of tools to self-regulate will allow them to coregulate their child, which strengthens the child's capacity to use the tools over time.

The Pause Script

The therapist pulls out the whiteboard or paper and draws a hill with a truck going down the hill. The therapist says, "Sometimes when we're triggered, we're moving outside our window of tolerance and into fight-or-flight so fast we're there before we know it. We're like a truck charging down a hill without the brakes, going faster and faster. If you're driving that truck, what do you do first thing so that the truck doesn't get out of control? _____ That's right. You want to push down on that brake and slow the truck down as early as you can. Well, our brains and bodies are like that truck. When we're triggered, we can get more and more worked up unless we put on the brakes and take a pause. How do we take a pause? We walk away and take a break. We may need to say, "I need to take a pause" so others know what we're doing. The pause helps us open our window wider and wider. Is the pause just for kids? _____ Right, it's for grown-ups, too. I have to use the pause a lot on some days. As we work together, I'll be reminding you about the pause. It won't be easy to take the pause when you find yourself getting worked up, but over time and with lots of practice, it will get easier."

Breathwork and Bodywork Activities

The following Breathwork and Bodywork activities are meant to be presented playfully and are just a start to helping the child or teen become more aware of their body and more proactive in shifting their state. The therapist prepares parents, explaining that the self-regulation activities will give their child more tools but won't replace their child's need for reassurance and coregulation from parents, based on the child's level of development.

Introducing Breathwork and Bodywork to Parents Script

Say to the parent, "Kids need their parents' help with managing upset feelings throughout their growing up years. We can't expect them to calm themselves like adults. However, the Breathwork and Bodywork activities provide kids and parents with a shared language and skills they can use at home to help manage those moments of dysregulation. Our goal is to make the activities fun and enjoyable to keep your child engaged. We won't tell them they have to practice activities as homework, because the word homework can be a trigger. And we certainly can't expect them to practice the activities when they're already in a highly dysregulated state, because that won't be possible. But it's okay to playfully practice the skills at home when your child is calm and receptive and to show them that you're practicing the methods for yourself. When your child is triggered, you'll want to focus on using the skills to keep yourself regulated so you can attune and connect."

When the child or teen joins the session, the therapist introduces the bodywork activities playfully.

Teaching Breathwork Script

Say to the family, "We can all can learn to breathe to help our bodies relax and to help us keep our calm window open. I'm going to show you an easy breath activity that can really help us calm down. Here we go. Everybody, take in a great big breath. Hold it, hold it, don't let it out, and now take an extra sip of breath, and then another sip. Okay, *now* blow it out in a big huff. Great! Let's practice again, okay? Here we go, big breath in. (*All practice together, then repeat once or twice. Invite everyone to notice how they feel.*) Let's try another one. Let's all lie back in our chairs (*or lie on the floor*). Everyone, place your hand on your stomach like this (*demonstrating*). Now practice breathing in, nice and big, so that the upper part of your stomach, called the diaphragm, fills up with air, like a balloon. Hold it, hold it, now let it out. Now just breathe nice and easy, in and out, and notice your hand moving with each breath. That's right. How do you feel?"

With younger children, you can place a toy on their belly and ask them to take a big breath, watching the toy move as their belly fills with air.

Bodywork Activity: The Cooked Noodle

Another fun skill is the Cooked Noodle. Younger children are fascinated by the therapist's comparison of the body with spaghetti noodles. The therapist can get the whole family involved in a playful demonstration. Even adolescents often enjoy the metaphor of the uncooked spaghetti noodle and the cooked spaghetti noodle.

Cooked Noodle Vignette With 7-Year-Old Maya and Her Dad

Therapist: Have you ever eaten spaghetti?

Maya: Yeah, I've eaten spaghetti.

Therapist: What does an uncooked noodle look like or feel like?

[It can be helpful to keep a package of uncooked spaghetti noodles in the office as a visual aid. Some cooked noodles can also be prepared ahead of time.]

Maya: It's hard.

Therapist: What happens if you bend a piece of uncooked spaghetti?

Maya: It breaks.

Therapist: You're right, and it usually flies all over the place. Now, let's compare an uncooked piece of spaghetti to a cooked piece. What's the difference?

Maya: The cooked piece is warm and soft.

Therapist: Can it bend?

Maya: Yeah.

Therapist: Let's imagine your body is a spaghetti noodle. (*The therapist instructs Maya to lie on the floor and invites her dad to come down on the floor next to her. The therapist asks Maya to stiffen her body and pretend to be an uncooked noodle. The therapist asks Maya's permission to lift Maya's arm and leg and see how stiff or flexible it is.*) What does your body feel like as an uncooked noodle?

Maya: I feel stiff.

Therapist: Is it a comfortable feeling or an uncomfortable feeling?

Maya: It's not comfortable.

Therapist: Okay, let's see if you changing your body to feel like a cooked noodle is more comfortable. Pretend your arms and legs and your whole body are like a cooked, squishy noodle. Maya, what does your body feel like now?

Maya: It feels comfortable. I could go to sleep.

Therapist: (*The therapist asks Maya's permission to lift Maya's arm for the cooked noodle test.*) Wow, look at that, your arm is so relaxed! (*The therapist explains to Maya and her dad that relaxing the body also relaxes the brain. The therapist explains that Cooked Noodle and the big breaths are different methods to make our window stay wider. Maya has trouble with sleep, and the therapist suggests Dad and Maya might enjoy doing belly breath and cooked noodle together at bedtime as an experiment to see if Maya sleeps better—but only if they both want to.*)

Optional Bodywork Activity: What Do You Notice?

Some kids with a history of abuse or neglect learned to dissociate from their body state to cope. Some kids have no awareness of being hungry or full or when they need to go to the bathroom, and they can't respond to questions regarding body sensations or where they feel an emotion in their body. The IATP-C therapist encourages the child or teen to observe various sensations, such as the sensation of various items against their skin, the body sensations associated with drinking hot chocolate or cold milk, and the sensations related to holding a rock versus holding a feather. The therapist teaches the child about all five senses and how the body experiences each of them.

The What Do You Notice? activity involves the therapist, parent, and child taking turns, sharing something they notice about any part of their body. It's playful and fun and a simple way to encourage body awareness.

What Do You Notice? Vignette With 9-Year-Old Latasha and Her Mother

Therapist: In this game, we all take turns just noticing something about a feeling in some part of our body. I'll start. Hmm, let's see, I notice my pants are tickling my ankles.

Mom: I notice I can feel my bracelet on my wrist.

Latasha: I notice my stomach.

Therapist: Is there anything that your stomach is feeling?
Latasha: Um, it's hungry.
Therapist: Hey, that's funny. My stomach is hungry too!
Mom: My arms and legs are kind of cold. I should have worn a sweater.
Latasha: I have on a sweater!
Mom: Do you feel warm in your sweater?
Latasha: Yes, I do!

Brainwork Activities

Brainwork assists kids with the mentalization skill of thinking about their thinking. The activities encourage them to pay attention to their thoughts, to reflect on them and to reason with themselves.

Thinking Brain, Feeling Brain Activity

The Thinking Brain, Feeling Brain activity is a beginning step toward mentalization. The IATP-C therapist creates a very simple drawing of the right and left hemispheres of the brain, explaining that the left front part is in general the logical, thinking part of the brain, while the right side is the center of big feelings—enjoyable feelings as well as upsetting feelings and upsetting thoughts. In the next part of the brainwork activity, the family therapist teaches the child that they can use their thinking brain to talk to their feeling brain rather than letting the feeling brain be the boss. The therapist can use themselves as an example and describe times when they talked to their feeling brain to cope with a difficult situation. They can also invite the parent to give their own examples. Figure 5.3 provides a visual aid for the Thinking Brain, Feeling Brain activity. The following vignettes illustrate this brainwork activity.

Thinking Brain, Feeling Brain Vignette With 13-Year-Old Anton and His Dad

Therapist: I'm going to draw an extremely simple version of the brain. (*The therapist draws a circle to represent looking down upon the right and left sides of the brain.*) This left front part of the brain is the logical, thinking part of the brain. This right side is more about feelings—automatic feelings that happen before we know it. We need our feelings. Feelings are very important and sometimes really enjoyable. Can you give me an example of when you were experiencing some enjoyable feelings?

IATP-C Foundational Family Therapy Activities 67

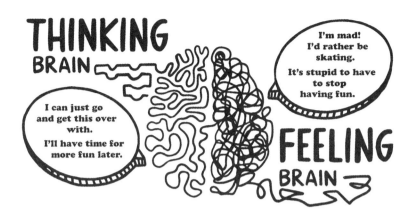

Figure 5.3: Thinking Brain, Feeling Brain

Anton: Yesterday, I did an awesome move on my skateboard.

Therapist: Very cool. I'll bet all your excitement and happiness circuits were all lit up in the feelings side, here. Sometimes feelings are not so fun and we have to manage them. Can you give me an example of an experience in which you had not-so-fun feelings?

Anton: *(Looking at his dad.)* Yeah. Probably just before we came here.

Dad: *(Nodding.)* Anthony was on his skateboard and didn't want to leave when it was time to come here for therapy. He had a small meltdown before he got in the car.

Therapist: Okay, this is actually a great example. I'll write down the feelings you had on the right side of this brain drawing of mine. Can you remember what they were, Anton?

Anton: Uh, like, mad, you know, I'd rather be skating, no offense, you're cool and all, but I'd rather be skating and it's stupid to have to stop doing something fun.

Therapist: That's it! I'm writing down on the feelings side of this brain drawing, "Mad. I'd rather be skating. It's stupid to have to stop having fun." Sound about right? *(Anton nods.)* And you had a bit of a meltdown, but then you calmed down, which is very impressive. Can you remember what was going on in your thinking brain?

Anton: Uh, I just knew Dad was going to make a big deal of it, and if I just came and got it over with, I'd have more time to skate later, you know?

Therapist: Your thinking brain kicked in there with some really helpful thoughts. I'm writing them down here on the left brain side: "I can just go and get it over with and have more time to skate later." Sound good? (*Anton nods.*) So, this is a great example of your right side feeling brain having some really upset feelings and thoughts and your left side thinking brain helping out with some very impressive logic.

The therapist next asked Anton for an example of a time when his feeling brain was hijacking his thinking brain, causing some troubles. Anton remembered smarting off to his algebra teacher because he didn't want to do the homework assignment, leading to a detention. The therapist wrote the upset thoughts and feelings on the right brain side of the brain drawing: "It's not fair! Homework is mean! I won't do it!" Next, the therapist asked Anton, "Can you write down some thoughts that might have been helpful over on the thinking brain side?" Anton wrote on the left side of the brain drawing: "Everybody has to do homework. I can ask for help if I need to." The therapist asked Anton how things would have worked out if he'd taken a pause and a breath and talked back to his feeling brain with the helpful thoughts.

Demonstration With Anton's Dad

Therapist: Dad, can you think of a time when your feeling brain got all lit up and you had a hard time managing a situation in the right way?

Dad: Sure, like when Anton wouldn't get in the car today, his feeling brain was lit up but mine got all lit up, too.

Therapist: (*Drawing a quick oval to represent Dad's brain.*) What were your big feelings and upset thoughts, Dad?

Dad: Well, I felt frustrated, that's for sure.

Therapist: (*Writing "frustrated" on the right side.*) And what were your frustrated thoughts?

Dad: My immediate frustrated thought was, "Anton doesn't respect me."

Therapist: (*Writing Dad's thought on the right brain side.*) Any other upset thoughts in your feeling brain?

Dad: I think my brain says, "I'm a failure as a dad."

Therapist: (*Nodding and writing the thought.*) A lot of parents get that upset thought. For all of us, when our feeling brain is activated, it can be helpful to take that pause, to step away for a few seconds and take a big breath as we've been learning, and then find those helpful thoughts. I try to do this myself, and it's not always easy but it can really help. Dad, if you could have paused, would it have helped?

Dad: Yeah, I think so. My thinking brain could have caught up to the situation and said, "I'm a good dad, Anton's a great kid, he's just having a hard time." I think that would have helped me stay calmer in the moment.

Optional Brain Activity: Stuck Memories

The IATP-C therapist uses clinical judgment to determine if or when the child or teen is ready for a simple teaching activity regarding stuck memories. The therapist uses the feeling brain, thinking brain drawing and explains that *upsetting* or *yucky* feelings and thoughts can get *stuck* in the downstairs part of the brain. Alternatively, the therapist can make a model of the brain with clay and use a small piece of paper inserted into the clay to represent the stuck memory, feelings, and thoughts.

Stuck Memories Vignette With 13-Year-Old Anton and His Dad

Therapist: Sometimes, when something very upsetting and confusing happens, the upsetting memory and the feelings connected to the memory can get stuck in the lower part of the brain, tucked in way back here. (*The therapist makes a quick clay model of the brain and then inserts a piece of paper into the clay to represent the child's memory stored in the downstairs brain.*) This piece of paper holds the memory of what happened along with the yucky feelings and thoughts. Are you with me so far? (*Anton nods.*) Okay, great. The word we use to describe really upsetting memories is *trauma*. Let's call this little spot in the back of the brain the trauma brain. When something happens at school or home, even something small and no big deal, it can remind the trauma brain of what happened before (*pulls out the paper representing the trauma memory*) and the yucky feelings and thoughts can get triggered. For example, you remember being hungry when you were little, right? (*Anton nods and the therapist sticks the paper back into the clay model of the brain.*) What happens when you see food in your kitchen at home?

Anton: I feel like I have to take it and hide it.

Therapist: That's right! Your trauma brain lights up and your feeling brain says, *I won't get enough of this food if I don't take it!*
Anton: Yeah.
Therapist: And right now, while you're sitting here with your dad and me, what does your thinking brain say about that?
Anton: Well, I do always get enough to eat.
Therapist: That's right! You do get enough to eat now, don't you? But when your brain is triggered, your feeling brain is like a bully to your thinking brain. It sort of overrules your thinking brain in that moment. Do you think the next time these yucky feelings and thoughts get triggered, you could take a pause? Could you step away, take a breath, and ask your thinking brain for help?

High-Alert, Low-Alert Language

When the window of tolerance is narrow and the sympathetic nervous system is on overdrive, our thoughts and perceptions will automatically match what is happening in our body. The High-Alert, Low-Alert activity facilitates mentalization. It encourages nonjudgmental language that helps traumatized children and teens with awareness of their internal state and provides parents with words to help them assist their child in a supportive manner. The high-alert, low-alert language is introduced by drawing what looks like a thermometer on a whiteboard or on paper and labeling "low alert," "medium alert," and "high alert."

The therapist, child, and parents discuss each term, identifying body sensations associated with each state. The therapist can take the lead, sharing how their shoulders might start to feel tight and their thoughts might race as they move toward high alert. They can also talk about the situation in terms of the feeling brain and thinking brain, noting that on high alert, the feeling brain assumes every situation is a big deal. On low alert, the thinking brain can recognize most situations are a little deal.

The therapist and child or teen can brainstorm strategies they might use to bring themselves to low alert, such as the pause, breath and bodywork, and talking to the brain.

Parents can use this neutral language at home to encourage the child to use skills by simply saying, "I think we're both moving into high alert as we talked about in therapy. How about we both take a pause and take a breath?"

High-Alert, Low-Alert Vignette With 8-Year-Old Jolie and Her Mom
>**Therapist:** It sounds as if your body and your brain go to high alert when the neighbor kids come over to play.
>
>**Jolie:** Well, they want to play tag, and I don't want to.
>
>**Therapist:** Well, what does your body look like and do when you don't want to play tag?
>
>**Jolie:** (*Starting to feel some shame, Jolie moves closer to her mother.*) I don't know.
>
>**Therapist:** Jolie, you are not in trouble. We're just trying to solve a problem. It looks like you want your friends to play with you, but sometimes your high alert gets in the way. We want to help make that better for you.
>
>**Jolie:** It looks like I'm mad, and I yell at them.
>
>**Therapist:** Okay, that's just your high alert turning on. Let's find ways to notice your high alert and practice calming down.

As the session progressed, the therapist drew a gauge on the dry erase board with high alert written at the top and low alert written at the bottom. The therapist, Jolie, and Mom brainstormed signs of high alert and low alert and calming thoughts and behaviors Jolie could practice to keep herself in low alert.

At the end of the session, the therapist asked Jolie and her mother to practice paying attention to the high-alert and low-alert signals in between sessions. A possible scenario of noticing high-alert signals was practiced with a role-play.

Facts About Feelings

Kids who've been unable or unwilling to receive emotional support from parents naturally learn to fear the emotions and sensations that arise inside of them. Obviously, this narrows their window of tolerance. The Facts About Feelings Activity can reduce their fear through the skill of mindful, nonjudgmental, awareness of feelings and increased confidence that their feelings aren't dangerous.

Conducting the teaching activity in the context of the family session allows parents and kids to speak the same mindfulness language and encourages parents to use mindfulness skills for themselves.

Facts About Feelings Script

Say to the family, "I want to talk with all of you about some really important facts about feelings."

If the child* can read, write a simplified version of the facts on the whiteboard:

1. *Everyone has feelings.*
2. *They don't hurt us.*
3. *Feelings come and go.*
4. *We can ride out our feelings.*

Point to fact number 1. "Everyone has feelings. Feelings are not good or bad."

Point to fact number 2. "Feelings don't hurt us. Feelings can be uncomfortable, but when we have feelings, we're still okay."

Point to fact number 3. "Feelings come and go like waves of the ocean. We can ride out our feelings like riding out waves in the ocean with a surfboard. They sometimes get really big for a time, but in a while, they'll grow smaller, and then our bodies will calm down and they'll go away."

Point to fact number 4. "We can ride out our feelings until they get better. If we take a pause, we can use bodywork and brainwork to help. We can ride out the wave more easily when we use big breaths, use cooked noodle, talk to our brain, or ask a parent or other grown-up for help."

Feelings Faces

The therapist can use cards with faces of kids or animals illustrating various feelings or make drawings of various faces and hold up one face at a time to talk about each one, naming the feeling, imagining the situation, and reminding the child of the facts. This is a nonthreatening way to help children gain comfort with feelings.

Feelings Faces Script

Say to the child, "What is the puppy on this card feeling? _____ How can you tell? _____ What do you suppose happened to cause the feeling? _____ Does everyone have this feeling sometimes? _____ Yes, that's

---

* IATP-C therapist Teresa Brown and Jason Williams created a book titled *Feelings, Feelings, Feelings* to help very young children with facts about feelings. See Appendix H for a list of books to use with very young children.

right, they sure do. I know I do. Feelings are not good or bad, they're just feelings. Can this puppy have this feeling and be okay? _____ Yes he can, can't he? The feeling won't hurt him, and the feeling won't stay. Feelings come and go like ocean waves. They get big and then they get small. What might he do to help him with this feeling? _____ You're right! That would help a lot! What might happen to change this feeling? _____ Yes, that would change his feeling!"

Facts About Feelings Teen Script

Say to the teen, "Perhaps you can notice all the feelings that you have the rest of today. See if you can put words to the feelings and notice how long they last. If you don't like a feeling, see if you can help the feeling by talking to your brain or working with your breathing skills. We can talk about what you noticed next week."

Recognizing Their Biggest Kid Self

Chronic attachment trauma interferes with developmental maturation. Furthermore, kids who experienced chronic attachment trauma have had little opportunity to internalize a positive view of themselves as reflected by an attuned and nurturing parent. The *biggest kid self* activity is designed to help children come to recognize and strengthen their most mature state by asking the child or teen and parents to describe moments in which the child was operating from their biggest kid self. The child or teen and parent are encouraged to really celebrate these positive moments. Reinforcement of this positive state encourages the child to stay grounded and more confident about managing events day-to-day and develop a more positive self-image as seen through the eyes of their parent. This activity is repeated throughout treatment to provide further reinforcement of the biggest kid self and reduction of patterns of regression or dissociation. (Later, the biggest kid self is strengthened with slow bilateral stimulation [BLS] as part of the EMDR foundational activities.)

Vignette With 8-Year-Old Lala and Her Grandmother

Therapist to Lala: We all have times when we feel bigger and more confident. We feel more sure that we can handle things in a good way. We all have other times when we don't feel big and it's harder to handle things. What I've discovered is that we can strengthen our biggest self so we can handle things better. Lala, let's start today by helping you think about your most 8-year-old self. Would that be okay with you? (*Lala nods.*)

Therapist to Grandmother: Grandma, what is an example of a time you noticed Lala was in her biggest 8-year-old self? Perhaps a time when she was making good decisions and handling something in a good way?

Grandmother: I'd say yesterday when she got up for school. She got dressed and ate and brushed her teeth without any fuss. I almost took her temperature to see if there was something wrong with her!

Therapist to Grandmother: But you weren't unhappy, were you?

Grandmother: No, I felt happy and proud.

Therapist to Lala: Do you remember how you were getting ready in your most 8-year-old self yesterday? (*Lala nods.*) How does it feel inside when you think about that?

Lala: Good. Like I'm more grown-up.

Therapist to Lala: When you think about yesterday morning, how does it make you want to hold your body?"

Lala: (*Sits up very straight.*) Like this. I feel taller.

Therapist to Lala: Do you like how that feels? (*Lala nods.*) I'd love to help you have this great 8-year-old more grown-up feeling more often. Do you think your window might stay more open when you're in your biggest 8-year-old self? (*Lala nods.*) So do I!

Therapist to Grandmother: Grandma, perhaps you could help her notice when she's in her 8-year-old self at home and remind her how wonderful it is for you to see. Would you be able to do that? It could be really helpful. (*Grandma agrees. The therapist and Lala make a sand tray picture about her big 8-year-old self and Lala wants to write a short story about it.*)

Introducing the Biggest Kid Self to Teens Script

Say to the teen, "Can you think of a situation in which you felt like you were in your most mature self, feeling more competent and confident? _____ Can you tell me about it? _____ When you think about that situation and your most mature self, how does it make you feel? _____ What body posture do you think is most associated with your more mature, confident self? _____ In a situation where you were having a hard day, like maybe at school, do you suppose it could help to think of this mature self and find that confident body posture? _____ It might be really interesting to experiment with it. Do you suppose you might try, and let me know what happens?"_____

NAVIGATING THEIR INSIDE WORLD

Children and teens are confused by their feelings, their struggles, and their past experiences. The activities in this section help kids gain compassion for themselves as they look at what babies need, how babies learn to trust, and what can go wrong. If they're ready, the therapist can provide additional adaptive information to help kids gain a simple, nonjudgmental understanding of the struggles of their parents to give them what they needed when they were little. This brief look at their early life (without too much detail) leads into the Smaller Child on the Inside activity in which parents and kids gain understanding that early thoughts and feelings are carried into present day as the smaller part of self on the inside.

What Babies Need

This activity involves teaching kids and their parents about what babies need and why some babies learn to trust and some babies learn not to trust. The IATP-C therapist is careful to take a compassionate approach when it comes to explaining the reasons why some parents can't give babies what they need. In the case of children who are placed outside of their biological homes, parents may need some reminders during one-on-one time regarding the importance of taking a nonjudgmental approach toward biological parents.

With younger children, a baby doll may help with the discussion. With older children and teens, the therapist can list what babies need on a whiteboard. The therapist invites the parents to contribute to the discussion regarding what babies need. During the discussion, they are guided to recognize that the baby is good and lovable no matter what, although the baby may feel to blame.

What Babies Need Vignette With 9-Year-Old Lisa and Her Mom

Lisa was neglected as an infant in her biological home. The therapist brings out a baby doll wrapped in a blanket to use as a prop during the discussion.

    Lisa: What are we going to do with the baby?
    Therapist: Well, I thought we could spend some time thinking about what babies need. What do you think babies need, Lisa?
    Lisa: They need a bottle.

Therapist: Yes, that's right, they do need a bottle. Do they just need one in a day or how many do you think?

Lisa: They need three.

Therapist: Only three . . . did you know that a tiny baby eats every three or four hours? Plus, they need to be held and cuddled to feel warm and feel safe.

Lisa: Wow, I didn't know that.

Therapist: Yes, they do. What else do babies need?

Lisa: Clean pants.

Therapist: Yes, that's right. How does a baby ask for what it needs? Does it say, "Hey, Mom, I'm hungry"?

Lisa: No, a baby can't talk. It cries.

Therapist: Yes, you are so smart. Did you know that a mom and a dad learn to understand the baby's cry? They can tell if the baby is crying because the baby is hungry, or tired, or needs some attention.

Lisa: That's cool. (*Turning toward her adoptive mom.*) Did I do that?

Mom: Well, Lisa, you didn't live with me when you were a tiny baby, but I know that is what you did. If I'd had you as a tiny baby, I know that I would have known why you were crying.

Therapist: That's right, Mom, I bet you would have. When moms or dads know what babies need and give them food and blankets and fresh diapers and cuddles, their babies learn they can trust grown-ups to take care of them, and they learn the world is pretty safe. But sometimes moms and dads have troubles that cause their brain to be mixed-up about how to care for their babies. Then their babies think that they can't trust any grown-ups to care for them or keep them safe, and that's kind of hard for those babies. How about we pretend to give this baby doll everything she needs so she can learn to trust?

Lisa: Can I give her this bottle?

Optional: Providing Information About the Biological Parents

In the case of foster or adopted children and teens, the therapist uses clinical judgment to determine if, at this early stage of therapy, the child is ready for the therapist to directly tie What Babies Need to the child's early life experiences. If so, it may be a time to provide a little more information related to their biological parents' inability to care for them. Some kids are struggling with misunderstandings and confusion about their past and need some simple adaptive information sooner rather than later. The therapist should keep the explanations simple, compassionate, and brief to avoid triggering trauma and related feelings at this point. During one-on-one time with the parent, the therapist emphasizes the importance of showing compassion for the child's biological parents despite their mistakes. When adoptive or foster parents show judgments, kids often believe they must pick a side, which increases confusion and anger. Kids relax when their adoptive or foster parents reassure them that it's okay to feel love for all the parents in their lives.

The following are some sample scripts for some of the situations with kids affected by attachment trauma.

Early Maltreatment Sample Script

Say to the child or adolescent, "I want you to remember that you were born lovable and loving. Your first parents couldn't give you all the good care that all babies need because they had struggles with their thinking and feeling brain. They *[had addiction, mental illness, intellectual disability; didn't learn good ways to care for kids when they were kids; were so young]*. People recognized what was happening and found you a safe place. You were a wonderful little child and you deserved to have everything you needed."

Explaining Other Causes for the Early Trauma

In the case of relinquishment of care, the therapist may explain, "Your parent knew they wouldn't be able to give you what all babies need, and they loved you too much to let that happen, so they made a plan for you."

In situations where the child lives with biological parents who have worked on themselves and made changes, the therapist may say, "Your mom/dad is very concerned that they didn't give you what you needed back then. They loved you and worked hard to get better, and now they're doing a much better job meeting your needs, but it's still hard for them sometimes and it's still hard for you to trust. We'll all work together to make things better."

In the case of medical trauma, the therapist may say, "Your parents did everything they could, but your medical needs got in the way. You were suffering and the doctors and your parents were working hard to help you, but you were just a baby and didn't understand what was happening. You might have thought your parents didn't care about how bad you felt."

Recognizing and Appreciating the Smaller Child on the Inside

We all have feelings and perceptions from our childhood years stored within our memory networks that can get activated at times, causing a shift in our emotions or thoughts. For kids with attachment injuries, this can easily cause pronounced shifts in affect state and perceptions we conceptualize as a hurt younger part of the self or ego state. Helping the child or teen reflect upon the smaller child on the inside is a compassionate and gentle way to address the phenomenon. This smaller part of the self lacks time orientation and operates from an earlier time period when life wasn't safe. Both parents and kids tend to instinctively understand this concept, and they are encouraged to work together to help the smaller child on the inside. A hands-on method of helping the child or teen understand this important concept is through the use of nesting dolls as a visual aid. (These dolls can be found at some toy stores or through an online toy company. In our offices, we have traditional nesting dolls as well as nesting penguins, nesting owls, nesting dinosaurs, and more.) The therapist takes the nesting dolls apart and lines them up from biggest to smallest while explaining the concept of the smaller part of self on the inside. The therapist emphasizes compassion and appreciation for the younger self while emphasizing time orientation and safety in present day.

The IATP-C therapist encourages the child or teen to provide reassuring and compassionate messages to the vulnerable younger part of themselves. The therapist describes "what I would want your smaller self to know" and also invites the parent to talk about what the parent would want the smaller self to know. This may include reassurance that the child is bigger now, that the child is safe now, that the child is good and lovable, and that the younger part of self doesn't have to be vigilant anymore.

The IATP-C therapist conceptualizes behaviors such as taking things without permission, lying, or aggression as behaviors that the smaller part of self discovered as a way to feel safe when life was hard. This compassionate understanding for the behaviors simultaneously diminishes the child's shame and guilt while encouraging mindful awareness and reflection. It also increases attunement and compassion within the parent. The therapist can encourage the child or teen to give messages of appreciation for whatever the smaller part did to survive while reminding the smaller part that the bigger kid self is learning better ways.

Smaller Child on the Inside Script

Say to the child or teen and parent, "We all tend to carry hurt or sad or scared feelings from when we were very little inside our hearts. The old feelings of the smaller child part of us get triggered sometimes, and at those times, it's not unusual to feel like that littler child again. Look at these nesting dolls. When I take them apart, I find littler ones on the inside. Do you want to help me line them up from biggest to smallest? _____ So the biggest one is like your biggest self, as you are here in my office today. (*If needed, the therapist can assist the child with accessing the biggest self through a confident posture or a positive memory.*) These littler dolls are like the littler parts of us on the inside who sometimes get triggered. When that happens, it's very common to feel the feelings of the littler child on the inside. Sometimes the smaller part of us learned they had to protect themselves by showing anger or taking things or making up lies because people around them made them feel unsafe. Later on it can be hard to give up the old ways. Do you think you might have done any of those things when you were little?" _____ "We need to be kind and patient with this littler one. I appreciate the younger part of you for trying to feel safe that way. Mom/Dad, do you appreciate how the younger part tried to feel safe back when things weren't safe?" _____ "Perhaps we can all say thank you to the younger part for trying to feel safe. We can also let the smaller part know that those things aren't helpful anymore, and we're working on new ways you can feel safe. We also want this smaller part to feel good and know that today everything is okay. You can just think these things in your mind if you like or you can say them aloud." (*Therapist models and dialogues aloud to the smaller part.*)

Smaller Child on the Inside Vignette With 9-Year-Old Emily and Her Mom

Emily was severely neglected and malnourished before moving to her adoptive home at age 2 ½. Emily's mother entered the session very frustrated that Emily took food from the kitchen and hid it in her room. The family therapist had previously used the nesting dolls to teach Emily and her mom about the smaller child parts on the inside. Now the therapist initiates compassionate dialogue with the younger child part.

Mom: This week, when I went in Emily's closet to put away some shoes, I found an empty box of graham crackers—again! We had just bought the box of crackers a couple of days before.

Emily: (*Hanging her head.*) I got hungry the other night, and you were too busy on the computer, Mom, so I just took the box of crackers into my room, and now they're all gone.

Therapist: Mom, were you too busy to answer Emily's question about the crackers?

Mom: No, of course not. Emily knows that she can always ask me for things. She may have to wait a minute, but I always have time to help her.

Family Therapist: (*Setting out the nesting dolls.*) Let's use these dolls again and see if we can figure out what is going on. (*Picks up one of the smallest nesting dolls.*) Emily, I'll bet 2-year-old Emily inside your heart still worries about whether or not there's going to be enough food. I think the little Emily felt hungry a lot. (*Speaking to the 2-year-old Emily doll.*) Is this true, little Emily?

Emily: (*Nodding.*) Yes, that's true. My mom sometimes forgot to feed me.

Therapist: (*Still addressing the little Emily doll.*) Little Emily, now that you're living with this mom and dad, do you still think that sometimes you have to sneak food and eat it in your closet because you're worried that this mom is going to forget to feed you?

Emily: (*Speaking for the 2-year-old doll.*) Yes, that's true. She is too busy to feed me.

Therapist: (*Picking up the 9-year-old Emily doll.*) Is this true, 9-year-old Emily?

Emily: (*Shrugs her shoulders, and the therapist waits quietly.*) No, that's not true. I know I can ask my mom if I can have a snack.

Therapist: I think the little Emily still gets scared and worried that there won't be enough food, and this is when she goes and gets things for herself without asking.

Emily: I think so, too.

Therapist: (*Handing the 2-year-old Emily doll to Mom for her to hold.*) Mom, what would you say to little 2-year-old Emily?

Mom: (*Speaking to the little doll in her hand.*) I would say, "Emily, you don't have to worry anymore. I'll always remember to feed you, and if you are still hungry, no matter what I'm doing, you can always ask me for food."

Therapist: Emily, did you hear what your mom said to little Emily? Do you think little Emily thinks this is true?

Emily: Yes . . . I don't know.

Therapist: Let's let the 9-year-old Emily talk to the little Emily and remind her that it is true that her forever mom will always feed her, and that she can ask for food when she's hungry. (*Picks up the 9-year-old Emily doll and pretends that the bigger doll is speaking to the 2-year-old Emily doll that the mom is holding.*) "Little Emily, it's okay. Now you're safe with your forever mom and dad who love you and will always feed you. Little Emily, it's okay to ask for food if you're hungry. You're safe now." (*Emily watches and listens intently. The therapist looks at her.*) Okay, big 9-year-old Emily, can you talk to little Emily?

Emily: (*Speaking to the 2-year-old Emily doll.*) "Okay, little Emily, you're safe now. You can ask for snacks and you don't have to sneak stuff."

Therapist: (*Setting the dolls aside.*) Now, let's practice for real. Nine-year-old Emily, please ask your mom for a snack.

Emily: Mom, can I have a snack?

Mom: Of course, you can. What do you think would be a good choice?

Emily is encouraged to experiment with asking for snacks at home from her biggest kid self.

Expressing Appreciation Vignette With 16-Year-Old Davey

Davey was easily triggered and grew angry when he was corrected by his mom. He had experienced abuse from his biological mother. The IATP-C therapist helped Davey address the behavior through the smaller child part on the inside.

Therapist: Davey, what do you suppose was the trigger when you blew up at your mom this morning?

Davey: Mom told me to hurry up and get in the car. I think it was her tone of voice that triggered me. I thought she was being mean.

Therapist: What do you think about that right now?

Davey: Well, I guess that Mom just wanted me to be on time for school. I guess she was trying to help me.

Therapist: Do you think those mistrusting feelings might have been coming from toddler Davey?

Davey: Yeah, toddler Davey is a real pain.

Therapist: No, toddler Davey really is not a pain at all. Let's remember that the toddler part of you had to be wary of grown-ups, because some of the grown-ups in your life back when you were little weren't always safe to be with. The toddler part of you used anger as a way to try to stay safe. I think we should thank the smaller Davey on the inside for working so hard to stay safe. We need to help him understand that today he is safe and let him know that he can stay in the safe place, and that big Davey can handle life now.

Attuning and Nuancing Language for the Individual Child or Teen

The IATP-C therapist always attunes to the individual child or teen. For example, if the child or teen is not receptive to discussing a smaller child part on the inside or not able to comprehend the concept due to developmental deficits and inability to comprehend abstract ideas or create a mental picture, the IATP-C therapist can adapt their language and instead refer to the biggest kid part of the brain and the smaller kid part of the brain. The therapist may say, for example, "Here's another way to explain this that you might like better. You have a biggest kid part of your brain. That part of your brain may know, for example, that it's a good thing to finish homework or brush your teeth. The smaller kid part of your brain may sometimes get triggered, though, and forget about the things that are helpful. But we'll work together to calm that smaller kid part of your brain and help you stay in your biggest kid brain to think and solve problems."

STRENGTHENING THEIR RELATIONSHIPS

The activities in this section help strengthen closeness and safety between kids and parents through relational games, through helping kids understand the why behind the actions of their present-day parents, and through communication skills and other day-to-day skills for improved relationships.

Relational Games

You may have a number of relational games you love and use regularly. Please incorporate any playful activities you find helpful for creating positive and playful feelings of connection between kids and parents. Encourage parents to incorporate relational games at home to create a sense of connection and security at any time, but especially during daily transitions in which kids and parents are separating or coming back together, such as first thing in the morning, after school, and at bedtime. The following are some of the activities we love to use:

- *Rock, paper, scissors.* Who hasn't played this one while growing up? Parents can use it later to keep a positive connection while sitting in a waiting room, waiting in line, or waiting to be served at a restaurant.
- *Guess what I'm drawing on your back?* Parents and kids take turns drawing shapes or letters with their finger on each other's back.
- *Pretend face painting.* Parents and kids take turns fake painting one another's faces with a finger as they describe the colors and shapes their pretending to create.
- *Mirroring games.* Parents and kids take turns making faces or making movements with their whole bodies and being the mirror, following along.
- *Noncompetitive board games.* For example: *Obstacles, Hoot Owl Hoot, Dinosaur Escape, Feed the Woozle, Mermaid Island,* and *Chicken Soup for the Soul.*
- *Creating with blocks, Legos, or clay.*

The Jobs of Moms and Dads

Kids with attachment injuries are often driven by negative beliefs such as "My mom is mean" or "My dad is mean" and "I can't trust them." The result is an assumption that their parents are not on their side but are out to get them. The child or adolescent interprets directions, corrections, or requests as evidence they don't care about their happiness.

Parents typically have no idea their child holds such beliefs and so they become frustrated, angry, and often punitive, which reinforces the negative thoughts. The Jobs of Moms and Dads activity helps the parents understand their child's negative assumptions and helps the child or teen recognize the positive reasons for their parents' actions and words.

During one-on-one time with the parents before the session, the therapist explains the activity and lets the parent know that articulating their intentions will help build trust. Parents often protest initially, saying something like, "I've done so much for my child, there's no way he thinks like this." The therapist reminds parents that their parenting behaviors automatically trigger their child's trauma brain, which hijacks the child's logical thinking brain. Essentially, the child is operating as if the past traumas are not over. The IATP-C therapist says

"EMDR therapy will help heal those old memories, but first, we have to front-load your child's brain with the correct information."

When the child or teen joins the session, the family therapist involves the parent and child in making a list on the whiteboard identifying the Jobs of Moms and Dads. The therapist gets as much input as possible from them before providing the information directly. The list will look something like this:

They keep me safe
- Riding in the car
- Crossing the street
- Safe house
- Safe neighborhood

They keep me healthy
- Brushing teeth
- Shower
- Doctor appointments
- Medicine
- Healthy food
- Enough sleep

They teach me how to get along with others
- Sharing
- Taking turns
- Listening
- Polite words

They teach me how to take care of my things so I can live on my own someday
- Chores
- Cleaning my room and putting things away
- Organizing

They provide for my needs
- Clothing
- House

- Food
- Transportation

They help me have a smart brain
- Getting to school on time
- Doing my homework
- Encouraging cooperation with my teachers
- Attending parent–teacher conferences
- Managing screen time

Jobs of Moms and Dads Vignette With 15-Year-Old Andres
Some of Andres's sessions are individual sessions without either of his mothers present due to his desire for independence. This is a session conducted one-on-one, without his moms in the room.

> **Therapist:** Now that we have our list, let's think about a situation from this week when you were triggered by something one of your moms said or did. Can you think of something?
>
> **Andres:** Uh, probably when Mom was on my ass when I was putting my phone at the charger station last night.
>
> **Therapist:** Great example! Looking at the list, can you see how Mom was doing her "Mom job"?
>
> **Andres:** Yeah, I guess it was the whole let's make your brain smarter thing. It's still annoying, though.
>
> **Therapist:** Yes, I can imagine it's still annoying, but at least it's good to know that it's all for a good cause, right?
>
> **Andres:** I suppose.
>
> **Therapist:** Would it be okay with you if next time we show this list to your moms? It might help them to have the words to explain why they say the things they say, instead of just telling you "You have to because I said so."
>
> **Andres:** Yeah, I guess so.

Who Has the Floor? Communication Game

One crucial skill that almost all kids and parents need assistance with is the skill of communication. Some common mistakes are making accusations and communicating with "you" statements, raising voices, and becoming defensive. The therapist notices the unhealthy patterns of communication, conveys a curious, nonjudgmental attitude, and uses language such as "Hey, here's something I'm noticing," pointing out their communication struggles and stating "This is an excellent opportunity to develop some new skills."

The skill of communicating involves truly listening to the other with an open mind and expressing our feelings with reason and a calm demeanor. The Who Has the Floor? communication game is traditionally used in couples' therapy. Kids and parents take turns as speaker and listener. The therapist holds up a toy microphone or a pen as a pretend microphone and instructs the family that they can't speak unless they're holding the microphone. After a family member speaks, the therapist invites the listener to recap the speaker's message. The speaker then is asked to rate the recap—for example, "You understood about half of what I said. The part you missed is. . . ." Then the roles are switched, and the child or adolescent gets to be the speaker while the parent practices listening.

Encourage the parent and child or teen to speak directly to one another, not to the therapist. If the child doesn't make actual eye contact, that's okay. Eye contact can be too intense and dysregulating for some children. Encourage both the parent and child to make "I feel" statements as much as possible. During the game, the therapist may have to coach the family members to use the I feel statements and may have to be directive to prevent the parent and child from interrupting one another. The therapist hands the speaker the toy microphone and playfully commands, "Only the person who holds this microphone can be heard right now. But don't worry; each of you will have your turn with the microphone so you have a chance to be heard."

Who Has the Floor? Vignette With 14-Year-Old Bree and Her Dad

Bree: Dad, you're always harping on me in the mornings and I can't stand it.

Dad: Well, you're absolutely impossible and disrespectful and I can't stand that.

Therapist: (*Holding up a hand.*) This is a good chance to practice the pause with a couple of deep breaths so you can both bring yourselves down into that window we talked about. (*Bree and Dad grumble and take a couple of breaths.*) This is also a great opportunity to develop some healthy communication skills. One thing I noticed there is that you both used the word *always* with each other. The words *always* and *never* are surefire trigger words for all of us, because they're very black and white. (*Bree and her dad nod in agreement.*) Can we figure out what words you might use instead?

Bree: How about *sometimes*? Like *sometimes* I'm impossible. I *am* sometimes. But not *always*!

Dad: (*Nodding.*) And sometimes I harp. I can accept that.

Therapist: That's a great idea. Another thing that would be helpful is trying to start your sentences with "I feel." It's a lot easier to empathize with one another when you use feeling words. Bree, what could you have said to dad about the morning thing starting with I feel?

Bree: Dad, I feel annoyed when sometimes you harp on me.

Therapist: Dad, how is that?

Dad: Well, that's a lot better, I don't feel so defensive.

Therapist: Awesome, and if Bree forgets and says "You always do such and such," how could you respond?

Dad: Well, I guess I could say, "I feel triggered when you say it that way."

Therapist: Bree, how would you respond to that?

Bree: Well, I think that would be better. I think I'd probably take a pause.

Therapist: Let's practice these skills we're talking about with a game I call Who Has the Floor? You'll each take a turn talking about your feelings regarding a topic, holding a pen as a microphone. When you're done, you hand it to the other person and they give a recap of what you said. You evaluate the recap and tell anything that was missed. Then you switch roles. (*Therapist picks up a pen and hands it to Bree.*) Here's the microphone, Bree. Now remember, as much as possible, use I feel statements.

Bree: (*Turning to look at her dad while holding the microphone.*) I feel you're on my butt all the time to do homework right after school, and that's just a time when it's not possible for me and you don't get it. It makes me mad.

Dad: Can I say something here?

Therapist: Hold on, Dad, you'll have the microphone in a minute. Bree, I'd like to invite you to tweak your message just a bit to help dad with attuning to your feelings. Instead of "I feel you are on my butt," can you give your dad an actual feeling word?

Bree: Okay, I feel friggin' frustrated and criticized and I feel you don't understand that I'm feeling exhausted after a hard day at school. I'm so stressed by the time I get home from school I can't think straight, and I need some time to relax before homework.

Therapist: Dad, are you okay with Bree saying the word "friggin' "? (*Dad indicates it's okay.*) Okay, I'm going to hand the microphone to you now, Dad. Dad, can you recap what you just heard?
Dad: Sure. You said you're too stressed and tired to do homework right away after school. You should have told me that before. I didn't know.
Therapist: Well, I think it's a skill that doesn't always come easy for kids or adults. The good news is Bree just did a great job with it. Bree, how did your dad do with the recap?
Bree: Yay. He got it 100%.

Skills Practice

Early attachment injuries and the subsequent chronic sympathetic nervous system arousal and/or dorsal vagal shutdown add up to missed opportunities to learn and grow in the social, emotional, and cognitive arenas. The IATP-C therapist reminds the parents throughout the course of therapy that the skill deficits are real and that their child will continue to need teaching, coaching, and patience throughout their growing-up years. Kids born with some type of neurodivergence, effects of fetal alcohol exposure, or other substance exposure have additional brain-based factors for nontypical skill development and may always need assistance and accommodations in the home (see Chapter 11). As skill deficits are identified, the therapy moves into teacher mode. Which skills to teach depends entirely upon parent and therapist observations.

Even when parents understand that their kids have skill deficits, they can still have a hard time tolerating their frustration and managing the reality of the deficits in daily situations. It's common for a parent to say something like, "My child is 12 years old—she should know how to behave in this situation!" The IATP-C therapist models a nonjudgmental, matter-of-fact approach to the recognition of missing skills. Here are just some of the skill deficits that IATP-C therapists observe regularly:

- Making friends
- Social skills such as sharing, taking turns, reacting to winning or losing a game
- Asking for help with a task or problem
- Seeking comfort appropriately

- Accepting help or comfort when offered
- Accepting the answer "no" appropriately
- Accepting redirection or feedback
- Using manners in conversation or at the dinner table
- Restaurant behavior
- How to care for pets
- Bathroom behaviors like wiping, hand washing, hanging a towel
- Organizing their things

The IATP-C therapist stays matter-of-fact, reminding the child or adolescent and parents that lots of kids need help with these skills. The therapist calls upon their creative side to teach and reinforce the skills. Drawings, sand trays, stuffed animals, action figures, and live role-plays can be used to demonstrate and practice skills. Some social skills can be practiced during board games and card games. The therapist finds what works most effectively with each individual child with consideration for their cognitive abilities, emotional maturity, and learning style.

Skill Vignette With 9-Year-Old Bette and Her Mom

Bette was adopted from abroad. She had very poor frustration tolerance and issues related to waiting for anything. Her mom was very triggered by the child's habit of interrupting her, and it was causing numerous arguments in the home.

> **Therapist:** So let's talk about this interruption thing, shall we? (*Bette nods.*) Tell me, what does interrupting mean, anyway?
>
> **Bette:** It means someone else is talking or doing something, and another person butts in.
>
> **Therapist:** That's right. Do you think you do it a lot?
>
> **Bette:** (*Thinking.*) I do it a lot . . . I guess . . . I don't know. I just want to say something or tell someone else something.
>
> **Therapist:** Do you think it's hard to wait?
>
> **Bette:** No.
>
> **Therapist:** Hmmm . . . I wonder about that.
>
> **Bette:** Well, maybe. (*Smiling.*)

Therapist: It's hard to wait sometimes. I know I have a hard time waiting. I think all people do. Do you think you interrupt your mom a lot?

Bette: (*Looking at her mom's face.*) Yes, I know I do.

Therapist: (*Addressing the mother.*) Is this true? Does she interrupt a lot?

Mom: Yes, it's true.

Therapist: How do you feel, Mom, when she interrupts you?

Mom: I think I feel frustrated. Sometimes, I think if she would only just let me finish my sentence, then she would get her answer or understand what I am trying to tell her.

Therapist: Oh, that is interesting, Mom, can you give us an example?

Mom: Well, the other day, she asked me if she could go to a friend's house after school. I was trying to tell her that on that particular afternoon, I had to go to a meeting at the church, but before I could finish, she interrupted me and started arguing. She didn't even know what I was going to say.

Therapist: (*Asks Bette.*) What happened then?

Bette: Well, we got into a great big argument, and I couldn't go.

Therapist: You didn't get to go because . . .

Bette: I argued.

Therapist: What would have happened if you'd let your mom finish talking about this meeting?

Bette: I would have known that her meeting wasn't going to get over until 5:30, and I would have to ask my friend's mom if it would be okay if I stayed that late. If it was okay with my friend's mom, I guess I would have been able to go.

Therapist: What do you think your brain is thinking or doing when it's interrupting?

Bette: I think my brain thinks . . . I have to talk.

Therapist: I think you're right. What do you think might be the upsetting thought?

Bette: I hate waiting.

Therapist: Well, that's a true thought, for sure. I wonder about the thought, "I can't wait."

Bette: Yep, that's it.

Therapist: Now, what do you think is going to happen to you if you have to wait?

Bette: I'm not sure. I just don't like it.
Therapist: Let's think about it for a minute.
Bette: I know—I think I won't get what I want.
Therapist: Okay, so your thought is that if you interrupt, you'll get what you want . . . like, in this case, wanting to go to your friend's house, right?
Bette: Right, but it didn't work. (*Sighing.*)
Therapist: Yes, that's true, isn't it? Maybe this upsetting thought is really getting in your way. Do you think we could practice waiting to talk when your mom is talking? Mom, would you be willing to practice?
Mom: Sure.

As the session progressed, Bette, her mother, and the therapist role-played a variety of different scenarios in which Bette had to wait until her mom finished speaking. Her mother was willing to practice her attunement skills when she noticed that Bette was becoming anxious during the role-play. Mom and Bette came up with a plan. Mom would point out what she had observed by saying, "Bette, I'm noticing that you're getting anxious about this conversation. Remember to tell your brain, 'It's okay to wait and let Mom finish.'"

CONCLUSION

The IATP-C therapist's demeanor is playful, curious, and nonjudgmental. The therapist provides a safe and secure environment through listening and attuning to parents and their children. Children and teens are embraced within a collaborative, nonjudgmental environment that helps them gain the ability to trust the world again. Therapists, kids, and parents become part of the same team, working together to build a healthy, regulated family and a healthy, regulated child.

The family therapy foundational activities assist parents and their kids with widening their window of tolerance for distress through self-awareness, self-regulation, and coregulation. The activities provide adaptive information about the child's *outside world* and *inside world*, teaches skills for communication, and helps with other skill deficits through playful methods and role-plays.

The IATP-C is a direct and active model that also allows for flexibility in response to the specific needs of children and families. The therapist is free to use clinical judgment and intuition regarding the choice of activities for the session, depending upon the needs of kids and parents. Although there is a general flow to the family therapy activities in this chapter, when kids have serious deficits, the therapist may repeat activities as needed and incorporate additional skills practice during family therapy sessions.

The EMDR foundational activities described in the following chapter are conducted in tandem with the family therapy foundational activities.

CHAPTER 6

IATP-C Foundational EMDR Therapy Activities

> Through reading this chapter, you'll gain skills for implementing the following EMDR activities:
>
> **BUILDING A RESOURCED STATE**
> – Introducing EMDR
> – Safe Place Activity
> – Strengthening Their Biggest Kid Self
> – Finding Their Power Animal
> – Optional Butterfly Hug
>
> **ATTACHMENT RESOURCE DEVELOPMENT (ARD)**
> – Messages of Love (With Optional Games)
> – Magical Cord of Love
> – Circle of Love
> – Safe Place for the Smaller Child on the Inside
> – Optional Songs and Playful ARD Activities
>
> **SELF-REGULATION DEVELOPMENT AND INSTALLATION (S-RDI)**
> – Coaching With Slow BLS
> – Optional Coaching With Photographs and Games
>
> **FUTURE REHEARSALS**
> – Role-Plays and Mental Movies

EMDR therapy facilitates a natural associative process to move disturbing memories and triggers to adaptive resolution through eight phases: (1) history taking and treatment planning, (2) preparation and stabilization, (3) target assessment, (4) desensitization, (5) installation, (6) body scan, (7) closure, and (8) reevaluation. EMDR is a three-pronged approach, addressing past events, current triggers, and future templates.

When kids experience trauma with a foundation of attachment security, they typically need only a short preparation phase prior to processing traumatic events. They're willing to remember and reflect on the past, ready to rely upon their parents and therapist for support, and armed with a store of adaptive information for successful EMDR reprocessing. However, kids who've experienced chronic adversity within their attachment relationships have a different situation. They're frequently mistrustful and resistant to talking about the past. Their behaviors in the office can be challenging. They lack the capacity to reflect, reason, and process information and lack adequate information to support the reprocessing phases. They need a much stronger preparation phase to overcome these challenges.

The IATP-C Stage 2 EMDR foundational activities in this chapter are provided in tandem with the Stage 2 family therapy activities in Chapter 5 to build internal resources, skills for self-awareness and self-regulation, and capacity for trust and closeness. The combined family and EMDR therapy activities increase trust, security, regulation, and adaptive information for improved outcome during Stage 3, Healing Triggers and Traumas.

ENGAGING CHILDREN AND TEENS IN EMDR FOUNDATIONAL ACTIVITIES

In general, kids respond positively to the EMDR therapist who is gentle, patient, and attuned. With younger children, the therapist should be curious about everything the child does or says and sit fairly close, without invading the child's space, perhaps pulling the chair up close to keep the child's attention. Of course, with younger children the EMDR therapist should be willing to get on the floor as needed, move about, and be silly, all the while remaining cognizant of the child's shorter attention span, cognitive limitations, limited selfawareness, and limited capacity to verbalize thoughts and feelings. The therapist should avoid the use of metaphors and use concrete vocabulary with all kids who lack capacity to comprehend abstract ideas.

Because of their size and age, younger children generally can often be enticed into sitting on their parent's lap or snuggling close. Some older kids are willing to sit close or sit with their parent's arm around them for some of the EMDR activities that follow. Children with attentional issues can often be encouraged to participate by assuring, "First we'll do my activity, and then you and I and your mom/dad can play." A game, sand tray time, or floor time with toys is a nice reward and helps extend the positive feelings of connection with the parent. With older children and adolescents, it's important to attune to their desire for independence and autonomy. They may be more fully entrenched in an identity built on a view of the self as independent and strong. With teens who avoid closeness, it's important to use a casual demeanor and more adult language that supports their self-concept. The therapist should give the avoidant teen personal space in the office and avoid a soft voice tone or concerned facial expression. One teen told me, "I hate it when you use your warm, fuzzy voice!" I eliminated any warmth or softness from my tone and the teen became more cooperative.

With the avoidant teen, the therapist may need to avoid talk of goals for "closeness" and "connection," but the same teen may cooperate with the goal of "getting along better" at home and school. Providing fidget toys or drawing tools improves cooperation with many avoidant teens. The EMDR therapist should also acknowledge their independence by incorporating some one-on-one sessions, without the parent in the room.

Considerations Regarding Bilateral Stimulation (BLS)

The EMDR foundational activities are designed to build the child's internal resources for positive states involving connection, calm, or confidence. Although bilateral stimulation (BLS) while reprocessing traumas or triggers involves fast passes and longer sets (typically 15 or more passes) to facilitate associations and shifts the foundational resource work is designed to deepen a positive state. To avoid stimulating processing or linkage to new material during the resource work, we typically use short sets (3 to 4 passes) of soothing, slow BLS (Shapiro, 2018, p. 118). However, there are some kids with ADHD or younger kids who don't like slow BLS and insist on fast BLS for the resource activities. When this is the case, it's most important to attune to what the child likes. My colleagues and I prefer the use of tactile or audio stimulation versus eye movements for resource work because in our experience this type of stimulation is more soothing for kids.

The therapist and child or teen can play around with various methods ahead of time and find methods the child enjoys. In our experience, many kids find the alternating vibrations of the "buzzies" (otherwise known as "tactile pulsars" or "tappers") in their pockets, socks, or shoes to be comforting. Some kids who are sensory sensitive dislike the buzzies but enjoy alternating pressure or squeezes on hands or arms or feet. Some children and teens are more relaxed wearing headphones and listening to bilateral tones or music. Many younger children find comfort and connection by sitting on their parent's lap while the parent sways them gently from side to side at the therapist's cue.

During the activities, many children are more cooperative and relaxed by using a weighted blanket, sucking on a lollipop, playing with a fidget toy, holding a stuffed animal, or sitting on a yoga ball while doing the work.

INTRODUCING EMDR

By introducing EMDR therapy to parents and kids through simple language, the therapist helps them feel comfortable with the idea. We find that most parents are relieved to hear that EMDR addresses underlying traumas and helps integrate the child's brain.

Explaining EMDR to Parents Script

Say to parents, "We know that trauma is stored differently in the brain than other experiences. It gets stored in the brain in a form that is easily activated, even subconsciously, leading to negative thoughts, feelings, and behaviors. EMDR therapy is a method that involves specific steps along with bilateral stimulation and eliminates or reduces the stuck negative emotions and thoughts. The first step involves some easy and fun activities that create good feelings for your child. We'll use some slow, relaxing methods of bilateral stimulation to strengthen those good feelings."

Explaining EMDR to the Child or Teen Script

Say to the child or teen, "I'm going to show you something I do and lots of therapists do called EMDR therapy. EMDR therapy helps good feelings get stronger and upset feelings get smaller. To start with, we'll just focus on making good feelings bigger. Would that be okay with you? _____ One part of EMDR therapy involves getting our right brain and left brain to work together to help with our feelings. Let me show you some fun ways we can do this." (*The therapist demonstrates and lets the child or teen very briefly experience the various forms of BLS.*)

With very young children or children with developmental delays, we can simplify the explanation further.

Say to the child, "I'm going to show you how we can use *[toys/tapping/lights/buzzies]* to make good feelings bigger and yucky feelings smaller." (*The therapist demonstrates and lets the child very briefly experience the various forms of BLS.*)

BUILDING GOOD FEELINGS

The first set of EMDR activities accesses internal resources of the child or teen to begin strengthening a present-day, positive state.

Safe Place Activity

Most EMDR therapists help clients develop a safe or calm inner place or state to increase the client's capacity to self-calm (Shapiro, 2018, p. 118). This may be challenging with severely traumatized kids who've never experienced safety. It's helpful to encourage the child or teen to think of a place that is completely imaginary, for example, a place out of a book, a television show, or a movie. The imaginary place helps prevent negative associations. If thinking of a *safe* place is difficult, it may indicate the word safe triggers thoughts of being unsafe. The word *calm* or relaxing may be more readily accepted. To engage the child by making it more fun, the therapist, child, or current caregivers can work together to create a picture of the safe or calm place through a drawing or painting, by cutting out pictures from a magazine, or by choosing a place from images found on the computer. Kids with difficulties paying attention do best if the therapist provides a guided visualization, emphasizing what they can see, hear, smell, and touch, while the therapist applies slow bilateral stimulation. I find it is safe to apply the slow bilateral stimulation for perhaps 7 to 20 passes, as long as I stop the BLS as soon as I stop describing the details of the safe place. If it goes well, I ask the child to relax for a few more moments, enjoying the safe place, while I add one more slow, short set of BLS (3 to 4 passes). If I ask the child to stay with the image or the good feeling any longer than that, I risk losing the child's attention. For the child who is uncooperative initially with BLS, guided visualization can be provided without any BLS at all. The IATP-C therapist always attunes and paces according to the needs of the child or teen.

Safe Place Vignette With Kennu

Kennu: My safe place is an island in the middle of the ocean with a coral reef and lots of tropical fish where I can go snorkeling.

EMDR Therapist: Wow, that sounds amazing. Can you describe the fish you see when you're under the water? (*Listens to a description of the fish.*) Imagine you're there right now. You can close your eyes if you want to. I'm going to turn on these buzzies just the way you like. (*Very slow BLS.*) Now you can feel the temperature of the water. It's just right. You can see the sun streaming down, making beautiful patterns in the water. There are beautiful rocks and seaweed, and beautiful white and pink coral everywhere. It's so quiet and peaceful. Your body is relaxed and calm. You spot some little orange and black fish that look like Nemo and . . . (*Continues describing more sights and the feel of the water. Stops BLS.*) How did that go? (*Kennu gives a positive report.*) I'll run them just for another slow, short set as you notice how relaxed you are in your arms and your legs. There you go. (*Slow, short set of BLS.*)

If the child's report is positive, the therapist can ask them to notice the calm feelings once more and add another slow, short set. If the child reports a problem, the therapist should change or alter the safe place as needed.

Kids affected by attachment injuries typically have little confidence for many everyday activities due to interrupted developmental trajectories. Resource development and installation (RDI; Korn & Leeds, 2002) procedures can be applied with ease in a simple way to help kids gain confidence. As with the safe place activity, the following resource activities involve slow BLS (adjusted to the preference of the child or teen) applied in tandem with a positive visualization that accesses the positive characteristic.

Strengthening the Biggest Kid Self

The child or teen is engaged in strengthening the biggest kid self after they're assisted with recognizing their biggest kid state in family therapy. After the child, teen, or parent has identified situations in which the child or teen was operating from the biggest kid self, the EMDR therapist asks the child or teen to talk about one of the recent times the child or teen was thinking and acting from their biggest kid self. (The memory can be as simple as making a good decision or accomplishing a task at home or school earlier in the day.) The therapist asks the child to think back to the memory and notice their biggest kid self body posture. If the child or teen has a positive response, the therapist applies a slow, short set of BLS while noticing the good feelings. Alternatively, the therapist can draw out the activity by guiding the child's focus with more detailed imagery and applying slow BLS throughout the dialogue. For kids who are more concrete, the therapist or parent can role-play the good memory with the child or teen.

Future rehearsals can be conducted by suggesting the child or teen bring their biggest kid self to some common challenging situation and think of responding in a good way. The child or teen may be challenged by very ordinary everyday situations such as dealing with a strict teacher, handling the word "no," completing a hard assignment, or picking up their room. A slow, short set of BLS can be applied to reinforce the good feelings associated with the positive response.

For kids who are more concrete thinkers or for younger kids it's more helpful to create a little play and act out the challenging situation with their biggest kid self. The slow BLS can be applied throughout the role play or briefly after the role-play.

Any future session throughout treatment can begin on a positive note by asking the child, teen, or parent to talk about a situation from the week when they made a positive choice and functioned from the biggest kid state and reinforcing positive affect with a slow, short set of BLS. The activity doesn't take long, and celebrating a success each week in this way gradually builds a stronger sense of self.

Vignette With 6-Year-Old Jane and Her Mom

Therapist: Jane, I would like you to think of a situation or something you did that made you feel like a big 6-year-old girl.

Jane: Yesterday, Mom asked me to pick up my shoes and my backpack, and I did it without whining.

Therapist: That is really great.

Mom: Yes, I was shocked.

Therapist: (*Applies slow hand taps while guiding the child in thinking about the entire scenario.*) Put yourself back in that situation now. Think about what your mom asked you to do, and how you just walked right over there and picked those things up without one word, and how mature and grown-up you were. Picture your mom's face when she felt surprised and happy. Notice how your body feels right now as you remember back to yesterday. (*Stops the hand taps.*) How did that go? (*The child gives a positive answer, and the therapist reinforces the positive big-girl feeling with one more short slow set of BLS.*)

Vignette With 16-Year-Old Rocky and His Foster Mother (Who He Calls Nan)

Therapist to Foster Mother: Can you talk about a time this week when you could see that Rocky was operating from his most 16-year-old self?

Nan: Yes, he had a big algebra test yesterday, and the night before he sat down at the table and did the practice problems without any nagging from me at all.

Therapist: What did you feel, Nan?

Nan: Well, I was proud of him. I know how much he hates algebra, and so for him to sit down and get to it without my help was really something.

Therapist to Rocky: Rocky, as you think about the state of mind you were in the other night, opening your book and getting right to it—how would you describe it?

Rocky: Uh, determined, I guess. I just decided to go for it. Actually, to try for a change.

Therapist: (*Getting out the buzzies.*) Rocky, let's see if we can deepen this determined, diligent most 16-year-old self. Can we do that?

Rocky: Sure.

Therapist: Can you hold these like before? (*Turns on the buzzies at a slow speed.*) I'm going to run them just slowly while you remember being in your most 16-year-old, determined self. Strong, focused, mature. (*Turns them off.*) How are you feeling right now?

Rocky: Good. Like I've got my crap together, you know?

Therapist: Yes. Notice that and I'll turn these on again just for a few seconds.

Strengthening Their Power Animal

Kids love animals. Animals can be a powerful way for kids to find a sense of safety and connection when people don't feel completely safe. A simple EMDR resource development and installation (RDI) can be applied to help kids feel connected to their own personal *power animal*. Developing a relationship with their own personal power animal naturally helps kids access feelings of confidence, wisdom, and worthiness.

Kids often know their power animal right away, but if not, they can be assisted with finding their personal power animal by looking through an animal book or animal cards, looking at animal pictures online, or choosing an animal from sand tray figures.

Power Animal RDI Script

Say to the child or teen, "Another way we can find our most wise, confident, and strong self is developing our own personal power animal. We can choose a special animal to be by our side who will help us remember that we are wise and good and strong. Would you like to choose your power animal? We can look through these *[pictures/sand tray figures]* to help you think about which animal you would choose to have as your power animal. (*Take time to discuss the various animals. When one is chosen, continue.*) Imagine your animal is right here with you, by your side, supporting you, reminding you that you are wise and good and strong. If it's okay, let's add some *[taps/buzzies]* while you think about your power animal."

After the resource activity, the power animal can be utilized to help access the biggest kid self at any time or used to help with any future rehearsals, future templates, or role plays. The power animal can also be accessed with cognitive interweaves to assist kids if they get stuck during reprocessing.

Optional Butterfly Hug

The Butterfly Hug (Shapiro, 2018, p. 245) can empower the child or teen to bring up any of their positive resources (safe place, biggest kid self, power animal) and take time to feel the good feelings when they're at home or school. The EMDR therapist teaches the child or teen to think about their resource and then bring in the good feelings with their arms, folding themselves into a big hug and tapping slowly back and forth on their upper arms or chest. The EMDR therapist cautions the parent to allow the child or teen to be in charge of when or if they want to use the Butterfly Hug at home.

The therapist may choose to use a different name, depending upon the personality of the child or teen. Alternative names we've used include The Mummy (arms crossed like a mummy), The Gorilla (pounding on chest like a gorilla) or simply self-taps.

Butterfly Hug for a Child Script

Say to the child, "I want to teach you something you can do that might be helpful called the Butterfly Hug. It's something you can do on your own at school or at home or anywhere. If it's okay with you, let's try it out with your safe place (or by thinking about your bigger kid self) for a moment. (*Provide the child or teen with some guided imagery.*) Notice those good feelings inside. Now, wrap your arms around you like this, holding those good feelings inside, and move your hands like butterfly wings to make the good feelings stronger. (*Demonstrating for the child.*) I'm going to think of my own safe place and tap my arms too. (*Demonstrating as the child follows along for 5 to 6 slow passes.*) How do you feel?

Lots of kids like to do the Butterfly Hug as they picture their safe place at night to help them fall asleep and have nice dreams. Or they use it at school, even tapping underneath their desk. It's totally up to you, but lots of kids say it really helps."

Butterfly Hug for a Teen Script

Say to the teen, "I have a trick for making good feelings stronger inside of you when you're at home. You can think about the safe place we made, or you can think about your most mature competent self and then do self-taps, tapping back and forth on your own arms, like this. If you're at school, you can even do this in a way that no one will notice, like giving yourself taps on your knees underneath your desk or moving your toes inside one shoe and then the other. How about we practice it together. I'll use my own safe place while I do my self-taps. It will only take a few moments."

ATTACHMENT RESOURCE DEVELOPMENT: TAPPING INTO LOVE WITH ARD

Attachment Resource Development (ARD) creates experiences of closeness for the child or adolescent with the parents and then uses slow tactile or audio stimulation to deepen the feelings of trust, safety, and connection. In some cases, ARD may be the sole focus of the EMDR sessions for 3 or 4 weeks or even more. Once EMDR reprocessing of memories and triggers commences, some ARD can be repeated, even just briefly, at the beginning or end of sessions as needed.

Relearning through ARD involves restructuring their brain and nervous system to have a new response. This takes effort, time, patience, and repetition.

Preparing the Parent for ARD

The IATP-C therapist explains to the parent that the ARD activities create experiences of closeness and connection for the child and hopefully for the parent, too, and that the sense of closeness is deepened for the child or adolescent with application of slow BLS. The therapist reminds the parent that their child doesn't have a strong sense of trust and connection, which leads to fight-or-flight responses and difficult behaviors, and that improved trust over time leads to a calmer, more enjoyable child. The therapist explains that although the activities are designed to help both the child and parent gain closeness, it's not unusual for either or both to feel uncomfortable with the activities in the beginning.

For the child or teen, there may be a temporary increase in reactivity afterwards. For example, a stern look or a redirection from the parent in the week following ARD may trigger a meltdown and a belief that the closeness is over and will never return. With both child and parent, the therapist may use the analogy of the feeling when a vacation comes to an end. Remind parents that these side effects are a natural response to closeness and connection when it feels new. As the child or teen comes to believe that the connection will continue, the aftereffects will lessen.

The therapist may ask the parent if they would be willing to experiment with a very simple EMDR self-help activity to help them feel more comfortable with the attachment-related activities. (The activity is similar to activities described by Francine Shapiro [2012] in her book for lay people, *Getting Past Your Past*.) Although one shouldn't provide individual therapy with a parent without a proper intake that establishes the parent as a client, suggesting a self-help tool is an appropriate and safe way to be helpful. The therapist explains that the first step is to imagine a characteristic or quality that would help them participate fully in the connecting activity with their child (e.g., the quality of patience, acceptance, or compassion). The second step is to identify a figure of some sort (e.g., someone they know or someone famous or spiritual) or even an animal figure that inspires the desired quality. The third step involves inviting the parent to visualize the figure there with them while crossing their arms and applying a few slow taps on their upper arms or upper chest. Suggest to the parent that they hold onto thoughts of the resource figure during the attachment resource activities with their child. The following is a script for offering the RDI self-help tool.

Optional Self-Help RDI for Parents Script
Say to the parent, "Participating in attachment activities that involve closeness with the child can be really challenging for lots of parents at this stage of therapy. I have a little trick that a lot of parents find helpful. The first step is to think of the quality or characteristic you want to call upon right now. What quality or characteristic would you like to rely on to help you? _____ Okay, the next step is to think of a figure—somebody you know or somebody famous from history or movies or books—or even an animal or a spiritual figure—who would inspire you or support this quality for you. Take your time, and then tell me who or what comes to mind. _____ Briefly close your eyes and imagine that figure at your side, bringing you encouragement, inspiration, and support. Get a sense of how it feels to have that figure here with you now. (*Pause.*) If it feels positive, go ahead and cross your arms and tap back and forth just 3 or 4 times on your upper arms or upper chest. (*Applies taps.*) How are you feeling? _____ See if you can hold onto the felt sense of this, and I'll bring your child/teen in to join us now for an activity."

This activity with the parent might naturally lead into a discussion about engaging in individual EMDR therapy to remove the emotional charge from their triggers, increase positive feelings, and lessen anxiety and stress. (See more about helping parents in Chapter 12.)

Preparing Resistant Children and Teens Script
A helpful way to disarm the resistant child or teen is to begin any of the ARD activities with a paradoxical prompt by saying, "You're lucky today, because you get to just settle back and relax. Your parent has to do most of the work today. You can listen, or you can not listen; it's completely up to you."

Offering a lollipop to suck on or snack of any type, bringing out clay or paper and markers, or getting down on the floor with toys may also reduce anxiety and improve cooperation, allowing the child or teen to listen in during the ARD activity. The therapist may also suggest a compromise: "After we do this activity for a short time, we can do something fun." If the child or teen is resistant to the BLS, the activities can be implemented without BLS, with a gradual addition of the stimulation as the anxiety begins settling down.

Messages of Love Activity

My preference is to conduct the Messages of Love activity with one parent at a time to optimize feelings of closeness and avoid distractions that can happen when the parents are engaging with one another during the session. Parents can be prepared for the activity together or one at a time. The parents should be prepared for the activity without the child or teen present.

The therapist explains that the Messages of Love activity enhances positive feelings of closeness and trust. The therapist goes over the Messages of Love Parent Prompts below and helps the parent reflect on their potential responses. Some parents like to write down what they want to say. Not all prompts need to be used. Find out which prompts the parent likes the best. Explain that physical closeness during the activity is helpful but not a requirement. Ask about the parent's comfort level with sitting together or snuggling up together.

Occasionally, parents who are capable of providing Messages of Love will have an objection to the activity related to a feeling that the child hasn't earned positive messages. The parent may believe the child should change before being rewarded with connection and affirmations. In this case, more psychoeducation may be needed to help the parent make the important shift from old school thinking to the new view from the attachment and trauma lens.

Vignette With Susan's Grandmother, Jeanette, Shifting Her Perspective

Jeanette: So you're asking me to give Susan positive messages? That's really backwards, isn't it? It's not the way life works! I don't want Susan to learn that she can act up and be mean to people and then get rewarded with all kinds of warm fuzzies. When we misbehave, it is a natural consequence that people don't want to be close to us!

EMDR Therapist: I understand your concern, Jeanette. A lot of parents come in feeling this way. But remember, Susan is functioning with an overactive fight-or-flight brain and stuck trauma keeping her in fear and mistrust. Susan's brain is stuck in hyperarousal probably 90% of the time. The hyperaroused brain is unable to learn. That's why all of the behavioral modification techniques you've already tried haven't created any lasting change in Susan's behaviors. We need to calm her brain by creating trust and connection with you before she can develop new patterns of behavior. The best way we know to accomplish this is to wrap

Susan in a cocoon of safe and nurturing messages from you. Using slow bilateral stimulation to strengthen the new positive memory networks of love and safety will begin to calm her firing brain.

Jeanette: Okay, what you are saying makes sense. But I might have to fake it a little bit, is that okay?

EMDR Therapist: That's okay. A lot of parents have to fake it 'til they make it.

Parents can be invited to bring in photos and mementos related to positive memories with their child and memories of first getting to know their child to supplement the Messages of Love activity. Biological parents can be invited to bring in baby books and baby blankets to assist them in talking about positive memories.

Messages of Love Parent Prompts

- "Tell me about the first time you met _____. What do you remember thinking? What do you remember feeling?" (In the case of biological children, the therapist asks about the parent's memories of the pregnancy and the birth.)
- "Let's hear about some of the other fun memories of the early days." (The therapist can ask the parent to bring photos and other mementos to the session to spark positive early memories about the child.)
- "I would love to hear more fun memories about the child's *[first words/first steps/first friends/funny moments/first trips/first holidays/favorite activities, etc.].*"
- "Tell me about some of the qualities and characteristics that you enjoy about _____."
- "I'd love to hear about moments you've felt proud of _____."
- "What are some activities you've enjoyed doing with _____?"
- "What are some things that the two of you have in common?"
- "What are some of your future hopes and dreams for your relationship with _____?"

(Be sure the parent's hopes and dreams don't focus on academic, sports, or job achievements. This is the time for parents to describe their desire for a happy relationship with the child when they are older. For example, they may describe going fishing or camping together or spending holidays together when the child is older.)

As long as the parent is speaking positively, the therapist reinforces the experience for the child or teen with relatively slow bilateral stimulation. Occasionally, throughout this exercise, the therapist brings the child's attention to the feelings of calm or connection by saying, "Notice the good feelings inside right now," or "Notice that sense of belonging and connection," adding another slow, short set of BLS.

Children and Teens Who Lack Permanency

In the case of kids who are wards of the state residing in foster care, group homes, or residential treatment, a committed foster parent, relative, or staff member can provide warm messages of positive regard for the child or teen. They can note positive traits, positive behaviors, and hopes for the child's future, while the therapist reinforces the child's feelings of connection, safety, and sense of worthiness with bilateral stimulation. For kids in residential care, this exercise can be conducted almost daily, strengthening the child's sense of self and connectedness to others at the facility. Although a guardian, foster parent, or staff member cannot talk of a personal future with the child or teen, they can still say something like, "You'll always stay in my heart and in my thoughts. I want a wonderful future for you full of friendship and love."

Messages of Love Through a Doll or Stuffed Animal for Resistant Children

With the dysregulated and resistant child, it can be helpful to provide the Messages of Love indirectly through a stuffed animal or doll. The therapist can explain the plan to the parent before the child joins the session. The therapist and parent can talk with each other while the child snuggles with the parent and/or plays with a fidget toy or draws. The following is a vignette involving 7-year-old Graham and his grandfather. Graham would cover his ears and become dysregulated when the therapist attempted to implement the Messages of Love activity. The therapist talked with the grandfather about providing the Messages of Love through a bear.

Vignette With 7-Year-Old Graham and His Grandfather

(*Graham is sitting near his grandfather playing with a fidget toy.*)

Therapist: Grandpa, would you like to hold this cute bear? Isn't this a wonderful bear?

Grandpa: This bear is handsome and strong. I'll bet he's a fast runner, and very smart.

Therapist: Yes, he is handsome and strong and smart. Do you think he was born with a good and lovable heart?

Grandpa: Oh, yes, I think he was born with a good and lovable heart.

Therapist: Let's help him take in this good stuff. Graham, can you help us out and hold these buzzies on the bear's paws? (*Graham shrugs and holds the buzzies on the paws while the therapist and Grandpa repeat the loving messages to the bear.*)

Therapist: Grandpa, does this bear remind you of Graham at all?

Grandpa: Now that you mention it, yes, this bear is just like Graham!

The therapist feels Graham has had enough exposure to loving messages for the day and so switches to another playful activity for the remainder of the session.

Optional Games for Tolerating Messages of Love

For some kids who have a hard time tolerating Messages of Love, it can help to make it more playful. Use a simple game like Tumbling Towers or Pick-Up Sticks. Explain that on the parent's turn, they will provide one positive memory about their child, one thought about something they enjoyed doing with the child, or a future hope or dream about the child. So, for example, the mom might share this as she places a block: "I remember falling in love with Dimitry the first time he smiled and I saw that adorable dimple."

The therapist can run the tappers slowly and say "Notice that you can handle the good message. It's safe to take it in. It's safe to feel good."

Magical Cord of Love Activity

Kids who have not developed secure attachments tend to have very little object constancy when it comes to sensing connection and love, especially when parents are not present or their parents are frustrated with them. Developing a Magical Cord of Love reinforces a sense of constancy. Like many of the other activities, the Magical Cord of Love is not one and done; it needs to be reinforced a number of times and referenced throughout treatment. Slow, relaxing

BLS is implemented while the child or teen relaxes or snuggles with the parent and the therapist guides their thoughts with the visualization.

Magical Cord of Love Script

Say to the child, "Does love exist? _____ Can you see love? _____ No, that's right. It's invisible, even though it's there. I believe love connects us, heart to heart, like an invisible magical cord. What color do you think love is? _____ That's a good love color. (*Applies slow BLS throughout the remaining dialogue.*) I'd like to invite you to close your eyes and picture the magic invisible cord that is connecting you to your mom/dad right here, right now, heart to heart. The cord is made of a beautiful light, the light of love. The color _____ is a wonderful color for your cord of love. Picture this beautiful _____ cord, like a shimmery light. This cord is magical because it can stretch, so no matter how far away you go, and no matter how far away your mom/dad goes, it can stretch and stretch, so you're always connected. Right now, the love is pouring into your heart from your mom's/dad's heart. And no matter how much love they send you, there's always more. Just notice the good feelings as you relax/snuggle there with your mom/dad. Mom/Dad, just notice how comfortable and close you feel to _____ right now."

Next, the therapist and child draw situations in which the child typically feels insecure, rejected, or unloved (e.g., when the parent is giving attention to a sibling, frustrated with the child, at work, or unwell). The therapist asks the parent to talk about how they still love the child in these situations while the child draws the cord connecting them heart to heart.

Short sets of slow BLS are applied while the child looks at the picture and the parent reminds the child, "Even in those times that I'm *[frustrated/away/busy]*, my love is there. The love cord is always there, connecting us heart to heart. You are always in my heart and in my mind."

The parent can be invited to help the child hold the buzzies or apply the taps for the child, reinforcing the sense of connection through the slow BLS for the parent as well as for the child.

Optional Cord of Love Activities for Younger Children

The therapist can take the younger child outside the office and then knock on the door and say to the parent, who is still inside the office, "Can you see

_____?" "So you can't see _____, but is he still in your heart?" *(Adding slow taps to the child's shoulders.)* _____ "So the Cord of Love is going right through the door!"

The therapist may also suggest that the parent describe fun items they might send to the child through the Cord of Love. For example, the parent can send the child teddy bears, unicorns, or peppermints over the Cord of Love. The parent can remind the child what they will be sending each day when they drop the child off at school to reinforce the child's sense of connection throughout the school day.

Modifications for Teens, Resistant Children, or Children Without Permanency

For teens or children who are wards of the state with no stable placement, the magical cord of love can be reframed as the *cord of love* or the *cord of caring*. The cord of caring activity can be conducted with the help of a committed foster parent, a court-appointed advocate, or a residential facility staff member who is willing to describe feelings of care and commitment to the child without a placement. The child can visualize a beautiful cord of caring, connecting them heart to heart to the adult who is committed to the child's well-being.

Circle of Love, Circle of Caring Activity

To expand a sense of connection in the world, the therapist can invite the child or teen to help make a list of all the people who care about them. These individuals can include relatives, caseworkers, teachers, siblings, friends, and so on. With children who have no stable placement, this exercise can be conducted as the Circle of Caring, utilizing the names of friends or professionals who are concerned for their welfare. The child or teen may be invited to add pets, as well.

Next, the therapist asks the child or teen to draw a very simple stick figure drawing of all the people in their caring circle surrounding them. Alternatively, the child or teen can make the Circle of Love, Circle of Caring in a sand tray or by creating a circle of stuffed animals on the floor surrounding the child. Next, the therapist deepens the sense of connection and safety by adding slow, comfortable BLS.

Circle of Love/Caring Script

Say to the child or teen (adding pleasant, slow BLS), "Look at all of the people in your circle. Think about how crowded this room would be right now if each one of them were here in this room right now, surrounding you with their care and their love for you. Picture their loving care as a beautiful light filling the room. Notice its color. Notice how you feel inside."

Safe Place for the Smaller Child on the Inside

The concept of the smaller child on the inside is first introduced during a family session early in treatment (see Chapter 5) using nesting dolls. If the child or teen was receptive to the concept of the smaller child on the inside, EMDR resource work can enhance safety for the child part of the self. The therapist begins the session by asking the child or parent to describe a situation from the week in which the child was in their biggest kid self and applying a slow, short set to deepen the biggest kid self. This ensures that the child or teen is operating from their present-day biggest kid self while creating the safe place for the younger part.

Next, the therapist invites the child or teen to create a special or safe place for a baby part or younger child part on the inside. The therapist uses language that insures the child or teen understands that the safe place exists inside the child's heart in present time and that they are not visiting the past.

The therapist asks the child or teen to identify an age of the self that needs a place of safety and comfort. (The EMDR therapist may wish to allow the child to line up nesting dolls as the child reflects on an age.) The therapist invites the child to make a special, safe place for that younger part of themselves that exists inside their heart. The therapist suggests the child make a place from their imagination to avoid using a place they've been that may end up having negative associations. The therapist explains that it's okay to make any kind of a fun, relaxing, and wonderful place that their creative mind can imagine, and it's okay to give their younger self anything at all they might need or want.

The therapist invites the child or teen to show the special place for the smaller child part on the inside by making a picture or a sand tray, which helps make the place more concrete. The parent can be invited to participate in thinking about what the younger part might need or want but the child or teen should have the final say. Sometimes the child wants the parent to actively help make the drawing or sand tray, and that's okay if it's what the child wants. Some children or teens struggle with being imaginative and respond well to choosing images from the internet related to nature or to nurseries or playrooms.

Don't worry about whether items in the special place are truly appropriate for the age level of the smaller part on the inside. If the parent is concerned because the child or teen wants a baby part of self to have a cotton candy machine or a trampoline, reassure the parent that it's entirely okay because this is a special place in their imagination and anything they want to happen can happen there. As the child or teen looks at the picture or sand tray representation, apply a short set of slow BLS to deepen positive affect.

Internal Attachment Repair

The Safe Place for the Smaller Child activity can enhance internal feelings of safety but also provides a chance for parents to make up for deficits related to nurturing and protection in the child's earlier life. Biological parents have a chance to make up for earlier neglect related to their own earlier untreated mental illness or addiction. Adoptive or foster parents can help make up for unmet needs in early life before the child came to them. Meeting the unmet needs of the smaller child part of the child through the child's present-day parents (or through the biological parents who now have capacity) is truly healing at a deep level and helps move the child down the continuum toward attachment security.

To initiate internal nurturing, the therapist invites the parent to picture themselves entering the newly created safe place to care for the smaller child self. They are reminded they are not going back in time, that the safe place exists in present time. The parent is invited to talk about what they imagine doing for the younger part in the present time in the safe place. Throughout the parent's dialogue, as the parent describes what they are doing for the younger child part in the safe place, the therapist adds slow, comforting, tactile BLS.

Lastly, the therapist invites the child or teen to say what they want the smaller child on the inside to know (e.g., "You're safe," "You're a good kid," "Everything's okay now.") The therapist can help out with suggestions if the child struggles to answer. The therapist asks the child to notice how it feels to think of the younger part hearing the positive message and applies a slow, short set of BLS. The therapist keeps a copy or photo of the Safe Place for the Smaller Child part so that it can be revisited and reinforced periodically through treatment.

Safe Place for the Smaller Part Script

Say to the child or teen, "I know that in your family therapy session, you learned how we carry hurt smaller parts of us inside of our hearts. You identified a hurt little _____-year-old part of you and a hurt little _____-year-old part of you on the inside. I think we should all work together to help those little parts of you know they are lovable, loved, and safe today inside your heart. Which of these little parts should we help to feel safe to start with? _____ Okay, let's work together to imagine a wonderful, cozy, and safe place inside of you this part will enjoy. We can put everything inside the safe place this part of you might ever want or need. Let's think about a place that would be relaxing and also fun and safe, and then we'll think about what toys, food, and other items we should add. You can take all the time you need to think about this. If you want, you can draw this place or make this place in the sand tray." (*Optionally, the child or teen may choose a place from images on the computer.*)

When finished, say, "How do you feel about this smaller part of you having this awesome place on the inside?" _____ (*If the response is positive, apply 3 or 4 slow passes of BLS.*)

Invitation to Parent to Care for the Smaller Part Script

Say to the parent, "Mom/Dad, here's the really fun part. You get to provide care to your child's smaller self, inside this cool safe place. Remember that we're not thinking about the past. This safe place is in the here and now, in the present time. You have the opportunity to meet your child's earlier unmet needs, to make up for what was missed. What do you imagine doing for that little one today?"

Say to the child or teen, "While Mom/Dad is talking, if it's okay, I'll apply some taps/buzzies." (*Applies slow BLS throughout the dialogue.*)

Dialogue With the Smaller Part Script

Say to the child or teen, "When that smaller part inside of you feels better, you feel better, too. What are the good things you think that smaller child on the inside needs to know?" (*The therapist may offer ideas such as "You're safe and loved. You're a good kid. You have everything you need and you're okay now." Slow BLS can be applied to deepen the positive messages.*)

Ten-year-old Tommy, who now lives with his grandmother, was severely neglected as a baby. Figure 6.1 is a picture like the one drawn by Tommy for the baby part of him on the inside.

Baby Tommy's safe place has elements that would not be appropriate for a baby in real life, but the therapist supports all aspects of the safe place for the

Figure 6.1: Safe Place for the Smaller Tommy on the Inside
Illustration by Theodora S. Malmud

baby self in Tommy's imagination. When Tommy's drawing was completed, the therapist asked Tommy to talk about the details of the safe place.

In the following vignette, Tommy tells the therapist and his grandmother about his drawing. The therapist also invites Tommy's grandmother to talk about what she is doing for baby Tommy and invites Tommy to talk to the baby part.

Vignette With 10-Year-Old Tommy and His Grandmother

EMDR Therapist: Tommy, tell me about this drawing of the safe place for baby Tommy.

Tommy: (*Pointing to the drawing.*) Baby Tommy can sit in his bed and watch whatever television show he wants. All he has to do is press the special button and any kid show will come on. The bed also has tons of blankets to keep him warm.

EMDR Therapist: I bet baby Tommy loves watching all those favorite shows and feeling warm. What is this button for, Tommy?

Tommy: This is the button that sends the baby food though the catapult [*drawn near the bottom of the picture*]. When he pushes this button, it throws him whatever food he wants and plenty of milk. The catapult is attached to a conveyor belt, and the food never runs out.

EMDR Therapist: That is so cool. Baby Tommy never even has to leave his bed for food or milk.

Tommy: (*Pointing to the picture.*) This is the button for the library.

EMDR Therapist: Tell me more.

Tommy: I push this button and whenever I want Grandma to read a book to me, she comes right into my room. I also have plenty of toys and clothes that match.

Therapist: (*Handing Tommy the buzzies.*) I'm going to run these buzzies, just a little bit, while you notice the good feelings you have about baby Tommy in the safe place, okay? (*Applies a slow, short set of BLS.*)

Therapist: Grandma, can you picture yourself there in the safe place with baby Tommy? You're not going back in time. This safe place for the baby Tommy part is in the here and now. What do you see yourself doing for baby Tommy today? Tommy, I'm going to run the buzzies slowly while your grandma talks about caring for the baby part in the safe place, if that's okay with you.

Grandmother: (*Tommy holds the buzzies, running slowly, as he sits next to his grandmother and leans against her shoulder.*) I love being inside the safe place with baby Tommy. We rock, and I sing lullabies and funny little songs I learned when I was a child. Today, I'm singing "This Little Light of Mine" to baby Tommy, and we're rocking and rocking. Later, we'll get down on the floor, and we'll roll a little car back and forth and make little car noises together.

Therapist: Tommy, what would you like the baby Tommy inside the safe place to know today?

Tommy: That he's safe, I guess—and that Grandma's there.

Therapist: So he's never alone, is he?

Tommy: Nope.

Therapist: Just notice your good feelings about that, and I'll turn on these buzzies just a short bit. (*Turning on buzzies.*)

This safe place drawing was brought out for Tommy to look at several times throughout treatment, with the reminder that here and now today, the baby part is safe and cared for by his grandma in the safe place.

Meeting the Needs of the Younger Parts at Various Ages and Stages

The child or teen may be assisted with creating safe places for many ages of younger parts at various times throughout therapy as early traumas are identified. For example, 10-year-old Darlene developed a safe place for her baby part on the inside because she suffered early neglect in her biological home, and later she developed a safe place for her 3-year-old part on the inside who suffered the loss of her biological family when she was moved to foster care. Later, when Darlene revealed abuse in her second foster home, she developed a safe place for the 5-year-old on the inside. Darlene's adoptive parents participated in providing loving care through guided imagery to each of Darlene's hurt little ones inside. Bilateral stimulation reinforced Darlene's experience of inner safety and love for these many vulnerable, wounded little parts of herself.

Optional: Nurturing the Smaller Child on the Inside Through a Doll

Another method for providing nurturing for the baby part on the inside is to use a doll to represent the baby. Often, children enjoy holding the buzzies (slow speed) on the doll's hands "to make the doll's good feelings even bigger." This is a lovely way to provide BLS to the child, while the child is feeling good about nurturing their baby part of the self.

Vignette With 8-Year-Old Bella and Her Parents

Therapist: Today we're going to take care of that little baby Bella who lives in your heart. Do you remember when Deb talked with you, Bella, about how we all have a little baby who lives inside our heart?

Bella: Yes, we used those red china dolls [*referring to the nesting dolls*], and the baby was very little. We put the baby back inside, nice and safe.

Therapist: Well, today all of us are going to take care of baby Bella. I have a baby right here, and we are going to pretend that she is baby Bella! (*Brings out the baby doll, wrapped in a blanket.*) We are going to hold her and rock her. We will talk to her and tell her how safe she is now. (*Cradles the baby doll and rocks the baby while speaking.*)

Therapist: Mom, would you like to hold baby Bella first?

Mom: Yes, I would love to hold Baby Bella. (*The therapist gently hands the baby over to the mother.*)

Therapist: Mom, what do you want to say to baby Bella? (*Bella sits between her adoptive mother and father on the couch.*)

Mom: I love you, baby Bella. You are safe now. No one is going to hurt you ever again. We keep you safe. (*Cradles and rocks the baby doll gently as Bella looks up at her mother and then back at the baby doll again and again.*) If you are hungry, we will make sure you have a bottle. If you are wet, we will change you. If you are scared, we will help you. The scary time is over now, and you are safe, baby Bella. You are safe.

Bella: (*Reaches up and touches the doll's head.*) You are safe now, baby Bella. Mom and Dad will keep you safe. We have a safe house and good dogs to protect us. Mom makes good food, too.

Dad: Yes, baby Bella, it's all okay now. We're so sorry you were so scared. You have a safe place now inside Bella's heart, where Mom and Dad are rocking you and taking care of all that you need.

Therapist: Bella, can you hold the buzzies on baby Bella's hands and make her good feelings get even bigger?

Bella: (*Holds the buzzies on the doll's hands.*) Baby Bella likes the tappers. They help her feel better. Shhh, baby Bella, it's okay now. You won't have any more bad dreams. Mom and Dad are here now to keep you safe.

Mom: Yes, we are here, baby Bella. We will be here forever, and we will never leave you.

Dad: That's right. We will never leave you.

Therapist: Gosh, I wonder how baby Bella feels on the inside right now?

Mom: I bet she is calm . . . she seems calm.

Dad: Yes, she seems calm and relaxed.

Bella: She's calm, but still worried about the nightmares. Mom, could you tell her that she doesn't have to have the nightmares anymore?

Mom: Yes, baby Bella, it's okay now. All the scary stuff is over and you can relax and be calm. You don't have to worry anymore about the scary stuff. We will help Bella with all of that.

Therapist: If baby Bella could talk, what do you think she would say?

Dad: I think she would tell us that she feels comfortable and warm and safe right now.

Bella: I think she'd say she's happy.

For about 8 to 10 more minutes, the three sat on the couch and continued to nurture and comfort baby Bella. The therapist continued to use interweaves to reinforce Bella's safety and to assist Bella in healing the hurt inner baby. This exercise helped Bella begin feeling the safe, holding environment of her new life with her new parents. The parents benefited from this exercise because they learned just how scared baby Bella was. At closure, Bella was guided in visualizing baby Bella in her safe place, and the picture was reinforced with the buzzies. Then the therapist engaged her mother and father in talking about "big 8-year-old girl" things Bella had done the previous week, while Bella held the buzzies to reinforce her 8-year-old feelings.

Creating Internal Safety and Nurturing for Kids With Unstable Environments or Problematic Dissociation

When an older child or teen is residing in a temporary placement and there are no stable adults in the child's life, the safe place for the smaller child on the inside exercise can be conducted, but with an imaginary ideal caregiver figure or spiritual figure taking the role of the nurturing parent, as described in the Potter and Wesselmann protocols for adults (Potter & Wesselmann, 2023, pp. 153–165). It's best to reinforce the visualization throughout treatment to help create stability and lessen any tendency for dissociation. The ideal caregiver figure can be an individual who has been a positive support in the adolescent's life (e.g., a grandparent, childhood neighbor, or teacher) or a spiritual figure (e.g., an angel, Jesus, Buddha). If the child or teen prefers, it can even be an animal figure or their power animal. Optionally, if the Circle of Caring activity has been completed, the child or teen can be invited to imagine all of the people or animals from the caring circle encircling the younger baby or child self. A drawing or sand tray can be used. Associated positive feelings can be deepened with a slow short set of BLS. The older child or teen can be invited to enter the safe place if they're willing, and to give the smaller child a simple hug or messages that it's okay to let go of worry, that they're lovable and good, that they're not alone, and that the past is over. Positive feelings are again deepened with a slow, short set of BLS.

Safe Place for Smaller Child Vignette With 16-Year-Old Annette

Annette has no stable figure in her life currently. She has drawn a picture of her 6-year-old self in a cabin in the woods, surrounded by flowers and friendly animals.

Therapist: How does it feel for your 16-year-old self as you look at your picture of your 6-year-old self, safe and sound in this beautiful place?

Annette: It makes me happy.

Therapist: Is it okay if I tap on you a little as you notice that good feeling? (*Annette nods, and therapist applies a short slow set of BLS.*)

Therapist: It would be wonderful to find a caregiver to watch over your 6-year-old self in this beautiful place. Who could it be, do you suppose? This might be someone who's been in your life at some point, or it could be a spiritual figure or even a special animal. (*Annette draws a beautiful angel figure in the safe place with the smaller child part.*)

Therapist: What do you suppose the angel is doing for the little one today in the safe place?

Annette: I see them in the meadow picking flowers together.

Therapist: That sounds wonderful. Can you look at your picture and think of your 6-year-old self, safe and sound, picking flowers with the angel? I'll add a few taps if that's okay. (*Annette nods, and the therapist applies a slow, short set of BLS.*)

Therapist: I wonder if you could imagine that your 16-year-old self enters this beautiful place. (*Annette nods.*) See if you can tell her that it's okay to just be a kid and play and not worry, that she's lovable and good, and she'll never be alone. Let her know the past is over and now it's time to heal—and anything else you want to say. You could even give her a hug if you want to.

Annette: I told her, and I gave her a little hug.

Therapist: Awesome. Does that feel okay?

Annette: (*Nodding.*) Yup. (*Therapist applies a slow, short set of BLS.*)

ARD THROUGH MOVEMENT, SONG, AND RHYTHM FOR YOUNGER CHILDREN

Bilateral stimulation can be implemented with toddlers and preschoolers in a fun way through rhythm, song, and bilateral swaying along with taps or buzzies. Infants and toddlers who are in a nurturing environment naturally experience a great deal of BLS through bilateral swaying and rocking. The infant who is held lying in the parent's arms and rocked in a rocking chair is experiencing BLS through side-to-side movement. A mother holding her infant upon her shoulder naturally sways her body from side to side, providing her infant with

BLS. In the 1950s, during Harlow's famous experiments with monkeys, it was discovered that the functioning of infant monkeys raised with wire mothers could be enhanced by placing them on contraptions that swayed them from side to side. As a form of ARD, toddlers and preschoolers can sit on the parent's lap facing the therapist, while the parent and therapist sway from side to side, rhythmically chanting or singing nurturing messages and positive ideas to enhance the child's trust and feelings of safety. Stefanie Armstrong wrote the lyrics that follow.

Sung to the tune of "Hush Little Baby"
> Hush little Isaac, we love you.
> Mommy and Daddy keep you safe.
> You are always safe with us.
> Learning every day that you can trust.

Sung to the tune of "Frère Jacques," a traditional French song (English version, "Brother John")
> Cali is safe, Cali is safe.
> Yes she is, yes she is.
> Her mommy and daddy, her mommy and daddy,
> Keep her safe, keep her safe.
> Cali is loved, Cali is loved.
> Yes she is, yes she is.
> Her mommy and daddy, her mommy and daddy,
> Love her very much, love her very much.

Sung to the tune of "The Wheels on the Bus"
> The love in mommy's heart never stops, never stops, never stops.
> The love in mommy's heart never stops, even when she's at work.
> The love in mommy's heart stays forever and ever, ever and ever, ever and ever.
> The love in mommy's heart stays forever and ever, even when she says No!
> Mommy whispers to Isaac, "I'll keep you safe, I'll keep you safe, I'll keep you safe."
> Mommy whispers to Isaac, "I'll keep you safe, forever and ever."

Sung to the tune of "Head, Shoulders, Knees, and Toes"
>(The parent or therapist begins the song by asking . . .) How much of Jacob does Mommy love? She loves him from his . . .
>Head, shoulders, knees, and toes, knees and toes. Head, shoulders, knees, and toes, knees and toes. Eyes and ears and mouth and nose . . . head, shoulders, knees, and toes, knees and toes.

Two-year-old Amy sat on her mother's lap, while her mother sat on the couch, facing the therapist. The therapist sat on the floor in front of Amy while her mother swayed side to side, and the therapist tapped on Amy's knees in synchrony with the swaying. The therapist led Mother in singing "Amy is safe" to the tune of "Frère Jacques." Amy loved the singing and swaying and tried to join in the singing. Amy and her mother continued singing and swaying as a nightly ritual, which appeared to calm Amy and help her feel safe and more securely connected to her mother. Amy's mother was also encouraged to play music and stand and sway while whispering nurturing and loving messages to her daughter.

OPTIONAL PLAYFUL ARD ACTIVITIES

Children who have difficulty remaining in their present-day self due to frequent dissociation or regression to a younger state may be unable to keep the Playing Baby game as a pretend activity. They may dissociate and have difficulty returning to the present-day, more mature child state. If you observe frequent dissociation or regression, the Playing Baby or lollipop games are contraindicated.

Playing Baby

Younger children through elementary school-age children may enjoy a pretend game of Playing Baby. Be sure to emphasize that it's a game in which they get to use their imagination and pretend to be a baby. Invite the child to cuddle or curl up on the parent's lap. Offer a lollipop as a pretend bottle, which the parent can hold for the child. The parent can be encouraged to talk playfully about how fun it is to care for the baby and act out rocking, feeding, and singing to the baby, and so on. The child can also be encouraged to place his or her ear over the mom's heart. The therapist can describe how the child's heart is syncing with the mother's heart, like two musical instruments playing in rhythm together. The therapist can also put on lullaby music or other soft music and dim the lights to encourage the child to relax and enjoy the closeness. The child may enjoy cuddling up with their old baby blanket or stuffed animal or another cozy item During any part of this exercise, the therapist can place buzzies in the child's socks or shoes or tap slowly and rhythmically on the child's legs or feet to create BLS while calling attention to the child's sensations and emotions: "Notice how safe and secure you feel curled up in your mom's lap. Notice how relaxed your body feels while Mom is in charge of taking care of you."

The Lollipop Game was developed by Joan Lovett (2015), in which a lollipop is used in a playful game that encourages the parent to attune to the child's cues. Following is a Lollipop Game script.

Lollipop Game Script

Say to the child, "Sally, you and your mom/dad are going to play the lollipop game. You get to lie across your mom's lap while she holds the lollipop. Your job is to use your eyes and mouth to signal when you want the lollipop in your mouth and when you want the lollipop out of your mouth. Mom, your job is to watch your child's face and read her signals so you know when to give her the lollipop."

If the child crunches the lollipop, the therapist says, "I think you're telling us it's time to move on to another activity! That's completely okay. We can always do this again another day!"

At the end of the activity say, "Let's tuck the baby part away in the safe place now. Can you picture the baby part there? Now we want the biggest kid self back. Tell me about some of the big kid things you did this week."

SELF-REGULATION DEVELOPMENT AND INSTALLATION (S-RDI)

Children and teens with a history of attachment trauma have anxiety about their feelings. Anxiety about feelings can spiral quickly into panic and meltdowns or lead to compulsive, unhealthy coping behaviors. Chapter 5 describes the role of the family therapist in teaching and coaching children to widen their window for tolerating distress through several family therapy activities. Self-regulation development and installation (SRDI) is an EMDR preparation phase activity that utilizes slow BLS along with skills coaching during therapy sessions to reinforce the experience of coregulation, decrease panic and defense related to feelings, and widen the window of tolerance.

The EMDR therapist looks for opportunities that arise naturally in session in which the child or teen needs some coregulation help. The therapist always begins by attuning and validating the feelings of the child or teen in order to keep them engaged and maintain trust. Some common opportunities that arise naturally in sessions include:

- Becoming irritated in session with the therapist or parent
- Becoming impatient for the session to be over
- A sudden urge to pick or scratch at their skin
- Sudden hyperactivity related to some playful activity in session

The therapist may also initiate an activity to intentionally create a low level of distress, including:

- Making up a homework sheet or using an actual homework sheet from school to practice handling homework stress
- Bringing up a recent dysregulating experience
- Playing a game that includes waiting or following directions or some other difficult component
- Demonstrating facial expressions associated with various emotions or examining pictures of animals or people showing emotions

Parents should be prepared for the S-RDI activities prior to the session.

Introducing S-RDI to Parents Script

Say to the parent, "I'm going to begin taking advantage of situations in which your child becomes dysregulated in session to provide coaching with the various skills we've learned. If it goes well, I'll reinforce the experience of moving to a calm state with buzzies or taps. At times, I might even create a tiny bit of dysregulation with a role-play, a challenging situation in a game or with pictures. Remember, the capacity to self-calm doesn't develop overnight, and we all struggle with it sometimes, even as adults. But every time you or I help your child's nervous system calm through attunement, empathy, and coregulation methods, your child is internalizing the skills just a little bit more."

Introducing S-RDI to Kids Script
Say to the child or teen, "Yes, it's so hard to *[wait for something/have an urge to scratch or pick/handle mad feelings]*. It can cause our bodies to get all worked up, and that's no fun. I'd like to help your body calm down a little if I can. If we can help your body be more comfortable this situation will be easier to handle."

Coaching With Slow BLS
When the therapist notices the child or teen is experiencing some dysregulation, the skills developed in the family therapy sessions are used to coach the child through the feelings. If the child or teen seems to be receptive or somewhat receptive, the therapist also applies a soothing method of BLS such as alternating gentle squeezes of their shoulders, gently swaying with the child from side-to-side, or placing the buzzies in their pockets or shoes. The therapist suggests the child or teen notice how it feels as their body calms down. The parent also benefits by witnessing the therapist coaching the child.

Sometimes kids reject any type of coaching or coregulation efforts during an episode of dysregulation. In that case, the therapist holds the space for the child, staying calm and patient, with very few words, perhaps just letting the child know their feelings are okay. This, too, is useful for parents to observe.

The following are some scripts for coaching the child or teen during S-RDI with the various skills learned during family therapy sessions. The therapist can use one or more of the following ways of coaching the child or teen. The experience of shifting from dysregulated to regulated is deepened with their preferred method of slow, soothing BLS.

Facts About Feelings Coaching Script
Say to the child or teen, "Having feelings can be really hard sometimes. Remember, all your feelings are normal and okay, though. We all have all kinds of feelings throughout the day. If it's okay with you, I'm going to add some *[preferred method of BLS]*. Sometimes they wash up on top of us like a big ocean wave, but we can have the feelings and still be okay. If we ride out the feelings for a bit, they gradually wash back out to sea. Feelings are just feelings, they're not right or wrong, good or bad. They just are. You can have any feelings and still be okay."

Talking to the Brain Coaching Script
Say to the child or teen, "You're having some big feelings right now, and I know that can be really hard. I'd love to help you feel a little better. If it's okay with you, I'm going to add some *[preferred method of BLS]*. I wonder if your thinking brain could remind your feeling brain, 'I don't like this feeling right now, but it's all going to be okay, and I can handle it. It's a thing I can manage.' Can your thinking brain help out your feeling brain this way?"

Talking to the Body Coaching Script
Say to the child or teen, "I notice your body is full of big feelings today. That can be really hard. It looks like maybe your feet are having a hard time. Can you talk to your feet and tell your feet everything is okay? If it's okay with you, I'm going to add some *[preferred method of BLS]*. Maybe you can let your feet know it's safe to calm down; there's nothing your feet have to do right now."

Breathwork and Bodywork Coaching Script
Say to the child or teen, "I can see you're having big feelings, and all your feelings are okay. But I'd like to help your body feel a little calmer and better. Here, let's both lay down on the floor, okay? We can each place one of these little toys on our belly and take some good big breaths. See how we can make them move up and down. If it's okay with you, keep breathing, and I'm going to add some *[preferred method of BLS]*. (*Leads the child in taking some more deep breaths.*) Now let's make our arms and legs relaxed, like cooked spaghetti noodles."

Talking to the Smaller Child on the Inside Coaching Script
Say to the child or teen, "I wonder if that smaller child on the inside is having big feelings. Can you remind that smaller child on the inside that you're safe today? Remind the smaller child on the inside they can stay inside that wonderful safe place and relax and play. See that smaller self safe and sound there?" (*Add a preferred method of BLS as the nervous system calms.*)

Breathwork and Bodywork Coaching Vignette With 7-Year-Old Kaya and Her Mother
Seven-year-old Kaya entered the EMDR session in an agitated state after another child had mocked her in the waiting room. She sat down next to her

mother, bumping her mother's sore shoulder with her head. When her mother asked her to stop, she became increasingly tense and irritated, kicking, hitting the couch, and growling.

> **Therapist:** Kaya, it looks like you're having a little bit of a hard time right now, and I'd love to help you. I'm wondering, are you feeling like you need to get the anger out by hitting or kicking? *(Kaya nods and begins hitting the arm of the couch with her fist.)* But Kaya, it seems like this way isn't working right now, it seems like your body is getting a little more worked up. Would it be okay if we try to help your body and brain some other way?
>
> **Kaya:** I guess. *(Still hitting the arm of the couch.)*
>
> **Therapist:** *(Invites Kaya to lie down next to her on the floor and places a small doll on Kaya's belly and on her own.)* Let's see if we can breathe air into our bellies and make the doll move up. We'll hold it for a minute and then blow it out and watch the doll go down. *(Pauses as they both take big belly breaths and blow them out.)* Just like you learned in Stefanie's office. Wow, you're doing even better than I am.
>
> **Kaya:** My doll is getting a fun ride on my belly.
>
> **Therapist:** Yes she is! Can I add some foot squeezes while you notice your body relaxing? *(Kaya nods and the therapist applies alternating squeezes with Kaya's feet.)* I wonder if you can make your arms and legs floppy like cooked spaghetti noodles?
>
> **Kaya:** Can you do the cooked noodle test?
>
> **Therapist:** Sure! *(One by one, she tests Kaya's limbs to see if they are relaxed.)* Wow, Kaya, that's impressive. I'm going to do some more foot squeezes to help your brain notice your calm body if that's okay with you. *(Gently applies foot squeezes as Kaya continues to belly breathe and relax on the floor.)* Just think, you're helping all the big waves of feelings get all washed away.

Speaking to the Smaller Child Vignette With 10-Year-Old Derek

Ten-year-old Derek was very triggered each time his adoptive mother paid attention to others or talked on the phone. His mother stepped out to take an important call during the therapy session and Derek started squirming and making growling sounds that continued when his mother returned to the room. Derek had experienced a great deal of neglect and being left alone for lengthy periods of time when he was 3 years old.

Therapist: Do you think that alone feeling you were having when Mom was on the phone was coming from little 3-year-old Derek who lives in your heart? Take a moment to think of the feeling.

Derek: (*Nods.*)

Therapist: That makes sense, doesn't it? And the 3-year-old Derek inside probably learned to manage the alone feeling years ago by getting attention any way he could. I am so grateful to that little part of you for trying to help. But he doesn't need to do that anymore, does he? Mom, what would you want 3-year-old Derek to know right now?

Mom: I want the little Derek part to know that he's not alone. I want him to know that he doesn't have to be scared anymore. My love doesn't disappear when I'm distracted. I always love him no matter what.

Therapist: Derek, what do you suppose big Derek can say to 3-year-old Derek to help him right now?

Derek: Tell him we're not really alone? We have a mom who cares no matter what?

Therapist: I think that would really help little Derek. Why don't you hold the tappers and think about that in your head or say it out loud, whichever you want. (*The therapist applies slow BLS while Derek speaks to the little Derek inside his heart.*) Can you visualize little Derek in his safe place with Mom and Dad? (*Slow BLS is applied to reinforce the safe, nurturing image.*) Your body looks more calm now. Notice how you helped your body calm down today. (*Therapist applies another slow, short set of BLS.*)

Reinforce Positive Experiences of Self-Regulation From the Week

When the parent reports that the child used skills to calm down or allowed the parent to assist during the previous week, the therapist can give the child a high-five, offer the buzzies, and then, while applying slow BLS, ask the child to think about how it felt to calm down. The therapist should encourage the child to remember the sensation of his or her body moving from high alert to low alert and to think about how good that feels.

Optional S-RDI Activity: Coaching With Photographs

To reduce the child's fear of feelings, the therapist uses feelings cards/faces or finds photographs on the internet showing various faces with emotions, animals showing emotions, or situations in which people are showing emotions.

Next, the therapist reminds the child about the facts about feelings while the child looks at the picture, allowing the child to reflect upon the emotion without taking on the emotion.

Coaching With Photographs (With Slow BLS) Script
Say to the child or teen, "The feeling the animal or person is having is temporary. The feeling will come and go like waves of the ocean. This feeling is very normal. They can have this feeling and be okay. The feeling won't hurt them, and the feeling won't stay."

Optionally, the therapist can ask the child to think about how or why the feeling might change. For example, while looking at a picture of a lion looking sad, the child may create a story of the lion feeling better after talking to a friend. The child thinks of the lion's new feeling of happiness while the therapist adds another slow, short set of BLS.

Optional: Coaching With Tumbling Towers Games
This fun, optional activity was developed by Stefanie Armstrong, who also gives credit to Joan Lovett (2009) for the idea of using bilateral stimulation to reinforce positive cooperation in play. Children or teens who have experienced attachment trauma commonly have difficulty relying on caregivers and trusting them to be in charge. They have difficulty asking for help or tolerating "no." The games provide some opportunity for S-RDI during small moments of dysregulation. During the games, the therapist coaches the child or teen through the moments of stress, adding the slow BLS to deepen the child's awareness of the positive shift.

The Tumbling Towers activities can be played with any Tumbling Towers or Jenga game. Follow the general rules of the game (stacking the blocks, taking a block from the stack, and putting the block on top of the tower) while adding the intervention below. Explain the games to the parent before introducing the games to the child. As the therapist, parent, and child talk, they can sit on the floor and build a tower with the blocks together.

Tumbling Towers Vignette With 8-Year-Old Torey and His Mom
Therapist: Today we're going to play Tumbling Towers. However, we will play it differently than you've probably played it before. Torey, I know it's hard for you to rely on Mom and Dad and trust them, so we're going to

play a game today that will help you practice. That way, you'll have less upsetting things happen during your week. To show you how to play, I'll roleplay with your mom's help. I'll pretend to be you. Okay, let's get started. Mom, I'll tap on some blocks to see how loose they are, and then you'll tell me yes or no whether I should take that block. I'll then take that block and put it on top while saying, "Okay, Mom." It might be a little hard for me to be patient during this part. I might have to take a deep breath or talk to my brain. After I move the block, Mom will say "Thank you for doing exactly what I asked you to do, exactly the way I asked you to do it." [This phrase was borrowed from work by Joan Lovett (2009).]

At this point, the parent and therapist model it one or two times. The therapist demonstrates taking a deep breath or talking to their brain to stay calm. Next, it's the child's turn. If using buzzies, place them in the child's shoes or pockets. Alternatively, sit next to the child and apply taps on the child's shoulders. It's important to tell the child and the parent the two main rules: (1) The child practices saying, "Okay, Mom" and (2) the parent practices saying, "Thank you for doing exactly what I asked, exactly the way I asked you to do it." The therapist can motivate the child by saying, "Let's see how tall you and your mom can make your tower, as you cooperate together." If the child gets frustrated with following Mom's directions, the therapist coaches the child with skills and then says, "Notice how you're managing that feeling!" while adding a slow, short set of BLS.

The therapist's coaching may include:

- "Remind your brain that you can trust your mom to be in charge."
- "Just notice the feeling inside as you have success with saying okay."
- "Just notice the uncomfortable feeling and remind your brain, 'It's safe to let Mom be in charge.' Remember, feelings come and feelings go."
- "Just notice how it feels inside to relax and let Mom be charge."
- "Just notice how connected you and your mom are right now."
- "Notice how connected you and your mom are when you are working together."
- "It's safe to trust your mom and rely on her."

After approximately 10 to 15 minutes, the therapist can stop the activity and encourage the child and parent to get comfortable and sit close to one another.

At this time, the therapist can ask the child to remember and just notice the good feelings of trusting and being close to Mom as the buzzies run.

FUTURE REHEARSALS WITH NEW SKILLS

EMDR future rehearsals can be conducted to practice handling challenging situations using any resources installed during EMDR resource development work. Future rehearsals can also be conducted to practice handling challenging situations using skills learned in family therapy sessions. The new skills utilized for the future rehearsal may include any new skills learned such as the *please and thank you skill*, the *getting ready for bed skill*, the *waiting skill*, or the *taking turns skill*.

As the parent, child, or teen reveals challenges and difficulties from the week, create a play and act out the situation, modeling the skillful response. Next, act out the situation and ask the child to try using the skill. Suggest the child notice the good feelings, and apply a slow, short set of their preferred method of BLS.

CONCLUSION

The EMDR and family therapy foundational activities in IATP-C Stage 2 bring stability through increased self-awareness and self-regulation, interpersonal skills, a more resourced state, and strengthened bonds with caregivers. Even after EMDR reprocessing is initiated, the therapist can return to the foundational activities as often as needed to reinforce positive gains.

Part III

IATP-C Stage 3: Healing Triggers and Traumas

CHAPTER 7

Addressing Present and Future Through Integrative Family and EMDR Therapy

> Through reading this chapter, you'll gain skills for implementing the following:
>
> Family therapy activities:
> - The Dominoes Activity
> - Detective Work
>
> EMDR reprocessing methods:
> - The Trigger Tolerance Protocol and effective processing strategies
> - The EMD to EMDR continuum
> - Future templates
> - Integrating healthy responses through songs
> - Processing unhealthy compulsive behaviors

IATP-C Stage 3 addresses the past, present, and future. Although the standard EMDR sequence is to first address the past and then the present and future, kids and adults with complex trauma often benefit by starting with resource work and future templates as previously described followed by reprocessing of present triggers and future templates before addressing the past (Shapiro, 2018, p. 292). The IATP-C clinician often begins EMDR reprocessing with present triggers so the child or adolescent can experience the process with a less threatening target and also to develop increased coping for the present before addressing the past. Therefore this chapter covers family therapy and EMDR therapy strategies for addressing the present and future. Chapters 8 and 9 describe EMDR therapy strategies for addressing the past.

UNDERSTANDING TRIGGERS THROUGH FAMILY THERAPY ACTIVITIES

Because attachment injuries interfere with optimal development of mentalization, the family therapy Dominoes activity and Detective Work activities play an important role in improving kids' capacity to recognize their triggers, emotions, feelings, thoughts, and actions and put them into words. The activities provide insights and self-awareness that improve success for EMDR reprocessing of their triggers and future responses with EMDR therapy.

A concept used in dialectical behavioral therapy (Linehan, 1993), the behavior chain analysis, examines the thoughts, feelings, and actions leading to a problem behavior in an effort to discover where the path could be interrupted by implementing a skill. Potter (2011) has used the term domino effect to describe a similar process with families to help parents, children, and teens reflect upon the thoughts, emotions, sensations, and actions each has contributed to any crisis experienced during the past week.

The therapist demonstrates the domino effect in the office by standing real dominoes in a line and asking the child or teen to tip the first domino. (Some teens may prefer a discussion without the demonstration.) The therapist explains that the dominoes represent thoughts, feelings, and actions and points out that meltdowns and other big behaviors are the end result of toppling dominoes. The therapist then places the dominoes in standing position again and asks the child to remove a domino toward the beginning of the chain before toppling the dominoes again. This leads to a discussion of how we can interrupt the cascade of falling dominoes and prevent the bigger problems at the end by removing just one of the dominoes along the way.

Next, the therapist uses sticky notes that can be placed on the wall or a big whiteboard to chart out the dominoes (i.e., events) that led up to a conflict, meltdown, or other problem behaviors at home during an interaction with the parent who is present in the session. Both child and parent are encouraged to identify the following key elements for themselves:

- Factors that increased vulnerability, such as hunger, fatigue, or other stressors
- Triggers (activating events or situations)
- Emotions
- Negative thoughts
- Body sensations
- The final domino before the conflict, meltdown, or behaviors

Figure 7.1 illustrates a sample chain of child and parent dominoes.

The following is a vignette in which the therapist helps 9-year-old John and his adoptive mother interrupt the domino effect. (This was not the first time John and his mother had participated in the Dominoes activity.) John was adopted from Ethiopia at 2 years of age, and he had entered therapy with symptoms of defiance and aggression. John was continuing to engage in challenging bedtime behaviors that had culminated in a physical confrontation the previous evening. Before John was invited to participate, his mother was helped to look at her part in the domino cascade and discover her own trigger as the parent. After this exercise, she was able to change her thinking, become more mindful, and successfully guide John through the bedtime routine.

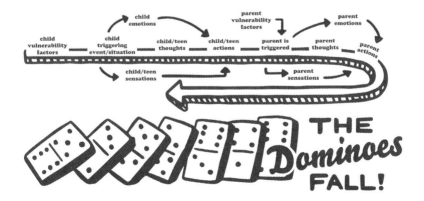

Figure 7.1: Sample Dominoes

Dominoes Activity Vignette With 9-Year-Old John and His Mom

Therapist: So, let's take a closer look at what's going on at bedtime.

Mom: Every night is a battle. Last night was awful. John came flying out of the bathroom and hit me several times.

Therapist: Before we bring John in here, let's do a domino exercise to see if we can discover the factors that led up to the outburst.

Mom: Okay.

Therapist: (Begins writing down each domino—each negative thought, feeling, sensation, or action—on the whiteboard, as John's mother recalls what happened in detail. In the middle of the exercise, Mom remembers that her son had been in the bathroom singing.)

Mom: (*Staring at the board.*) That's it. I'm triggered by his singing.

Therapist: Singing? Tell me more about that.

Mom: When he sings, I think he isn't listening to me and doesn't care about what I have asked him to do. (*Discovering her own negative thought.*) He doesn't care what I say. He's just in there singing. He's just standing there doing nothing.

Therapist: (*Gently.*) Do you know for sure that he's not brushing his teeth and washing his face?

Mom: No.

Therapist: (*Addressing the negative thought very gently.*) Is it true that he never listens to you?

Mom: No, that's not true. (*Now smiling.*) But sometimes it's true.

Therapist: (*Laughing.*) Of course, our children don't always listen to us, do they?

Mom: No, I guess that singing is just a trigger for me. I think that if you're in the bathroom doing what you need to be doing, there should be no singing.

Therapist: (*With a smile.*) That's understandable, but it could be true that in between song verses, he's getting it done.

Mom: True . . . I guess I will let the singing thing go and try not to worry about it.

Therapist: Yes, let's see how that goes. If he starts singing tonight, just notice how you're feeling, consider your thoughts, and don't say anything. Just let the feeling pass. Now, let's bring him in, so we can go through this same event with him. If you're comfortable with it, I'd like

you to share your trigger, how it makes you feel, and we'll see what he comes up with.
Mom: Okay. You know, I just want the very best for him.
Therapist: I know.

As the session continued, the domino exercise was repeated with John. As the therapist and John walked through the evening's events, Mom revealed her trigger. In addition, John figured out that he was triggered whenever his mom told him what to do. John identified his negative thought as "I should get to do what I want. I'm in charge of myself." The therapist discussed this thought with Mom and John, noting that "while it's true that you can do some things by yourself, like brushing your own teeth and washing your own face, don't you think that it's a good idea for Mom to help you remember that there is a bedtime, because getting enough sleep is important?"

Though he recognized that this statement was logically true, John had a hard time really believing it deep down. The family therapist described what John had discovered regarding his trigger and negative thought to the EMDR therapist. The EMDR therapist now had good information to assist with beginning EMDR reprocessing of John's negative thought, emotions, and sensations related to the trigger.

Dave Examines His Dominoes

Dave was guardian to his 14-year-old grandson, Nick. Dave and Nick had yelled at one another the night before after several weeks of IATP-C in which the relationship between them had shown very encouraging signs of improvement. Dave had come into the session feeling very discouraged. Luckily, Dave had developed a trusting relationship with the family therapist and together they examined the falling dominoes. Dave was able to recognize that both he and Nick had been highly vulnerable due to a stressful month in which the family had moved and Dave had had to place his elderly mother in a nursing home due to her failing health. Dave also noted that he was suffering from a fatigue headache when he had been triggered by some back talk from Nick. Because of his vulnerable state, he had immediately experienced some negative thoughts, such as, "Nobody appreciates me or cares about me." His thoughts had led to anger and yelling. Dave agreed that yelling is a big trigger for Nick, who experienced a lot of verbal abuse from his biological father as a younger child. Dave recognized that both he and Nick had entered a high alert state in which they lost their ability to reason or problem solve. The following is an excerpt from the one-on-one time with Dave.

Dominoes Vignette With Nick's Dad, Dave

Therapist: Dave, where do you think you might have been able to pull some of your own dominoes last night? Remember, the point in doing this exercise after the fact is so that you might be able to change the course of things next time.

Dave: First, I should have realized that I was mentally exhausted from all that has gone on just recently. I probably should have told the family up front that I felt awful, and I should have gone to bed right after dinner with that headache.

Therapist: That would have stopped the dominoes from falling right there, wouldn't it?

Dave: Yes, and otherwise, as soon as Nick started talking back to me, I should have told myself to pause and take some space. I might have said to Nick, "We're both stressed and tired. I know I'm too tired to talk rationally right now. Let's do some problem solving in the morning."

DETECTIVE WORK: EXPLORING TRIGGERS

Detective Work in sessions is another way to explore behaviors and triggers. During one-on-one time with parents, they often report on challenging interactions from the week. Before the child or teen enters the session, the therapist reminds the parents that feelings of shame on the part of their child will activate their downstairs brain and shut down their capacity to reflect from their *upstairs brain*. The therapist promotes a collaborative, nonjudgmental approach, emphasizing that their child's triggers are to be expected considering their history of traumatic events.

When the child or teen joins the session, the therapist explains that all kids with difficult experiences in the past have a self-protective trauma brain that goes into fight-or-flight mode very easily and that this can interfere with the thinking brain and lead to actions that aren't helpful. The therapist invites the child or teen and parent to put on their detective hats and work together with the therapist to identify the child's negative thoughts, emotions, and sensations related to the trigger.

Introducing the Detective Work Script

Say to the child or teen, "All kids who've had some hard things happen have a very self-protective downstairs brain that lights up and goes into fight-or-flight mode really easily when there is some sort of trigger. Unfortunately, when the downstairs brain lights up it causes unhelpful thoughts and actions instead of helpful thoughts and actions. Let's do a little Detective Work with that trigger you've identified. Let's put on our detective hats and work together to figure out what your brain was thinking when this trigger happened." (*The therapist and child or teen discuss possible negative beliefs.*) "How about we work together to figure out what your brain could think instead?" (*The therapist and child or teen discuss ideas for helpful thoughts.*) "What emotions and body feelings go along with this trigger? (*The therapist and teen discuss possible emotions and sensations the child felt at the time and feels right now just thinking about the trigger.*) "Let's think about how you wish you could respond and what skills you might need to help you." (*The therapist and child or teen discuss ideas for helpful responses.*)

Detective Work allows the child or teen to move easily into EMDR reprocessing with the triggering situation later on.

Vignette With 15-Year-Old Devoney

The family therapist invited Devoney, age 15, to do a little Detective Work to help learn more about her triggers and figure out more helpful responses. The family therapist conducts the work without the parent present after observing tension between Devoney and her mom in the waiting room.

> **Therapist:** I wonder if we could do a bit more Detective Work here. Would it be okay with you if we do a bit of brainstorming together? (*Devoney nods.*) When you think about your frustration related to the trigger of Mom telling you to pick up your shoes in the hall? Can you identify your frustrated thought?
>
> **Devoney:** I don't know, I just think that people are always trying to control me, that's all.
>
> **Therapist:** It makes sense that you're on high alert. Even if it doesn't seem possible to think anything different, is there another thought that might be helpful? Down the road, perhaps?

Devoney: Mmm, maybe that my mom thinks she's doing a good thing by nagging or whatever.

Therapist: Yeah, that's a great one. Like, she thinks she's doing a good thing because she's trying to do her job as a mom. I could see that would be totally helpful, if you were able to have that thought. Could we try to figure out a skill that could help you manage the trigger, even if the helpful thought doesn't come right away?

Devoney: I just need to walk away, to get a breather. I'm afraid my mom will think I'm just being a jerk if I walk away.

Therapist: Maybe we could get your mom in here and talk about this idea so she'd be more on board with it, what do you think?

Kids, like adults, want to believe their feelings matter and they have choices. Therefore, obtaining Devoney's consent assured that Devoney stayed more reasonable in the problem-solving discussion with her mom. The therapist offered to role-play the situation with her mom, and then encouraged the two of them to role-play. Later, the trigger and negative belief were targeted and reprocessed with EMDR.

EMDR THERAPY: GENERAL SUGGESTIONS FOR KIDS WITH ATTACHMENT INJURIES

Kids with a history of attachment trauma need a container at the outset of reprocessing. The therapist should also have an assortment of engaging BLS methods available and take some special precautions when it comes to virtual work.

The Container Activity

Before commencing reprocessing, the child or teen develops a container that can hold any feelings, thoughts, or memories that are bothering them. This provides a method that empowers the child or teen to be able to set memories and feelings aside before they're ready to work with them. It can be an imaginary container that exists only in the mind's eye, such as a magic box or treasure chest. For kids who are concrete thinkers, the therapist offers an actual container such as a file drawer or brings in a jar or box the child can decorate.

Container Script
Say to the child or teen, "You get to pick what kind of a container you want. The great thing about this is that you can choose to send worries, bothers, memories, or feelings to your container anytime you want. When we work on different things, we'll just take it one thing at a time and leave everything else in the container. Anytime something comes up in between our sessions that you don't want to think about, you can send it back here, into your container. I'll hang onto it for you."

Optional Container Activity
Glass marbles, shells, or stones can be placed in the container to represent the contained feelings or memories.

Explaining How EMDR Will Help Script
Say to the child or teen, "This EMDR thing we've been doing to make your good feelings bigger can also make yucky or uncomfortable feelings get smaller. I use this method with lots of kids, and they find it really helps. You and I will identify a situation or event to work on first, and then we'll identify thoughts and feelings. You can draw the situation, or make it in the sand tray if you want, and then we'll use those buzzies or some tapping or you can do eye movement by watching these lights or by watching me move a toy from side-to-side. (The therapist should allow the child or teen to try out various methods and choose what they prefer.) We'll do some taps/buzzies/eye movements and then I'll check on what you're thinking or feeling. Then we'll do a little more and then I'll check in again. We'll keep going a bit and in the end, I think you'll find you have some better thoughts and feelings about whatever was bothering you."

Bilateral Stimulation Strategies
BLS through fast eye movements are most recommended for EMDR reprocessing of triggers or traumas, although other methods of fast BLS are effective for reprocessing as well (Shapiro, 2018). For kids with attachment trauma who still have some measure of mistrust, we want to use the BLS methods they like the best to keep them engaged and willing. It's helpful to keep a basket or drawer of little brightly colored puppets and toys and light-up wands to keep it lively by switching it up between fun ways of moving the eyes. Lots of kids

enjoy watching lights on an eye scan machine or watching bilateral movement of images or lights on a computer app.

For kids who don't stay with the eye movements, there are many fun options for tactile BLS. Many kids like to join the therapist in shaking maracas or beating a drum with alternating hands or engaging in hand-clapping games. Kids with lots of energy or processing mad feelings benefit from BLS involving running in place or stomping. A very popular method of BLS involves holding a giant metal Slinky toy in both hands and moving the metal rings back and forth between right and left hand in tandem with the therapist, who also has a Slinky. Many kids like buzzies in their pockets or shoes, which keeps their hands free to suck a lollipop, draw, work in the sand tray, or use a fidget toy. Other kids prefer hand taps or alternating pressure on their legs or hands or shoulders, applied by their parent or therapist. The therapist can change it up frequently, alternating methods or modalities within the same session to keep it playful and engaging.

A Word About Virtual Therapy

Virtual EMDR therapy is a viable option that allows families access to care who otherwise would be unable to get help due to logistical barriers. EMDR virtual therapy is indeed effective, but there are some challenges. To prevent problems with keeping kids contained and engaged when they're not in the therapy office, the therapist should first explain to the family the importance of having a quiet, private space out of earshot of others. The therapist should work with the family on creating seating that allows the therapist to be seen and heard and allows every family member to be seen and heard by the therapist. Ground rules should be established about staying on camera throughout the session and requiring others in the household to stay outside the room.

The therapist should work with the child or teen to establish preferred methods for the BLS. The following are a few options:

- The child or teen watches the therapist move their hand or a playful object from side to side.
- The therapist leads the child or teen in applying butterfly taps or leg taps.
- The therapist leads the child or teen in squeezing squishy balls, one hand and then the other.
- The therapist leads the child or teen in moving the rings of a giant metal Slinky from one hand to the other.

- The therapist leads the child or teen in drumming on the table.
- The parent applies taps on the child's shoulders or hands at the therapist's direction.
- A younger child sits on the parent's lap facing the screen, and the parent sways the child from side to side.
- Use of one of the many available EMDR apps developed for virtual EMDR therapy.

TRICKY THINGS ABOUT TRIGGERS

The IATP C therapist can refer to the History-Taking Checklist (Appendix A) completed by the parents during the initial session to discover which child triggers the parents recognized at that time, although parents may not have insight regarding many of the triggers. Continuous Detective Work related to situations that came up between therapy sessions helps bring to light many of the child's triggers.

Some triggers are hard for parents to recognize because the parent's emotions have been activated, and because the child's trigger can be something that doesn't seem logical on the face of it. For example, if a parent gives their child a hug and their child says, "I hate you," the parent may assume their child truly hates them. The therapist can help the parent step back and look at the situation through the attachment trauma lens to see that the child is triggered by affection due to fear that closeness is unsafe. Closeness with parents can trigger negative cognitions (NCs) such as "Closeness is unsafe," "Nobody could really love me," and "I have to keep up my walls to be safe."

Reassuring kids around triggers like this can be somewhat helpful but often is not enough because their reaction is so automatic. EMDR reprocessing is helpful because it goes deep, activating the neural networks and jump-starting the adaptive information processing system within the child.

THE EMDR TRIGGER TOLERANCE PROTOCOL

Note: Appendix F provides a review of the EMDR reprocessing phases with tips for working with kids. This chapter contains additional strategies for reprocessing triggers related to attachment trauma and challenging behaviors.

Attachment-injured children have sensitive limbic brains that are easily dysregulated by many triggers, large and small, at home, at school, and in the community. Some of their triggers are directly associated with their traumas, as is true for the situation of a teacher's angry face activating memories of early abuse. Some triggers are very indirectly associated with the early traumas, as is true for the situation of a difficult homework assignment activating underlying feelings of poor self-esteem. Either type of trigger can lead to quick dysregulation and maladaptive defenses.

When starting with trigger work, it's important to remember that the traumas driving the triggers are still maladaptively stored. Eliminating all emotional charge or addressing every trigger is unrealistic. However, we can reduce the intensity of their emotions related to their biggest triggers and widen their window for managing day-to-day feelings that they have by improving their capacity to think and solve problems during reprocessing. As their reasoning improves and their reactivity lessens, kids become more stable and more capable of addressing their past. Eventually, the IATP-C therapist moves back and forth between working with present triggers and working with the past. This slows the pace of the trauma work and continuously builds stability.

Our colleagues in the Netherlands who translated the first edition of this book began using the term Trigger Tolerance Protocol to describe what we were doing with EMDR and triggers (Schlattmann et al., 2023). We found the term to be appropriate and descriptive of our focus on building the capacity to manage and tolerate emotions and triggers rather than focusing on the unrealistic goal of eliminating all their triggers and emotional responses.

The IATP-C therapist explains to the child or teen (in the presence of their parents): "Our goal is to help you grow a stronger thinking brain and manage your feeling brain so you can stay calmer and figure out the best thing to do in hard situations."

Phase 3: Assessment Phase, Trigger Tolerance Protocol

To keep children and teens cooperative and engaged, the Phase 3 target assessment should be conducted with simple language, flexibility, and playfulness. As stated previously, for children and teens with attachment trauma, the trigger is often something quite ordinary, such as a hug from a parent or a parent saying no, losing a board game, bedtime, waking time, school time, homework, or feeling hungry before dinner. Many of the targets, NCs and PCs, have been identified during Detective Work and the Domino activity.

However, just because a target trigger has been identified doesn't mean the child is able to access the emotional components of the target in the office. Kids with poor capacity for mentalization often have difficulty visualizing a situation, and they're also in the habit of guarding themselves from their emotions. It can be helpful to role-play the triggering situation at the beginning of the assessment phase. Alternatively, a photograph can be used to help the child or teen access the memory components. For example, if a child or teen is triggered by moments of closeness, a family photograph of opening a present from a parent on their birthday may help access the memory and associated feelings of danger.

The therapist and child or teen should agree upon a neutral name for the trigger such as the *birthday trigger*. The therapist keeps the assessment phase questions simple (as described in the Appendix F review).

Remember that it's quite common for a child or teen to choose an NC that is other-referencing. Kids who struggle with trust and assume negative intent on the part of others often choose "My mom is mean," "My teacher is against me," or "The other kids are bullies." It's okay to use these other-referencing NCs because they really resonate for the child. The therapist can assume the NC is driven by the self-referencing NC "I cannot trust."

When targeting triggers before past traumas have been processed, a "process PC" may be most achievable for the child or teen. Process PCs are positive beliefs that are in process like "I am learning to trust" or "I can learn to take in good things."

The following are some assessment phase examples for kids with attachment injuries.

Latka, Age 17, Currently Residing in an Adoptive Home After a History of Foster Care

Trigger: "Messages of Love" activity with her mother
NC: "She's making it up. I don't trust her."
PC: "I can give this a chance. I can learn to take it in."
VOC: 3
Emotion: Anxiety
SUD: 8
Body sensation: Tension in arms and legs

Valenia, Age 6, Currently Residing in a Foster Home After Abuse in Her Biological Home

Trigger: Foster mom telling her "no"
NC: "She's mean to me." (This is the NC that resonated. It's not self-referencing, but the therapist knew the self-referencing interpretation would be "I can't trust moms.")
PC: "She's doing her mom job." (The self-referencing interpretation would be, "I can trust my foster mom.")
VOC: Hands halfway apart
Emotion: Mad
SUD: Hands wide apart
Body sensation: Arms

Jamal, Age 14, Currently Residing in a Residential Treatment Center

Trigger: Homework
NC: "It's too hard." (This is the NC that resonated. The therapist knew the self-referencing interpretation would be, "I can't do it. I'm stupid.")
PC: "If I let someone help, I can figure it out."
VOC: 4
Emotion: Frustrated
SUD: 8
Body sensation: Head

Corey, Age 10, With Adoptive Mother (Biological Grandmother) After Biological Mother Died From Substance Abuse

Trigger: Getting dropped off at school
NC: "I'm not safe."
PC: "My teachers are safe and they will help me."
VOC: 3
Emotion: Fear
SUD: 9
Body: Stomach

TRIGGER TOLERANCE PROTOCOL AND EFFECTIVE PROCESSING STRATEGIES

As previously stated, we're using the term trigger tolerance protocol because we're focusing on the goal of reducing emotional reactivity and widening tolerance, rather than the goal of eliminating all triggers. Realistically, the child will always experience situations that trigger a negative emotional response, but as we encourage mentalization, reflection, and problem-solving throughout EMDR reprocessing with present day triggers, they naturally build greater capacity to manage their emotions and cope with hard things.

Kids with a history of attachment trauma may be fast processors or they may have deficits in their capacity to reason and process, causing slow processing and a need for longer sets. It may be hard to tell when to stop the BLS and check in through their face or body. If they often respond with "I don't know" or "Nothing," say, "This time, I'll continue longer, and you look up at me when you have a thought or feeling to share." This allows the child or teen to be in control of the length of the set, and they know when they have a new thought or feeling to share.

Children and teens with a history of attachment trauma often need cognitive interweaves to help them through stuck places caused by deficits in their storage of adaptive information and their ability to reason. Don't worry if it's necessary to provide an interweave after every set. The BLS allows the child to make new associations with the help of the interweaves and achieve true shifts in their feelings and thoughts. The following section describes interweaves that are especially helpful for building tolerance to the many everyday triggers they encounter.

Cognitive Interweaves: Expanding Trigger Tolerance and Capacity to Reflect

Cognitive interweaves can do much more than simply get kids unstuck when they're looping on the same feelings and thoughts. Interweaves build kids' skills for mindfulness, distress tolerance, and reflection. The interweaves may be short questions or direct statements between sets. Interweaves may coach kids in the facts about feelings learned during the family therapy activities. Interweaves may invite expression of their internal state through words, actions, art, or a sand tray. Interweaves may prompt dialogue between the parent and their child (interactional interweaves) or prompt internal dialogue between the thinking brain and feeling brain or between the biggest kid self and the smaller child part. With an interweave question, the therapist may want to wait for the child's response before initiating another set of BLS, or the therapist may want the child to consider the question during the next set of BLS.

Interweaves when reprocessing present-day triggers can help children or teens with
1. Riding out the feelings
2. Accessing information they don't know or can't access
3. Zeroing in on an obstacle or stuck point
4. Increasing their capacity to reason and reflect effectively
5. Separating past situations from present situations

Methods of providing cognitive interweaves for triggers
- Coaching with facts about feelings
- Invitations to parents to provide helpful information or words (interactional interweaves)
- Brief questions or statements
- Invitation to child to access the thinking brain, biggest kid self, or power animal

Examples of cognitive interweaves to help them ride out their feelings (offered between sets or briefly during BLS)
- **Therapist:** "Just notice the feeling . . . It won't hurt you . . . You can ride it out."
- "Remember . . . feelings come and feelings go . . . The feeling won't hurt you."
- "It's just a normal feeling . . . .Talk to your brain . . . You don't have to act it out."
- "Take some deep breaths . . . It's going to be okay."

Examples of cognitive interweaves to provide needed information (offered between sets)
- (*To the parent.*) "Mom/Dad, what do you want _____ to know about this?"

- (*To the parent.*) "Mom/Dad, do you expect your child to do things perfectly?" _____ (*To the child or teen.*) "Do you believe what Mom/Dad just said? Think of that."
- "I'll bet you didn't realize that all kids struggle and need some help sometimes."
- "Why do you suppose Mom/Dad wants you to _____ [*Task such as doing homework/getting to school on time*]?"
- (*To the parent.*) "Mom/Dad, why do you ask your child to do this task? _____ [*Task such as room cleaning/doing chores.*] _____ (*To the child or teen.*) "Do you believe your Mom/Dad? _____ "Think of that."

Examples of interweaves that zero in on an obstacle or stuck point (offered between sets)
- "What feels most upsetting about this?"
- "What feels unsafe about this?"
- "What is the worst thing that could happen?"
- "What would be scary about cooperating with Mom/Dad/the teacher?"

Examples of interweaves that help kids mentalize and reason effectively by accessing the biggest kid self, thinking brain, or power animal wisdom (offered between sets)
- "What could your biggest kid self say to the littler you about this trigger?"
- "What does your power animal want your smaller self, feeling brain to know about this trigger?"
- "Can you bring your power animal to be right by your side? (*Pause.*) What helpful ideas come to you about this now?"
- "What does your thinking brain say to your feeling brain about this trigger?"
- "I'm going to be your feeling brain. You be the thinking brain and help me out." (*Therapist initiates role-play.*)
- "I'll take this puppet and be the feeling brain. You take this other puppet and be the thinking brain. Your puppet is going to help my puppet!" (*Role-play with puppets.*)

Examples of cognitive interweaves to help separate past from present between sets
- "Even though it may feel the same, how is this situation now actually different from the situation you had when you were little?"
- "How are the adults in your life different from the adults in your life when you were younger?"

If a past memory surfaces and the child or teen isn't ready to reprocess the memory (or there isn't time in the session), the therapist can invite them to move the memory into their container. The therapist can then use one of the above interweaves to separate the past from the present.

If a past memory surfaces and the child or teen is ready for it, it's okay to continue fast sets of eye movements and allow the memory to reprocess within the session.

Excerpts From Sessions Reprocessing Present-Day Triggers
Vignette With 11-Year-Old Eugene: Separating Past From Present Interweave

The trigger involves his teacher looking angry and using a stern voice. The NC = "My teacher is mean." (Interpretation = "I can't trust. I'm not safe.") The PC = "My teacher is trying to be a good teacher." (Interpretation = "I can trust her. I'm safe.")

> (The vignette picks up in the middle of reprocessing.)
> **Therapist:** What are you noticing?
> **Eugene:** I still think she's scary. I think she hates me.
> **Therapist:** Go with that. (*BLS.*) What's there now?
> **Eugene:** She thinks I'm bad. It reminds me of my first foster mom, when she used to hit me.
> **Therapist:** I'm so sorry that happened, Eugene. Would you like to put that upsetting memory in your container for now? And perhaps think about what is different in this situation?
> **Eugene:** Well, my teacher doesn't hit me. She's all bark and no bite.
> **Therapist:** Go with that. (*BLS.*)
> **Eugene:** We were all talking and not listening. I get that she was frustrated.
> **Therapist:** Go with that. (*BLS.*)

Eugene: I guess she was just trying to get us to listen.
(*Processing continues to closure.*)

Vignette With 7-Year-Old Maria: Thinking Brain, Feeling Brain Interweave

The target trigger is Mom telling Maria dinner will be ready in 20 minutes. The NC = "I can't stand it." The PC = "I can handle it." Partway through the session, Maria starts looping on "I can't stand it."

> **Therapist:** Think of when Mom said "wait" again and I'll run the buzzies. (*Fast BLS.*) What are you noticing?
>
> **Maria:** It's not fair. I just can't stand it when I have to wait to eat. Why can't I just eat right away?
>
> **Therapist:** I'm going to use this rabbit puppet and be your feeling brain, okay? You can be the dog puppet thinking brain. (*Picks up the rabbit puppet.*) It's not fair when I don't get to eat right away. I don't like being hungry, I can't stand it!
>
> **Maria:** (*Picking up the dog puppet and speaking to the rabbit puppet.*) It won't be that long. You can do it! You won't die, you know!
>
> **Therapist:** (*Speaking as the rabbit puppet.*) It seems like a long time! What can I do to make the time go faster?
>
> **Maria:** (*Speaks to the rabbit puppet with the dog puppet.*) You can always ask Mom if you can play a game on her phone for a while.
>
> **Therapist:** (*Turns to Mom.*) Mom, is that okay?
>
> **Mom:** Sure, that's a great idea.
>
> **Therapist:** Maria, think of that while I turn on the buzzies again. (*BLS.*)

(*Processing continues to closure.*)

Vignette With 16-Year-Old Harvey: Interweave to Zero in on Stuck Point

Harvey gets triggered and verbally aggressive when his foster parents tell him what to do. NC = "I'm trapped." PC = "There are things I get to do." He begins looping while processing the trigger of being given a curfew.

> **Therapist:** Let's have you go back to the trigger of your dad and the curfew and do another set. (*BLS.*)
>
> **Harvey:** Mad. No change. I hate it.

Therapist: If the mad feelings left you, would that be a bad thing?

Harvey: Yeah, it would be bad.

Therapist: How so?

Harvey: If I just accept this all passive like, my foster dad is going to think he can clamp down on all aspects of my life. I'll be a sitting duck.

Therapist: Ah, I see. This would be important to discuss with your foster dad before we continue working on this trigger. Let's take a pause and see if we can get your foster dad to come in so we can talk about this all together. We'll get back to this and finish it after that. Would that be okay?

Harvey: Yeah, I guess so.

In the case of Harvey, the interweave brought the blocking belief to light, and the therapist became aware that a family session was needed to address Harvey's fear. In the next session, Harvey's foster dad reassured Harvey that he had no plans for further restrictions other than the ground rules that had already been laid out. This removed the block and allowed Harvey to complete reprocessing of the trigger to complete closure.

The Trigger Tolerance Protocol and the EMD Continuum

The IATP-C therapist attunes to the child's window of patience for sitting still and attending throughout the trigger work and for tolerating any memory associations that may surface. If (1) the child's patience is low or (2) the child or teen is making associations to the past and becoming dysregulated, the therapist can switch to some version of EMD. See Appendix G, "The EMD-to-EMDR Continuum," to learn strategies for a contained method that reduces associations and shortens reprocessing sessions for kids with low tolerance.

FUTURE TEMPLATES

It's easy to become confused regarding the difference between future rehearsals and future templates. EMDR future rehearsals are a way to practice using new resources to help with challenging situations and can be conducted at any time. Slow BLS is applied to help integrate the new resources or skills.

Alternatively, future templates are imagined scenes or role-played scenes for handling the triggering situation in the future. With future templates, fast BLS is applied to help with any troubles that might surface. The following are strategies for future templates with kids who have difficulty staying focused or engaged.

Future Templates Made Easy and Fun

The therapist begins the future template by inviting the child and the parent to participate with the therapist in working out the best response to the troublesome trigger in the future. The therapist may be able to draw upon skills learned in family therapy sessions. Once the child or teen is happy with the planned response, they're invited to think about the helpful response along with a PC (perhaps the same PC installed during reprocessing of the trigger). If it goes well, the child is encouraged to think of the response and the PC again and the therapist applies a couple of short sets of fast BLS. If that goes well, the child or teen is invited to think of the PC and imagine watching the entire scene on a movie screen while the therapist applies fast BLS. With younger kids or kids who are more concrete thinkers, the therapist can replace the mental movie by creating a little play about the new response. The therapist and child or teen can act it out, perhaps also with the help of the parent, or use puppets or stuffed animals to act it out. The therapist can remind the child or teen of the PC and strengthen the good feelings with tapping or buzzies throughout the role-play or at the end. The therapist can observe the child or teen for clues regarding VOC or take the measure through a number line or demonstration with hands.

With young children or older kids who are developmentally young, the entire future template may be a simple role-play or actions with puppets or animals while reminding the child of the PC and application of taps or buzzies throughout. In some cases, it's helpful to coach the child throughout the role-play with several positive statements.

For example, after processing the trigger of the teacher's voice using EMD, I created a future template by asking the child to pretend they were at their desk in the classroom while the parent pretended to be the teacher repeatedly commanding the class to be quiet with a loud voice. Next, I applied fast taps while stating "Her voice is strong, but you're safe. You're fine. She's not going to hurt you. She's a nice person. She means well. You can handle it." The child was also encouraged to state out loud, "I'm safe. I'm fine. I can handle it." The therapist ran the buzzies throughout the role-play. At the end, the child reported her PC "I'm safe" as a 7 by pointing to numbers on a number line.

If the child or teen starts to show signs of disturbance at any point during the future template, attune with, "I notice something is bothering you right now. I wonder, could there be an upset feeling or thought of some kind?" It may be enough to talk about it and possibly do some problem solving or skill building related to the disturbance. In some cases, the therapist can invite the child to just notice the anxiety or other upset feeling and then add some short sets of BLS to reduce or eliminate the disturbance before continuing the future template. Alternatively, the feelings can be placed in a container and addressed in the following session by bringing up the future template and asking, "What makes it still hard?" followed by some collaborative problem solving.

Trigger Tolerance Work Phase 8 Reevaluation

For kids with attachment injuries and lots of triggers related to their parents, the reevaluation can be conducted first with parents one-on-one and then with the child or teen when they join the session. The one-on-one time with parents allows them to speak openly without leading kids to become defensive or dysregulated, and it gives the therapist another opportunity for coaching the parents regarding how to interact with their child with sensitivity and attunement. Often, uncovering triggers with kids uncovers issues related to the parents' methods of parenting.

Weaving Back and Forth Between Present and Past

Over the duration of therapy, I typically weave back and forth, addressing present-day triggers and future templates, addressing past traumas, then more triggers, and then the past again. Sometimes sessions are closed by repeating a foundational activity. This weaving continues to improve present-day functioning by reinforcing new skills and responses to present situations and provides breaks from the trauma work.

INTEGRATING HEALTHY RESPONSES TO PRESENT TRIGGERS THROUGH SONGS FOR YOUNGER KIDS

Credit to IATP-C therapist Teresa Brown for the idea of adapting the ARD songs to reinforce healthy responses to triggers. Songs can be made up to address almost any triggers. Slow BLS can be applied throughout with the buzzies in the child's pockets or shoes. Alternatively, the child can sit on the parent's lap facing the therapist, and the parent can sway the child side to side with alternating taps or squeezes on the child's arms. Here are two examples.

> ***Sung to the tune of "Wheels on the Bus"***
> *When Mommy says no she's taking care of me, doing her job,*
>   *helping me grow.*
> *When Mommy says no she's taking care of me, all . . . day . . . long.*
> *When Mommy says no I can handle it okay, handle it okay, handle it okay.*
> *When Mommy says no I can handle it okay and often times she says yes.*
>
> ***Sung to the tune of "Frère Jacques"***
> *Verse 1:*
> *Time for bed, time for bed, it's all okay, it's all okay.*
> *The cord of love connects us, the cord of love connects us,*
> *All night long, all night long.*
>
> *Verse 2:*
> *Time for school, time for school, it's all okay, it's all okay.*
> *The cord of love connects us, the cord of love connects us,*
> *All day long, all day long.*
>
> *Verse 3:*
> *When Mommy cares for brother, when Mommy cares for brother, she loves*
>   *me, too, she loves me, too,*
> *The cord of love connects us, the cord of love connects us,*
> *All day long, all night long.*

TARGETING UNHEALTHY COMPULSIVE BEHAVIORS

Kids with a history of attachment injuries often exhibit unhealthy compulsive behaviors. Common behaviors listed by parents who call for help for their child include compulsive behaviors related to stealing, lying, food, pornography, sex, or hurting younger children or animals. Many of the compulsive behaviors of children and teens develop early on as a misguided, maladaptive attempt to self-protect or get unmet needs met or as a defense to counter feelings of powerlessness and fear. The therapist makes sense of the behaviors as a way the child coped with the lack of nurturing or protection in early life. In the present time, the younger part of the self on the inside continues the behaviors because they are associated with survival, and the old fears are still stuck in the brain. The IATP-C can help create safety on the inside and new, adaptive ways to get needs met in present life.

Addressing Behaviors Script

Say to the child or teen, "You may not know this, but when little kids are trapped in a bad situation when they're little, they end up with stuck feelings of helplessness. Their brain tries to fix that by redoing what happened and making someone else be the helpless one. I think your brain may have tried to fix what happened to you this way. The things you did are not really part of who you are. You were born a good and lovable kid. I would like to help you stop doing this so you can find better ways to feel good."

Whether the behaviors are intentional or hurtful to others or maladaptive attempts to get their needs met or self-protect, I find the following three EMDR protocols for addictive or compulsive behaviors to be helpful. I often utilize two or all three of the methods with the same child or teen.

The therapist uses clinical judgment regarding inclusion of parents when using EMDR methods to help children or teens with maladaptive behaviors. If the therapist intuits that the child or teen will feel more ashamed or guarded with their parents in the room, the work can be conducted one-on-one with the child. When applying any of these methods with attachment-injured kids, it's important to have established a trusting therapeutic relationship.

The DeTUR Model

The DeTUR Model (Popky, 2005) begins with resource work including a positive picture of the future, free of the compulsive behavior. Next, situations that trigger the behavior are identified and reprocessed in order from mildest urge to strongest urge. Instead of a SUD, the Level of Urge (LOU) is identified for each trigger. Finally, the trigger is paired with the feelings of the future positive state.

With kids, I apply the steps of the DeTUR model with very simple language:

1. *Say*, "Let's list all the things that would be good about a future life free of this bothersome behavior." (*Child or teen and therapist collaborate to make*

Addressing Present and Future Through Integrative Family and EMDR Therapy   157

a list.) Let's pretend you can see your life in the future, up on a movie screen. Notice all those good things about it. (*Elaborate details for the child or teen.*) *If response is positive, say,* "Imagine stepping into the movie in your biggest kid self and notice your body posture and how that feels. (*Add a short slow set of BLS to deepen the good feeling.*)

2. *Say,* "Now let's make a list of situations, people, thoughts, or feelings that trigger you and make you want to do the bothersome behavior. (*Take time to make the list.*) Now let's rate them from smallest triggers to biggest triggers."

3. *Say,* "Let's start with this smallest one. How strong is the urge to do the behavior with this smallest trigger, from 0 to 10, with 10 being the strongest? (LOU)" *Alternatively, have the child or teen give a rating with hands together (small) hands apart (medium) or hands wide apart (strong).*

4. *Say,* "Think of the trigger and notice the urge, and let's do some fast taps or eye movements." *Check in between sets. Occasionally check the LOU. Sets are continued until the LOU is as low as it will go.*

5. *Say,* "Find your biggest kid self and think of handling that trigger in a good way." (*Add a short set of slow BLS to deepen the positive affect.*)

6. Target and reprocess each trigger, from mildest to strongest.

7. Later, past traumas are addressed with IATP-C methods.

If the child reports engaging in the compulsive behavior between sessions, the therapist responds with nonjudgmental curiosity and says, "Thank you for telling me. What happens in between sessions just gives us more helpful information. We'll reprocess each trigger that comes up until there are no more triggers."

Vignette With 13-Year-Old Abbie: Addressing the Urge to Steal

Therapist: Abbie, your stealing problem has really decreased a lot, but as long as it occurs occasionally, the quality of your life is not as good as it can be. Would it be okay if we do some work on this stealing habit?

Abbie: *(Nods.)*

Therapist: What would be good about your life if you were free of the urge to steal? (*Makes list, hands Abbie the buzzies, and turns them on slowly.*) Abbie, see if you can see yourself on a movie screen, living your life with freedom from the stealing habit at some point in the future when it's way easier. See your future self on the movie screen, confident and happy. Notice how your face looks, and how you are holding your body. See yourself with all your privileges, your parents trusting you, happy with you. See yourself hanging out with friends. See yourself at school, talking with teachers, happy and confident. See your teachers smiling, trusting you. (*Stops buzzies.*) How did that go?

Abbie: (*Nodding.*) Good.

EMDR Therapist: Great. (*Turning buzzies back on.*) Now imagine yourself, your biggest kid self, right there in the movie. Think about how it feels inside, how it feels to be in your body, at home, feeling confident and mature in your biggest kid self, with your parents smiling and happy. Think about how it feels to be relaxing, hanging out with friends. Now you are at school; notice how it feels to interact with teachers when they are happy and smiling, and notice how you are standing, walking, and holding your body.

Abbie: I feel tall. I feel relaxed, happy.

Abbie and the therapist identified several situations that triggered Abbie's urge to steal recently, including seeing a pretty necklace on her friend's nightstand, spotting some cash on the table at home, and seeing a pack of new pencils on her teacher's desk. Abbie decided seeing cash seemed to be the strongest trigger. No cognitions were identified. The therapist asked Abbie to imagine she was back in that situation, and she identified her Level of Urge (LOU) to steal was an 8. Sets of fast BLS were applied and Abbie reported her LOU was a 2. Eventually, all the triggers were addressed. In each session, a positive future template with her biggest kid self helped Abbie connect to a skillful way to handle the trigger.

Targeting the Maladaptive Positive Emotion

Jim Knipe (2005, 2015, p. 108) and Robert Miller (2019) view stored, maladaptive positive affect associated with past unhealthy behaviors as driving the compulsion to repeatedly engage in the behavior. By targeting and reprocessing the maladaptive positive feeling states associated with the compulsive behaviors using sets of fast eye movements, the association with the maladaptive positive feeling can often be significantly reduced or eliminated. Before initiating reprocessing, the part of the behavior most associated with the positive feeling state is identified, along with a description of the positive state. The client is then asked to think of the behavior and the positive feeling and rate the strength of the

Addressing Present and Future Through Integrative Family and EMDR Therapy   159

connection 1 to 10. Then, after instructing the client to think of the behavior and the positive feeling state again, repeated sets of fast BLS are applied until the rating for the connection is a 0 or 1.

With kids, it's important as always to use a matter-of-fact demeanor, showing no judgments when discussing the compulsive behavior, no matter what it is, to keep the child or teen willing and engaged. Targeting of maladaptive positive feelings can be conducted with kids using simple language from the therapist:

1. "Think about a recent time you engaged in the behavior. *(Pause.)* What part of that experience gives you the absolute best feeling?" _____

2. "How would you name or describe the feeling? You can use one word or more than one word. For example, it might be a giggly feeling or an explosion of happiness feeling. Whatever makes sense to you." _____

3. "Think of that part of the behavior you like the best and the _____ (*Using their words*) feeling and also notice the good feeling in your body. How strong is the feeling to you now from 0 to 10?" (*For kids who don't like or understand numbers, ask them to demonstrate how strong it is by holding their hands close together, somewhat apart, or wide apart.*)

4. "Think of that part of the behavior you like the best and the _____ (*Using their words*) feeling. Notice the good feeling in your body, and let's do some _____ (*Name the form of BLS such as taps or eye movements*)." Apply fast BLS and ask "What's there now?" _____ Wait for their response and then say, "Think of the behavior and the feelings and let's do some more _____ (*Name the form of BLS*)."

5. *Use your clinical intuition to guess when the strength of the maladaptive positive feeling has lowered and then say* "Think of the behavior and the good _____ feeling again. How strong is it now from 0 to 10? If the strength is greater than 0 or 1, continue reprocessing until the positive feeling is a 0 or 1. (If the strength of the connection to the good feeling does not reduce, stop the reprocessing and move to Steps 7 and 8.)*

6. *Identify any other maladaptive positive feelings or positive parts of the behavior and repeat Steps 2 through 6.*

7. *When all positive parts have been addressed, say,* "What is the negative

belief about yourself that causes you to need that positive feeling you've been going after? For example, some kids say they have a negative belief that they're not good enough or that they don't belong." _____ (*Brainstorm with the child or teen to identify the NC.*) "When in your life do you remember first feeling that way?" _____

8. *Use EMDR standard protocol on the identified memory or memories.*

In my experience, the strength of the positive feeling either begins reducing right away or it does not reduce at all. If it does not reduce, I stop the protocol and skip to Steps 7 and 8 and reprocess past traumas that led to the intense need for the positive feeling state. Then, when the child or teen is ready, Steps 1 through 6 can be repeated.

Vignette With 10-Year-Old Dionte: Addressing the Urge to Hit

Therapist: Dionte, the hitting behavior seems to be a habit you just can't break out of right now, am I right? (*Dionte nods and shrugs.*)

Therapist: I wonder if there is a super-great feeling connected to the hitting habit. Can you think about the incident yesterday where you came up and surprised your mom with a hit on her arm?

Dionte: (*Nodding.*) Uh-huh.

Therapist: What is the part of the hitting where you get the best feeling?

Dionte: Umm, I guess when she yells right away.

Therapist: Good thinking. So think back on that if you can. How would you describe the super-great feeling when you think back to yesterday?

Dionte: (*Smiling.*) Gotcha!

Therapist: Gotcha! Would you call it the "gotcha feeling"?

Dionte: Yup.

Therapist: How big is that gotcha feeling when you remember your mom yelling? This big? (*Shows hands wide.*) Or this big? (*Shows hands closer together.*) Or smaller? (*Shows hands even closer.*) (*Dionte indicates the feeling is very strong.*) Okay, Dionte, think of your mom yelling and that great gotcha feeling and follow this light-up sword with your eyes, okay? I'll even turn out my lamp so it really shines.

(*Therapist implements about 20 fast passes of BLS.*) What are you noticing? Thoughts? Feelings?

Dionte: (*Scowling.*) I don't know.

Therapist: Can we do it again? Think of the yell and the gotcha feeling, okay?

(*Another set of fast BLS.*)

Dionte: (*Grunts.*) It seems sort of stupid.

Therapist: What is it that seems stupid?

Dionte: The hitting. It's kind of dumb.

Therapist: Can you just notice that?

(*Processing continues until the gotcha feeling reaches a 0.*)

The Two-Hands Method

Another method that can be applied in a simple way with children and teens is Robin Shapiro's "Two-hand-method" (Shapiro, 2005). With the two-hands method, rational ideas or desires are placed in one hand and unhealthy urges or beliefs are placed in the other. BLS is conducted through either tapping on the hands or squeezing soft balls bilaterally, following the therapist's lead. The child or teen is asked to notice any sensations related to the hands or any thoughts or feelings that surface during the activity. Because in general the left hand is connected to the right brain, and the right hand is connected to the left brain, we like to place urges in the left hand and rational ideas in the right. I conduct the two-hands method with kids using simple language:

1. *Say,* "It seems that part of you would like to stop this behavior and part of you doesn't want to stop this behavior. Would you be willing to try something with me?" _____ *If the response is positive, say,* "I'd like you to imagine placing desire to continue the behavior in your left hand, because your left hand is connected to your right side thinking brain. Do you have it there?" _____ *If positive, say,* "Now imagine the part of you that wants to be free of the behavior in your right hand. Your right hand is connected to your logical thinking brain over on the left side. Do you have it there?" _____

2. *Say,* "Now we each get two soft balls. Just follow along with me. We're going to squeeze the balls back and forth. Just notice whatever you notice about your hands or any thoughts or feelings that come up. I'll check in with you after about half a minute. (*Therapist leads the child or teen in bilateral squeezes.*)

3. *After a set of 15 to 20 alternating squeezes, the therapist asks,* "What's there now? Any thoughts or feelings?" _____ (*Child or teen responds.*) "Just go with that." Continue with sets, checking in between sets for thoughts or feelings, until there is a positive shift.
4. (*Optional*) *I find it helpful to close by saying,* "Perhaps you can place your thoughtful right hand on top of your left hand, and just allow your right hand to reassure and support your left hand."

The child or teen usually reports thoughts and feelings regarding their problematic behavior that lead to new insights and awareness not previously experienced. The procedure can be repeated as often as needed.

If the child or teen has little to report, lengthen the sets and suggest, "Just signal me when you have a thought or feeling to share." If still nothing happens, ask what's scary about letting go of the behavior. Use standard EMDR processing to target and reprocess the underlying fear.

Vignette With 15-Year-Old Amir: Addressing the Urge to Bully

Therapist: Amir, would you say that a part of you wants to stop bullying, but a part of you doesn't want to stop bullying?

Amir: Yeah.

Therapist: I wonder if we could try something. I'm going to give you a squishy ball to hold in each hand, okay? Here you go. (*Places a squishy ball in each hand.*) I'd like you to imagine this left hand of yours is the hand that wants to bully. This left hand is connected to your right-side feeling brain. And let's put the part of you that wants to be free of the bullying behavior in the right hand, okay? Your right hand is connected to your left side thinking brain.

Amir: Okay.

Therapist: I'm going to squeeze squishy balls with my own hands, too. You can just follow my lead. Now, let's start by remembering what your right hand wants and remembering what your left hand wants. You got it? (*Amir nods.*) Okay, let's do some squeezes. (*Therapist and Amir do fast alternate hand squeezes for about 20 passes.*) What do you notice? Anything in your hands? Any thoughts or feelings?

Amir: (*Holding up his right hand.*) This one seems like it has more strength.

Therapist: Huh. That's interesting. Just notice okay? (*Another set of hand squeezes.*)

Amir: Weird. This right one is still stronger. But I feel like this left one is fighting it.

Therapist: Okay, how about just go with that. (*Another set of hand squeezes.*) What are you noticing? Thoughts? Feelings?

Amir: (*Holds up left hand.*) This hand doesn't want to give in.

Therapist: Go with that, okay? (*Another set of hand squeezes.*)

Amir: I think this left hand feels like if I'm not the bully, I'll be the one getting bullied.

Therapist: Interesting. Let's go again. (*Another set of hand squeezes.*) What's there now?

Amir: It's not a huge deal. Those other kids just have their problems, too. I get it.

Therapist: I wonder what might happen if you place your right hand over your left hand, just lightly, and just hold it there for a minute.

Amir: Hmm. I feel like the right hand part of me is like, "Hey, man, calm it down."

Therapist: Do you suppose you could do that sometimes when you're at school? To help keep that part of you more calm?

Amir: Yeah, maybe.

CONCLUSION

EMDR reprocessing of triggers is made possible by the work of Stage 1 and Stage 2 and the nonjudgmental, supportive environment of the therapist's office. A matter-of-fact approach to troublesome triggers and behaviors lessens shame and improves motivation and cooperation for addressing the past.

CHAPTER 8

Entering the Past Gently Through Timeline and the EMDR Therapeutic Story

> Through this chapter, you will gain skills for transitioning to trauma work through
> Therapeutic Story:
> – Past, present, and future activity
> – Beginning with a Timeline
> – Using the Timeline and outline to create the story
> – Writing in session or outside session
> – Reading of the story with BLS
> – Showing the story with animals

This chapter provides step-by-step directions for gently moving children and teens toward addressing past memories through the Therapeutic Story method. The method begins with a Past, Present, and Future activity followed by directions for engaging kids in creating a Timeline for their story. Finally, directions for writing the story and applying the Therapeutic Story method utilizing BLS are provided along with sample stories.

OVERVIEW OF THE THERAPEUTIC STORY METHOD

Children with attachment trauma are confused about the events in their lives. Even adults have a hard time making sense of their difficult experiences, and kids who suffer from mental disorganization and deficits in knowledge and reasoning are at a loss to understand why and how things happened. Kids come to us with the most heartbreaking histories, and they're not at a place developmentally where they can make sense of things without our help. Research tells us that individuals who naturally move from a nonsecure or disorganized pattern to a secure pattern have developed the capacity to tell their story in an organized and reasonable way, so the Therapeutic Story method can be a useful way of helping kids along the path toward attachment security.

The Therapeutic Story method helps kids put together a reasonable story that helps them make sense of what all happened, adding adaptive information to their understanding of the events. Kids with preverbal trauma in their past don't have stored pictures for what happened, but they often have a felt sense of events due to maladaptive storage of the events impacting their thoughts and feelings. The therapeutic story can help straighten out misinformation and clarify a child's preverbal story.

For kids who are fearful and resist addressing their past, Therapeutic Story is a gentle way to transition them into working on the past by providing adaptive information and desensitizing them to their story as a whole. With dissociative kids, the Therapeutic Story can help with grounding in the present while beginning desensitization for the past. In several case studies, symptoms of traumatic stress for children and adults with intellectual disabilities improved with EMDR, often using the Therapeutic Story method (Lobregt-van Buuren et al., 2019; Mevissen et al., 2011a; Mevissen et al., 2011b; Mevissen et al., 2012; Mevissen et al., 2017; Wesselmann et al., 2025b). Many of the children and teens also were on the autism spectrum.

Only Known Events

Only events that are known events should be included in the Timeline and story. Some events may be known to parents or therapists through case files, social workers, or relatives, and some events may have been described by the child. We can't make assumptions about the child's experiences based on the child's behaviors or issues. For example, if a child or teen has issues with masturbation or pornography, the therapist shouldn't make assumptions about sexual abuse. The behaviors aren't evidence, and children are all too easily influenced by the ideas of adults, leading to false ideas and beliefs.

If there is a two-therapist team working with the family, either therapist can engage in writing of the story. The EMDR therapist reads the completed story while applying BLS. Later, EMDR standard reprocessing can be applied to individual events in the story as needed.

Past, Present, and Future Activity

Past, present, and future are powerful concepts that can be confusing to traumatized children. By assisting children with reflecting on the actual meanings of these three words and understanding that the past is truly over, we can help them better separate the past from the present and keep them grounded. Of course, this is critical for successful EMDR reprocessing later.

Past, Present, and Future Vignette With 10-Year-Old Cade and His Parents

Cade was adopted 1 year prior by his paternal grandparents. He was removed from his biological mother at age 8 due to neglect. After adoption, he revealed past sexual abuse by an older cousin. He suffered from nightmares, severe anxiety, and frequent meltdowns.

> **Therapist:** Today, I'm going to pretend that I'm your teacher, and we're going to learn about three new words. (*Writes the three words on the whiteboard and asks the child about the meaning of each.*) What does the word past mean?
>
> **Cade:** (*Shrugging his shoulders.*) Something that happened a long time ago.
>
> **Therapist:** Yes, that's right. Can you tell me one or two things that you remember from your past that are good memories?
>
> **Cade:** Yes, my birthday last year—I had that really cool cake with cars on it. And I went swimming last weekend.
>
> **Therapist:** Yes, those are great examples. Those things did happen in the past, and when you thought about those things, what were your feelings?
>
> **Cade:** Happy.
>
> **Therapist:** Good. I'm glad there are things that happened to you in your

past that do bring back happy feelings. Now, let's talk about the next word: present.

Cade: Yeah. It's something you get at Christmas.

Therapist: You're right again, you do get presents at Christmas time. Does this word have another meaning?

Cade: (*Shrugs his shoulders.*)

Therapist: Well, where are you right now?

Cade: In therapy with you.

Therapist: Yep, you are. So this is happening in the present.

Cade: Yeah, I guess.

Therapist: So, the present is stuff that is going on right now. Tell me, where do you live right now?

Cade: At my mom's house.

Therapist: Right. You live in your forever mom's house right now. It's a nice, safe house, right?

Cade: Yes.

Therapist: What about the last word, future? What does that mean?

Cade: Something that will happen some other time, like when I'm older.

Therapist: Okay, can you name something that will happen to you in the future?

Cade: I'm going to be 11 on my next birthday.

Therapist: Yes, that's a good example. Sometimes our brains get mixed-up about what is happening to us right now in the present and what happened to us in the past. We have to remind our brain that we are in the present, living in a safe home with a mom and dad who are taking good care of us. Do you think you get confused sometimes?

Cade: Yeah, sorta.

Therapist: Mom, do you think he gets confused sometimes?

Mom: Yes, I think he does. Sometimes, I think he confuses me with his birth mom. Sometimes he expects me to do some of the mixed-up things she did.

Therapist: That does happen, doesn't it? Okay, Mom and Cade, what can you do if you think Cade's brain is getting confused?"

Mom: I could remind him . . . gently. Hey, it's me—your forever mom. I'm trying to be the best mom I can be for you.

Cade: I could talk to my brain and tell it that I'm in the present.

Therapist: Both of those are great ideas. And who will be in your life in the future?

Cade: My mom. This mom, I mean.

Therapist: Yes, that's right. We'll keep working on making sense of the stuff from your past, and we'll keep reminding your brain that the past is over, that you are safe now in the present, and that you have lots to look forward to in your future.

Creating a Timeline

A Timeline is a gentle way to create a brief overview of the events. The therapist should prepare the parents for the Timeline activity and discuss with them what should and shouldn't be included in the story. With more resistant or easily dysregulated kids, the Timeline and story should focus on just one small part of the child's life or include only one or two events to start. More events can be added later in therapy. The basic IATP-C rules still apply: Keep it simple, keep it playful, stay attuned to tolerance and mood, and be flexible and supportive.

The therapist may use a large sheet of paper on which to draw a horizontal line, using spaced vertical lines to represent each year of the child's life. The therapist invites the child or teen and parents to show on the Timeline where the child lived at various ages. The therapist may wish to use markers or crayons to color code the Timeline. If the child or teen wants to actively write on the Timeline themselves, they can be encouraged to do so. If the Timeline ends up a little messy, it makes no difference to the usefulness of the activity.

Next, the therapist asks about positive events, both recent and long ago, and places these on the Timeline. The child's birth is considered the first positive event in the child's life, no matter what the circumstances. After placing that, the therapist facilitates naming of the difficult things that happened, without looking for details. The therapist should surround the negative events with as many positive events as possible.

If the child or teen is tolerating the activity well, the therapist can do a little Detective Work by exploring the beliefs associated with the positive and negative events. The beliefs may be added to the Timeline above or below the appropriate events. The therapist can point out negative beliefs that are common for

Entering the Past Gently Through Timeline and the EMDR Therapeutic Story   169

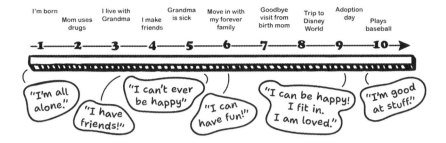

Figure 8.1: Sample Timeline

kids in these circumstances and reassure the child or teen that one goal is to help them develop more helpful thoughts about what happened.

Figure 8.1 provides a sample Timeline.

Creative Timelines
With younger children, the therapist may wish to draw small, simple stick figure pictures to illustrate the Timeline. Alternatively, the parent can bring in photos to tape onto the Timeline, as long as the photos aren't triggering. An engaging way to create a Timeline with younger kids is to draw a Candy Land game on a large piece of paper. The Candy Land path is the Timeline, with marks for each age of the child's life and events noted in the squares or illustrated with small simple drawings. Children love to decorate and color the Candy Land Timeline, which increases their cooperation with the activity.

Using the Timeline to Create a Therapeutic Story
We are grateful to Joan Lovett for assisting us in the creation of the following therapeutic story outline, based on her EMDR therapeutic story method as described in her book *Small Wonders: Healing Childhood Trauma with EMDR* (1999).

Third Person, Second Person, and Animal Characters
The story is usually written in third person to create some distance and lower emotional intensity. The therapist may ask the child or teen whether they want their name included or not included in the story. If they have very low tolerance for their memories, it may be helpful to go ahead and write the story without the child's help and without the child's name.

Although the Therapeutic Story is traditionally written in third person (e.g., "There was a baby who was born lovable and beautiful . . . "), kids who are very concrete may need to hear their story in second person (e.g., "You were a lovable and beautiful baby . . . "). Adler-Tapia and Settle (2023, p. 210) recommend the parent tell the child's story in second person for preverbal trauma, termed "Parent Narrative." The Parent Narrative is especially helpful when the story is told by a biological parent who was present for the preverbal trauma in the child's life. (See the Parent Narrative example later in this chapter.)

With younger children, it can be helpful to write their story in third person using animal characters in an animal setting. It helps them tolerate their story while keeping them very engaged. However, children with an intellectual disability, fetal alcohol syndrome disorder (FASD), or autism may be very concrete thinkers and may not make connections between themselves and the story about the animal characters. They may need a story that identifies them directly by name or a story told in the second person.

Sequencing the Story

The first part of the story grounds the child or teen in the present and includes positive information such as activities, talents, and strengths. As an example, the first sentence might read: "There was a boy who lived with his parents, his two dogs, and his two cats. He liked playing basketball with his friends, and he had a talent for drawing." For younger children, you may wish to begin with "Once upon a time. . . ." because it's a story starter that is familiar.

The next section, as recommended by Lovett (1999), normalizes the mix of positive and negative events. For example, this sentence might read: "Like everybody else in the world, the child/teen had experienced some wonderful/positive things and some things that were sad/difficult/confusing."

Next, the story describes a positive event in the past. For example, this part might read: "One wonderful thing was that this baby was born with a healthy body and a good brain. The baby was lovable and special."

Then the story identifies a negative event, negative feelings (optional), and a negative belief associated with the event. For example, the story might say: "One confusing thing was that the baby's birth mother couldn't stop drinking alcohol and that made her brain fuzzy so she didn't pay enough attention to her baby. If the baby could have talked, he might have said, "I must not be a good enough baby."

The story also includes the adaptive information needed to make sense of things. For example, the story might go on to say, "The truth was, the baby was a lovable, wonderful, and good baby. The alcohol caused the mother's brain to be confused. Luckily, the baby's aunt saw there was a problem and stepped in to help the baby."

The story continues with one to three more positive events and one to three more difficult events, depending upon tolerance. For a child or teen with very low tolerance, the therapist may wish to write about just one difficult event sandwiched in the middle of several positive events or fun facts about the child.

The story concludes with a short paragraph that is both realistic and positive. There is a short description of the present struggles followed by a description of how the child or teen is continuing to heal and grow with lots of help from all the people who care about them. For example, "Sometimes the child still struggles with believing she is safe and loved and worthwhile. Luckily, her parents and therapists are helping her feel better about herself, and she is gradually learning to trust her parents to keep her safe and love her each and every day."

Therapeutic Story Outline

There is a child/teenager who lives with . . .

Like all kids, they experienced some wonderful/positive things and some things that were sad/difficult/confusing.

A wonderful/positive thing was they were born . . .

A confusing/hard thing was . . .

If this baby/child could have put their thoughts and feelings into words, they might have said (NCs):

The truth is (or what we want them to know is) (PCs):

A wonderful/positive thing that happened was . . .

Another confusing/hard thing that happened was . . .

The child felt . . .

If the child could have put their feelings into thoughts with words, they might have said (NCs):

The truth is (or what their present-day parent wishes the child could have known is) (PCs):

Then some other wonderful things happened . . .

(The story may include additional wonderful things and additional confusing things.)

Today, the child/teenager still struggles with believing . . .
But, they have a family who loves them and they continue to help them understand things.
Their parent(s) want(s) the child/teen to know, . . .
As they become older and wiser, they will gradually learn . . .

Writing in the Session or Outside the Session

Many therapists begin writing stories outside of the therapy sessions until they feel more confident about the writing process. Writing in session can be anxiety provoking for the therapist who is new to this therapeutic activity. Alternatively, the clinician may choose to write a rough draft or outline of the story outside of the family session and then complete the story with help from the parent and child or teen.

For a child or teen who is uncooperative or dysregulated by assisting with the writing, it's helpful to write the story outside of session or with just the help of the parent, and then invite the child or teen to help add the negative beliefs and feelings of the littler child in the story.

One 13-year-old female resisted helping with her story, and her parents couldn't contribute much because she had lived in an orphanage until age 11. I did the best I could with what I thought I knew, but when I read the story to her, she quickly got busy filling in the gaps of the story and making corrections to parts I didn't describe correctly. I learned a great deal about her story through the process.

Some younger children like making little books that they illustrate, or the therapist illustrates, as an alternative to a typewritten story. Some older children or teens prefer to write short chapters such as "The Baby Years," "The Toddler Years," and "The Preschool Years."

Reading of the Story with BLS

The child or teen is invited to listen while the therapist or parent reads through the story. The paradoxical approach, "You can listen or not listen, either way is okay," is a useful strategy for increasing the child's willingness to listen. We usually prefer reading the story versus asking the parent to read the story, because we can attune to the child and stick to easier parts of the story if the child's tolerance is low.

The application of BLS begins desensitization for the story as a whole and creates sequential organization along with adaptive information. Tactile BLS is applied throughout the reading of the story, using a speed and method preferred by the child or teen. Allowing the child or teen to choose what they like best improves their comfort and level of cooperation. Some kids choose to place the buzzies in their socks or shoes so they can play with a fidget toy during the story. Others choose to sit next to their parent while the parent applies bilateral taps or strokes on their shoulders or upper arms. Younger children may enjoy holding a weighted blanket or a stuffed animal or lying on the couch or floor during the reading and BLS.

With more resistant kids it can be helpful to negotiate reading just a small section of the story each week. If reading a partial story, the therapist should be careful to close by describing positive situations or events in the child's life or describing people who care about the child.

Because the therapeutic story includes adaptive information and children's positive, present-day situations in addition to earlier traumatic events, it provides what Lovett (2009) has referred to as "the light at the end of the tunnel" for the child.

Continued Readings

On subsequent readings, the therapist can engage the child to describe more about the child's thoughts and feelings with a series of questions: "What do you imagine the girl thought? What did she feel? What did she want? What did she need?" As the child imagines the wants and needs of her younger self in the story, the therapist can invite the parent and child to imagine giving the child what she wanted and needed. For example, if the child identified that she needed food, the therapist can ask the adoptive parent what they would have done if they'd been there and had known that the child was hungry. Then alternating bilateral stimulation can be used for resource enhancement as the child imagines her adoptive parent giving her the food she needed.

Later, the therapist can reread the entire story or just a portion of the story and then ask, "What part of the story did you like?" "What part of the story was hard for you to hear today?" The part that's still hard to hear can be used as a target for EMDR reprocessing. If the hard part is a preverbal event, the therapist can reread that part of the story and then ask, "When you hear that part of the story, what is the picture in your mind?" The picture becomes the target, and the therapist continues by identifying the negative words that go with the picture, the desired positive thought, and so forth, followed by desensitization, installation, and closure.

Using Stuffed Animals to Show the Story

For younger children (or developmentally young children), a simplified story can be effectively told impromptu by the EMDR therapist using puppets or dolls to play out the story during the telling.

The child can listen and watch from the parent's lap, while the parent sways the child side to side or gently taps. If the child wants to be down on the floor with the therapist participating with puppets or dolls to tell the story, the parents can apply taps on the child's shoulder or buzzies can be placed in their shoes or pockets.

Sample Therapeutic Stories for Some Heartbreaking Situations

Notice that the difficult events in the following stories are supplemented with adaptive information and sandwiched between ample positive events and information.

Story Involving Sexual Reactivity Subsequent to Sexual Abuse

There is a 13-year-old girl who lives with her aunt and uncle because they love her and want her to be safe. Her mom is doing the things the judge wants her to do so the girl can live with her mom again in the future. The girl has good friends and loves to play softball in the summer and basketball in the winter. Like all children, she had some good things happen in her life and some difficult things happen.

One happy thing was she was born with a strong body, a healthy brain, and a good heart. When she was very little, her parents gave her what she needed, and she grew bigger and was strong and smart.

Then when she was eight, a hard thing was that her dad started using bad drugs and her parents started fighting a lot. She believed, "Maybe if I can just be perfect enough, they will be happy and they will be like they used to be." She tried, but it didn't work, because the truth is, kids can't make things better for grown-ups.

Another hard thing was when her dad started acting strange. He did some touching stuff that made her body and brain very, very confused. She thought, "It must be my fault." Her brain and body got so confused about all this that one day she copied what her dad was doing and touched her sister. Her sister told her mom and her mom was mad. She thought she must be really bad. The truth is, she's very good. She was just too young to handle such confusing things.

A good thing was that the girl talked to her school counselor. She was brave and told the counselor about her dad. After that, she got a caseworker and went to live with her aunt. She had visits with her mom, but not her dad, because he had to go to jail. Her mom has a counselor, too. Her mom said, "I'm sorry I didn't believe you when you told me what was happening with your dad." Her mom wants them to live together soon.

The girl still struggles with thinking she's bad, but the counselor and her aunt and her mom say, "You're good. Your dad has a problem with bad drugs and problems with the way he thinks and acts, and what he did is not your fault. You copied his actions because your brain was trying to figure it all out. You're a good kid with a good heart. Now you're getting help and healing so you can have a wonderful life."

Story of Early Orphanage Care

There is a 9-year-old boy who lives with his forever mom and dad. The boy enjoys reading and math and he is a very good student. He has some good friends.

Like all children he had some good things and some hard things in his life. One good thing was that he was born lovable and smart. One hard thing was that his birth mom lived in a poor area and he was born with a condition called cerebral palsy. His mom didn't have money to help get him medical care or anyone to help with taking care of her baby. The mom brought her baby to an orphanage so he could be adopted by a family who could meet his needs.

The baby boy was taken care of at the orphanage for a year. There was a doctor, but there weren't enough people to hold him and give him the attention and love he needed. The baby was alone and sad. He believed he wasn't lovable and that he couldn't expect to have love. The truth is, he was lovable and special and his new mom and dad found out about him and they were working to bring him home. They wanted this little boy to know how special and lovable he truly was.

A wonderful thing was that the new mom and dad finally were allowed to bring their little boy home to their country. (The paragraph continues with more details about "the wonderful thing.")

Now the boy is nine and he still struggles with believing his parents love him or that he is meant to have love and care. Sometimes he thinks he's not good enough because he has cerebral palsy.

His parents want him to know that cerebral palsy doesn't change a thing. His parents want him to know that they love him so much. They want him to know they're not always as patient as they want to be. They want him to know that's not his fault, and they're working hard to learn how to be the best parents they can be.

Animal Story of Mother Keeping Custody of All but One of Her Children

There was a little boy wolf who lived with his bear mom and bear dad in a cave in the forest. The little wolf enjoyed life with his family except for one thing. Sometimes he had visits with a wolf mom they called his birth mom. She was his mom when he was first born. The wolf mom had some other little wolves, too. The other little wolves still lived with her in her cave. The little boy wolf asked his bear mom why he was the only one who didn't live in the cave with the wolf mom.

He asked, "Am I a bad kid?" The bear mom said, "Oh, no, you are a good kid. You were born lovable, healthy, and perfect in every way. You came to daddy and me because your wolf mom had a hard situation. Your wolf mom and her husband had three baby wolves before you were born. One day, they had a bad fight, and your wolf mom moved in with a boyfriend wolf. The boyfriend wolf helped make you. He is your dad, but when you were growing inside your wolf mom's tummy, she and the boyfriend wolf got mad at each other and he moved far away. Then your wolf mom and her husband decided to be together again. When your wolf mom gave birth to you, she was afraid her husband might not be nice to you because you had a different dad. Your wolf mom loved you very much and she decided to find a mommy and daddy who could love you like she did in a home that would be safe for you all the time."

The mommy bear said, "God wanted you to be born. You were meant to be. You're meant to be here with us. We may not be wolves, but Daddy and I knew you were meant to be ours. You are in our hearts forever. This is where you are supposed to be. We love you so much."

Story for a Child With No Permanency

There is a 12-year-old boy living in a place for kids who need extra help to feel better after hard things happened in life. The boy likes to shoot baskets and play video games. He has several staff members who truly care for him and want to help him have a good life.

Like all kids, he had both good things and hard things. A wonderful thing was that he was born with a good heart and a smart brain and like all babies, he was eager to love and be loved. A hard thing was that his biological mom had a mental illness. Her brain wasn't able to have helpful thoughts or understand things. She had behaviors that didn't make sense. The baby felt scared and alone. If the baby could have put feelings into words he might have said, "Adults are bad. I must be bad. I'm alone forever."

The adults in his life now want him to know that people in his life today care about him very much. They don't want him to be alone. They want him to know that what happened wasn't his fault.

A good thing was that some people who protect kids saw that the boy's mother couldn't give care to her son. They arranged for him to have foster parents.

In foster care, the boy's brain was stuck in fight-or-flight mode. It was hard for him to trust others because of all the hard things. His workers thought a residential center would be a good place for him to get more help. The boy thought, "I'm too bad to be helped. I'm being sent away."

The adults all around him want him to know that the fight-or-flight in his brain is causing his struggles, and his struggles are normal for a boy who had so many hard things. He is good and has a good brain and a good heart. The adults will keep looking for ways to help his body and brain calm down so he feels better. The people around him are thinking about him a lot and they are looking for ways to support him. They don't want him to feel alone. They are certain that as they work together with the boy, his life will get better.

Today, although he still struggles with trusting others to care about him, he is learning good things. The adults continue to help, and he continues to heal so he can have a happy life.

Second Person Parent Narrative for a Child With Preverbal Trauma

You are an amazing girl. Dad and I love watching you grow and learning to do new things like riding your trike and going to preschool.

Dad and I were so excited to meet you on the day you were born. It was a wonderful day. You were the most beautiful, lovable baby ever. Dad and I couldn't get enough of holding you and rocking you and being with you.

The hard thing was that you had to stay in the hospital for a while, because you were born a little early and you had some struggles. We took turns going into the hospital to hold you and rock you. But sometimes the doctors and nurses had to do things to help you get strong that probably didn't feel so good. You might have thought, "I'm not safe in this world with people poking me and checking me out all the time." You might have thought "My mom and dad don't care. They're not taking me away from here." The truth was, Dad and I loved you and the doctors and nurses were doing all the right things to make you well. We wanted our girl to be healthy and strong, and now you are! You grew and got stronger and stronger, and now you can ride a bike and run with all the other children! We love you so much. We want you to know you can trust us. We'll always try to do what's right. We'll keep you safe and take care of you forever and ever.

Making Sense of Other Hard Things

Following are single-paragraph excerpts from therapeutic stories describing other hard things.

Boy Relinquished by Adoptive Parents

Another hard thing was that one day the new mom and dad told the boy they felt they weren't the right mom and dad for him. They told the boy that they'd made a mistake. The boy thought there was something terribly wrong with him and he would never have a forever family. The truth was that his struggles were normal for boys in his situation. He had a lovable heart and needed the right care. They just were not the parents he needed. But the mom and dad did a good thing and found some people who helped kids find homes. They helped the boy find the right home with a mom and dad who understood about his struggles. The new mom and dad saw that he had a lot of hurt, and they wanted to give him the right kind of love and care and become his forever family.

A wonderful thing was . . .

Boy Who Lost a Parent to Suicide

Another difficult thing was that his dad had a mental illness that gave him very mixed-up thoughts and feelings. While he was suffering from his mental illness he took his own life. This is something some people with mental illness do, even when they have kids they love. Their mixed-up thoughts and feelings stop them from thinking right. When the boy found out, he was so sad, and he thought he should have been able to prevent his dad from doing that. The truth was, no one knew what his dad was going to do, and no one could have prevented it. The truth was, his dad loved him and he loved his dad. The boy also thought he'd never feel better. But the truth is that it takes time to get through all the sadness when a parent dies. The boy has many people who love and care about him, and they'll continue to help him with his sad feelings.

Girl Whose Parent Was Murdered by the Other Parent

Another sad thing was that her dad had a very bad addiction to some very bad drugs and a mental illness that caused very mixed-up thoughts and feelings. He started having explosions at home that were very scary to the little girl. One day a police lady came and got the little girl out of bed and took her to her aunt's house. The police lady and her aunt told her that her mother had died and that her dad had caused it and was in jail. Losing her mom was the saddest thing that had ever happened in her life. She thought she'd never feel happiness again. She was angry, too, at her dad. The good thing was that her aunt had always loved her so much. She wanted to give her all the love in the world to help her heal her sad heart. Her aunt told her it was okay to be sad and mad, too. Her aunt took her to a therapist to help her with all the feelings in her heart.

A happy thing was . . .

Child Who Was Bullied Due to Gender Identity

Another hard thing was that some of the other students in their middle school made fun of them for their short hair and the way they dressed. The students laughed and whispered. No one would sit near them on the bus or in the cafeteria. They felt all alone and believed they would never fit in anywhere and they would never be good enough for others. Their foster mom and their therapist want them to know that being nonbinary is a right and does nothing to change the fact that they're lovable and deserve to be treated with respect. The truth is that some kids find reasons to make fun of other kids to make themselves feel bigger or tougher. The truth is that kids who bully aren't healthy or happy kids. The truth is that kids who have a less common gender identity are just as good as anyone else.

A wonderful thing is they do have some good friends who are caring and accepting of them, and their opinions are the ones that matter . . .

Optional Therapeutic Story Activity: The Tale of the Hamster and the Porcupine Coat

The Tale of the Hamster and the Porcupine Coat is found in Appendix E. The hamster tale makes sense of what's happening, with compassion, for kids who learned to keep themselves safe by pushing people away. The therapist can change the gender of the hamster or reword the story to better match the particular details of a child's life. In the tale, a hamster that experiences trauma in early life finds a protective, spiky porcupine coat. The hamster continues to wear the coat despite a new, safe life, and it becomes clear to the child listening to the story that the coat keeps the hamster from experiencing closeness with the parents. BLS is applied throughout the reading of the story. The child is then asked to choose from two endings to the story—both endings are positive, but one is even more positive than the other. The chosen ending is reread while the child holds the tactile pulsars to reinforce the positive feelings associated with the hamster's new choices. The EMDR therapist can also use the positive ending of the story to help the child develop and reinforce a positive future rehearsal based on their decision to set aside the porcupine coat.

Vignette: Creating a Positive Future Rehearsal Through the Porcupine Story

EMDR Therapist: Sue Ann, can you tell me how you would be able to get along at school and at home if you were able to toss your porcupine coat in the closet?

Sue Ann: I would be able to stay in my classroom all day. My teacher would be really happy with me. The kids would want to play with me at recess. My mom and dad would be happy with me too, and they would let me have all my privileges at home. It would be more fun.

EMDR Therapist: Would you like to hold the buzzies while you picture a good movie about this? (*Sue Ann nods.*) See yourself at school without your porcupine coat. See yourself sitting at your desk doing your work; you are relaxed, and you have a smile on your face. Your teacher is

smiling at you as she walks by your desk. . . . (*Continues describing the positive future state movie while running the buzzies.*) How did that go?
Sue Ann: Good. I like this movie.
EMDR Therapist: Now I'd like you to put yourself right in the future movie and imagine how it feels in your body to be sitting in the classroom without your porcupine coat. Imagine how it feels to be smiling and relaxed while sitting at your desk; imagine how it feels to look up and see your teacher smiling. . . . (*Continues describing the positive future state while running the pulsars.*)

CONCLUSION

Kids are afraid of their stories and want to understand their stories at the same time. The examples provided in this chapter demonstrate how use of simple language and inclusion of abundant adaptive information soften the story to make a gentler transition to the traumatic past of kids and teens.

CHAPTER 9

Addressing the Hardest Parts With EMDR Trauma Work

> Through reading this chapter, you'll gain skills for:
>
> – Parent involvement
> – Motivation through metaphors
> – Choosing a memory
> – General strategies for reprocessing attachment traumas
> – Cognitive interweaves for reprocessing attachment traumas
> – Processing grief
> – Bringing closure to treatment

The same basic rules apply when addressing the past that apply when addressing the present when it comes to attachment-injured kids: Keep it simple, keep it playful, stay attuned to tolerance and mood, and be flexible and supportive. With trust and connection, the child or teen is more likely to bring down their guard and allow themselves to feel what they need to feel to heal.

By the time EMDR reprocessing of memories begins, the family therapy sessions can often be reduced or eliminated if parents' skills for coregulating and attuning are adequate. Even if parents need ongoing support to address the behavioral challenges or the child or teen needs ongoing skills work, the family therapy component can most likely be reduced in frequency.

See Chapter 7 for the general EMDR for kids—Phases 3 through 8 review.

This chapter will zero in on strategies for safe and effective reprocessing with kids' most difficult memories of attachment trauma.

PARENT INVOLVEMENT

When a child resides with a nonadoptive foster parent or guardian, this does not preclude implementation of trauma work if the caregiver is willing and able to commit to being an ongoing part of the youth's life and providing emotional support during therapy. Success in implementing the IATP-C for kids in long-term residential care depends largely upon therapeutic trust and the youth's willingness and emotion-tolerance skills. If there are committed adults involved in the child's life, they should be encouraged to participate in the therapy in person or through online video meetings.

The majority of parents who have a full understanding of the traumatic roots driving their child's behaviors can provide an attuned and compassionate presence. If the child or adolescent is willing, suggest that they sit to the side of the parent during the work, so they can physically feel the parent's presence but not be distracted visually by them. The parent's compassion and presence provide emotional regulation, grounding, and the safe connection many kids need to access their vulnerable emotions.

Some older children resist the presence of parents during reprocessing, because they worry about the parent's reactions or because they want to feel independent and strong. Some parents feel too overwhelmed at the thought of listening to details of their child's memories. In either of these situations, the therapist asks the parent to provide a supportive note or leave a transitional object such as the parent's sweater for the child or teen to keep during the trauma work and to provide extra support following the session. The therapist should offer concrete ideas for providing support, such as activities they can enjoy together between sessions.

For parents who are going to stay in the session, the therapist provides psychoeducation regarding how it will look and the goal of compassionate but silent support.

Explaining EMDR Trauma Processing to Parents Script

Say to the parent, "Before we begin, Mom/Dad, I want to explain that there may be some long silences during the EMDR. There is a lot of silence during the BLS because the BLS stimulates internal processes that access and integrate important thoughts and feelings for healing at a conscious and subconscious level. Between sets, I'll check in with your child regarding thoughts and feelings, and there may be long pauses because finding words can take quite some time for some kids. You and I will want to provide a mostly silent, supportive presence. We don't want to interrupt the natural shifts that are happening internally for your child. There may be some strong emotions at times and there may be times I provide some supportive words or I interject what is called a cognitive interweave, as much as possible without interrupting the processing. This is a nugget of needed information or a brief question for your child to focus on. Sometimes I will turn to you to provide that bit of information or to provide a positive thought or image. The important thing is to wait for my cue—I will let you know when I need you."

Motivation in the Closet Metaphor Script

Metaphors can be used to help motivate kids to participate in reprocessing their traumatic memories. The following is a sample script the therapist can use to present the Monster in the Closet metaphor:

Say to the child or teen, "Imagine that you are lying in bed and you hear a sound in your closet. You say, 'Mom, come here. I think there's a monster in my closet!' How would you feel if your mom came in and said, 'So you heard a sound in the closet? I'm not opening that closet if there's a monster in there. Just forget about it and go back to sleep.' Now, you're sure there really IS a monster in your closet, right? But what if you call your mom in and she throws open the closet door and says, 'Look, there's just a bunch of old junk in here. There's no monster.' Now you feel a lot better, right? Well, it's the same thing with your old upsetting memories. You think you have to keep the closet door shut because you have a bunch of monsters in there. But if we open the door and take a look—and use a little EMDR—you will come to see, as I do, that there's just a bunch of old junk in your closet, and then it will no longer have power over you."

Video Game Metaphor Script

Say to the child or teen, "Just like a character in one of your video games, you are on a quest. You are beginning a very important journey to conquer your memories. EMDR is your special power, and it will help you find the other special powers you need to zap each one of your memories, and then to put each of them inside a special, powerful container."

The therapist may add, "What special power can you find to help you with this memory?" or "What special power can you use to put this into your container today?"

CHOOSING A MEMORY

The standard method for choosing a memory for reprocessing is returning to the list of memories that were noted during EMDR Phase 1 history taking and EMDR treatment planning. For children and teens with attachment injuries, the initial list is generated with the help of parents to avoid dysregulating the child or teen at the beginning of treatment. The original list is often sketchy, however, as specifics regarding the child's traumatic past may be unknown to the parents. Fortunately, during the Timeline and therapeutic story activities, the child or teen frequently reveals more of their own recollections.

One way of choosing a memory for reprocessing is by returning to the therapeutic story. The therapist rereads the story, first instructing the child or teen to hold up a hand when the therapist reaches a part of the story that still has upset feelings attached.

Another method is to bring up a negative belief or feeling that is troublesome in the present day and help the child or teen explore the associated memories. The following is a script for finding a memory related to a theme or negative belief.

Finding a Memory Script

Therapist: "When do you think this yucky thought first got stuck in your brain? _____ "Do you have a specific memory about that? _____ Do you have any other memories similar to that one? _____

(or)

Therapist: "Can you think about a recent time you struggled with that feeling/upsetting thought? _____ (*If yes*) "Now let your mind go back to when you were littler and you might have felt/thought that way. Take your time. Just see what comes up in your brain."

ASSESSMENT PHASE TRICK

Appendix F provides a quick review of the assessment phase and the other reprocessing phases with tips for kids in general. However, kids with a history of attachment trauma may sometimes have very little capacity for noticing and mentalizing thoughts and feelings during the assessment phase. The following strategy can help.

For Kids Who Report No Thoughts During the Assessment Phase

As described in Appendix F, "A Quick Review of EMDR Reprocessing Phases With Tips for Working With Kids," the therapist can offer possible negative cognitions (NCs) orally or on index cards. However, some kids still have difficulty accessing and verbalizing the NC related to traumatic events. In this situation, the therapist can ask the child or teen to think about the picture or worst part of the memory and notice any thoughts that come up while the therapist applies a few fast hand taps or eye movements.

In the following vignette, 12-year-old Ted agreed to work on a memory of being left alone in an apartment at age 3. He was able to identify the "worst picture" as sitting in the middle of a small room alone, but he was unable to identify an NC, even with assistance from the therapist.

Vignette With 12-Year-Old Ted

EMDR Therapist: What is the yucky thought that goes with this picture in your mind, Ted?

Ted: (*Shrugging his shoulders.*) I don't have a thought.

EMDR Therapist: Ted, while you have the picture in your mind, would it be okay if I tap on your hands a bit? It might help you find a yucky thought. Remember, it's safe to think about this because it's all in the past. (*Ted nods.*)

Ted: (*After the therapist taps a few moments.*) Okay, I've got it. I think it's "I don't have anybody."

This method can also be used to assist kids who are unable to articulate an emotion. The therapist can ask, "How about I apply a few hand taps (or eye movements) while you think of the picture and just notice any feelings that pop up? Remember that feelings come and go, and this is all in the past."

STRATEGIES WHEN REPROCESSING ATTACHMENT TRAUMA

In addition to the information provided in the Appendix F review of the EMDR reprocessing phases that includes tips for kids, this chapter provides strategies specific to reprocessing attachment trauma for kids with developmental deficits.

Commencing Reprocessing With Kids Who Are Easily Dysregulated or Dissociated

For kids who are easily dysregulated or who have dissociative or regressive features, the therapist begins by briefly grounding the child or teen in present time in their biggest self and perhaps picturing their smaller child self in the safe place on the inside. In the following example, the EMDR therapist grounds Vince prior to commencing EMDR reprocessing:

Vignette: Grounding Vince in the Present Day
    Therapist: "Vince, I'd like to take just a moment to remind you of the picture we made of little Vince in the safe playroom. Remember how Mom said she was reading to little Vince and playing with him? Can you think about little Vince safe in the playroom inside your heart? (*Vince nods.*) That's great. Now, I'd like you to think about your biggest kid self and how you helped Mom when she had the flu last week. You were in your biggest kid self. (*Vince changes his posture.*) "Okay great. Now, can you bring up that upsetting picture of the babysitter memory, the words 'I'm a bad kid' and where you feel it in your stomach and watch the lights?"

Piecework: Adjusting to the Child's Level of Tolerance for the Work

Attachment-injured kids may have a pretty narrow window of tolerance for doing the harder work, even when they're trying to cooperate. They frequently struggle with sitting still and are eager for the session to be over. Besides being skillful with the procedures and activities, IATP-C therapists learn to stay entertaining and engaging and make adjustments to match the child's tolerance for the work.

The IATP-C therapist may need to negotiate time for a piece of work. Most kids with low tolerance will agree to do a piece of memory work for 15 or 20 minutes, followed by a fun activity. When working with kids with low tolerance, the therapist should be ready to initiate an incomplete closure at any point. Even when the child or teen has only engaged in EMDR memory processing for a short time, they usually have something helpful they can take home with them.

Closing an Incomplete Session Script

Therapist: "And what is the most helpful thought or idea that has come to you today?" _____ "That's wonderful. I'd like you to hold onto that and take it home with you. Put everything else in your container. I'll hold onto it for you here. If anything comes up in your mind about this in between, you can draw a picture about it/write it down or ask your mom/dad to write it down and tell me about it next time. Or you can just send it to the container here with me. Now, how about we do a fun/relaxing activity . . ."

Always remind parents to stay aware that processing can continue and the child or teen may need a listening ear or extra attunement.

Containing Associations With the EMD Continuum

Containing associations as needed through the EMD continuum is always an option at any point during reprocessing. (See Appendix G, "The EMD Continuum," for instructions.) The IATP-C therapist uses clinical judgment to determine whether containment strategies are needed. Full EMDR reprocessing with average or lengthy sets, allowing the child or teen to associate freely, is ideal for kids who can tolerate the associations, because lengthier sets give them the opportunity to achieve helpful insights and find new meaning regarding past events. On the other hand, if the child or teen shows signs of becoming overwhelmed by associations to other memories, the therapist is free to shift to EMD continuum strategies (shortening the sets of BLS and returning to the target memory more frequently) for additional safety.

COGNITIVE INTERWEAVES

As with reprocessing of present-day triggers, kids with a history of attachment injuries usually need assistance through interweaves due to developmental deficits in their capacity to reason, lack of adaptive information, and low tolerance for distress. It's important to remember that some children and teens with developmental deficits do process quite slowly. By providing longer sets of 20 or more passes and waiting patiently for their response after each set, many slow processors can make many helpful associations on their own. Sometimes it's helpful to let the child or teen signal when they have a thought or feeling to share. The therapist should stay attuned and balance the child's need for assistance during reprocessing with the need to stay out of the child's way.

Many kids with a history of attachment trauma do require frequent interweaves due to their developmental deficits. The good news is that even kids who require many interweaves can find healing through EMDR reprocessing of their traumatic memories.

Possible goals when using cognitive interweaves for attachment trauma
- Managing kids' intense emotions and helping them stay grounded
- Providing information they can't access or don't know
- Discovering the obstacle, feeder memory, or stuck point
- Increasing kids' capacity to mentalize thoughts and feelings
- Helping kids stuck in sadness or loneliness related to the past
- Empowering kids stuck in helplessness related to the past
- Helping kids connect to their emotions
- Helping kids release stuck emotions
- Helping kids stuck in shame for things they did in the past

Methods of providing cognitive interweaves for attachment trauma
- Words to keep the child grounded
- Coaching with facts about feelings
- Invitations to parents to provide helpful information or words (interactional interweaves)
- Brief questions
- Invitations to child to express feelings through words or body movements

- Invitation to child to access the thinking brain, biggest kid self, or power animal
- Invitation to child to address the smaller self on the inside.
- Invitation to child to use their imagination

After each interweave, if the child or teen's response is positive, say, "Notice that," "Go with that," or "Think of that," and continue sets of fast BLS. If the child doesn't respond to the interweave, it's okay to try a different one. Sometimes if the child or teen doesn't have an immediate response to an interweave question, it's okay to say, "Just think about my question during the *(eye movements/taps/buzzies)*."

The following sections provide sample interweaves.

Interweaves That Help Kids Manage Intense Emotions and Stay Grounded

Children who become emotionally dysregulated during EMDR may exhibit atypical behaviors such as agitation, excessive silliness and giggling, or hiding behind a pillow or blanket. These behaviors signal a need for interweaves that help the child stay emotionally regulated and grounded. In some cases, it may be necessary to take a pause and apply a Stage 2 activity to regulate the child before returning to EMDR trauma processing, but most often, processing can continue by using one or more of the following interweaves between sets of BLS:

- "Tell me where you are right now."
- "Name three things in my office you haven't seen before."
- "What is your favorite color?"
- "Tell me about your bedroom."
- "Feel the couch cushion with one hand and your shirt with the other. How are they different?"
- "You're safe here in this office."
- "Mom/Dad, I wonder if you could move a little closer so your child can feel your connection right now."
- "You can have these upset feelings and still know inside that you are loved, you are safe, and you are comfortable."
- (Movie metaphor.) "Picture yourself watching a DVD. You have the remote in your hand. You can push play, pause, fast forward, or fast

rewind, and you can push the off button whenever you choose. Remember, this is an old memory, so the DVD may be a little scratchy and fuzzy. You can watch the memory from the safety of your favorite chair, with your favorite blanket and pillow."
- (Photograph metaphor—use a sticky note, crumple it, and stick it on the wall.) "This memory is like an old photograph. Picture the photograph on this sticky note. It's old, so it's all crumpled up and faded."

Examples of interweaves that help with intense emotions through encouraging statements during BLS

"You know, you can have these feelings and still be okay."
"By feeling your feelings, you can heal your feelings."
"These feelings are temporary. They are like waves—they wash up on shore for a while, and then they subside."
"Let your feelings move on through your body."
"Notice your mom's arms around you."
"Can you push those feelings into this pillow with your fists/feet?"

Interweaves That Provide Kids With Needed Information

EMDR processing naturally stimulates associations to helpful information resulting in new perspectives and insights. However, kids who experienced chronic early trauma have less knowledge than other kids their age due to developmental deficits. In fact, they often hold erroneous information and ideas. For example, they may hold beliefs that they are responsible for the choices of their parents. They may not understand why things happened the way they did or how things are different in their lives today. The following are examples of informational interweaves that may be used between sets:

- "I'll bet you didn't know that children are never responsible for the actions of adults."
- "Mom/Dad, do you think a child is ever responsible for abusive behavior by adults?"
- "Mom/Dad, do you believe that children who are in foster homes/adopted are somehow less worthy than children who live with their birth parents?"
- "Mom/Dad, what do you want your child to know about how you keep them safe today?"

Interweaves to Help Kids Zero in on an Obstacle, Feeder Memory, or Stuck Point

Sometimes processing gets stuck in the middle of Phases 4, 5, or 6 and there seems to be some obstacle in the way, but it's not clear what it is. These questions can help zero in on what is creating the problem. The following are examples of interweaves used between sets of BLS:

- "Was there another time even earlier when you were made to believe this?"
- "What might be bad about letting these old feelings/beliefs go?"
- "Is there a smaller child part of you who thinks you don't deserve to feel better?"
- "Is there a smaller child part of you who thinks fear/anger will help you stay safe?"

Interweaves to Help Kids Mentalize Their Thoughts and Feelings

Poor capacity to mentalize is typical of children with attachment injuries and a frequent cause of getting stuck during EMDR reprocessing. During reprocessing, they may respond to the therapist query, "And what is there now?" with "I don't know," or "Nothing." The therapist should be prepared to offer interweaves that help kids observe and verbalize their thoughts and feelings. The interweaves are effective only in an emotionally supportive environment. The following are examples of interweaves used between sets of BLS:

- "I'll continue the eye movements, and you can just look up or signal me when you have a thought, feeling, or picture that you want to share."
- "Any changes in memory, thoughts, feelings, or in your body?"
- "Can you tell me a little more about this memory? And then what happened?"
- "You say 'nothing' right now, but what do you guess that smaller child part of you might think or feel?"
- "Wow, just thinking about what happened to you makes *me* feel sad [mad, anxious]."
- "Mom/Dad, if this had happened to you, what would *you* be feeling?"

- "Mom/Dad, how do *you* feel right now, just knowing what happened?"
- "I am imagining that this is me in the picture. Here is what I am getting right now . . ."
- "What is the most upsetting thing about this right now?"

Interweaves to Help Kids With Stuck Sadness or Loneliness

Kids who were emotionally neglected when they were young may loop in stuck feelings of sadness, loneliness, or shame. The following are interweaves used between sets of BLS:

- "Mom/Dad, could you talk about what you want the younger part of your child on the inside to know regarding the love that you feel?"
- "Mom/Dad, what else do you want your child/teen to know right now?"
- "What could your biggest kid self say to the smaller child in your heart about this?"
- "Imagine your power animal is right here by your side. What does your power animal want you to know right now?"
- "Perhaps you could place your hand over your heart and picture your younger self safe and sound in the safe place for a moment."
- "What could your biggest kid self do for the smaller child inside your heart right now?"
- "What can your thinking brain say to your feeling brain about this?"

Interweaves to Assist Kids Stuck in Helplessness

When adult clients reprocess traumatic childhood events, there is quite a distance of time between the traumatic past and the present. Adult clients have reached a life state in which they naturally have more power, independence, and control. Because kids are vulnerable and dependent upon adults, their presentday self may feel no more powerful than the younger self who was victimized. For this reason, they may get stuck and loop in feelings of powerlessness during EMDR reprocessing of past trauma.

The difference between the past and present for kids who are reprocessing past trauma is that someone has intervened to protect them at this point and their life circumstances have changed. The following are interactive rescue interweaves provided through the parent between sets of BLS:

- "Mom/Dad, if you could travel back in time, what would you do right now?"
- "Mom/Dad, what would you do to help your child in those earlier years if you could travel back to the past?"
- "Mom/Dad, could you take the little one to the safe place? What would you do for him/her there?"

The following interweaves empower the biggest kid self by encouraging them to help the smaller child self on the inside. The following interweaves are directed to the child or teen between sets of BLS:

- "Can you draw the upsetting picture that is stuck in your mind?" (*Draws picture.*) "Now you can draw the picture again, but this time, change the picture in any way you wish."
- "Can you arrange some things in the sand tray to represent the upsetting picture in your mind?" (*Creates sand tray picture.*) "Now you have permission to move the figures around and decide how you want the picture in the sand tray to look."
- "If you could get in a little car that flies back and forth through time, and you could fly back in time and bring along anyone to help you, who might you bring along and what would they help you do?"
- "If you could speak up and do or say anything you want with your power animal by your side, what would you do or say?"
- "What does your power animal want you to know?"
- "What does your thinking brain want your feeling brain to know?"
- "Is there something your arms want to do right now?"
- "Is there something your legs want to do right now?"

Interweaves That Help Kids Connect to Their Emotions

Sometimes, kids are disconnected from their emotions or sensations but they're not in a dissociated state. It may be that they've learned so well how to stay disconnected from their feelings that it's automatic. Successful processing requires access to the emotional components of the memory. The following are examples of interweaves used between sets of BLS:

- "It's safe to feel because you're here with your mom/dad and me and we all care about you."

- "Mom/Dad, what's going on inside your heart right now?"
- "What does the little one inside your heart feel right now?"
- "What might the little one inside your heart believe?"
- "Let's stop and act out what happened. I'll be _____." (*Playact the incident together or act it out with stuffed animals.*) "What feelings are you noticing?"
- "Let's pause so you can draw a picture or make a sand tray of what you remember." (*The child or teen draws or makes a sand tray.*) "Perhaps you can just look at the picture/sand tray while I do some taps."
- "Can you tell me about any words or sounds or smells or sensations you might remember?"
- "Can you imagine how you might have felt at the time this happened?"

Interweaves That Help Kids Release Their Emotions

Often kids have pent-up emotions that cause them to get stuck during reprocessing. If the child or teen feels safe in the office with us, we can help them get relief by releasing their emotions during EMDR reprocessing. The following are interweaves used between sets of BLS:

- "It might feel good to push that mad and scared feeling right out of your body. What do you think? Do you want to use arms or feet? I can hold up this pillow and you can push, push, until your arms are all the way out straight in front of you. In fact, you can push me all the way out this door, if you want! We can stop anytime you want to."
- "Do your hands want to do something right now? Like pound or push?" _____ "Let your hands/arms do that right now. I can hold up this pillow and you can pound/push."
- "Do your feet want to do something right now? Like stomp or run?" _____ "We can do that together." _____ After, say, "Notice how you feel now."
- "Would you like to make a quick picture or sand tray to show me your feelings right now?" _____ After, say, "Notice how you feel now."

Interweaves That Help Kids Stuck in Shame for Things They've Done

Chapter 7 offers three EMDR protocols we find useful to assist kids with present-day addictive or compulsive behaviors, including behaviors that are hurtful toward others.

However, even if the harmful behaviors are eliminated in the present, kids are negatively impacted by their memories of hurting others. Common NCs related to memories of past behaviors include:

- "I'm bad."
- "I'm evil."
- "I'm shameful."
- "I don't deserve to be loved."
- "I don't deserve good things."

Helpful PCs related to memories of past behaviors include:

- "I'm good in my heart, because I don't want to do those things anymore."
- "My heart is healing and I don't do those things anymore."
- "I know how to make better choices now."
- "I have better control of myself as my heart heals."
- "It is okay to make mistakes."

Helpful interweaves related to memories of past behaviors include:

- "I wonder if you know that a lot of kids do what you did to cope with the hurt they carry in their hearts."
- "I wonder if you know that kids who feel sad inside often try to fix their sad feelings with anything that they think will make them feel good or powerful."
- "You feel guilty about what you did. Do you think someone who was evil would feel guilty?"
- "Can you think of a special good deed you could do to make up for that past mistake?"

Completion of Reprocessing Phases

Due to the impairment in their self-reflective capacity, many traumatized children have difficulty recognizing a change in a SUD. Occasionally, a child will report a high SUD despite clearly observable relaxation and relief. In this case, the child may be interpreting a low SUD as equivalent to admission that the trauma or loss was unimportant. Traumatized children who experienced a lack of validation from caregivers early in life need clear validation regarding the enormity of what they've suffered. The therapist might say, "What happened to you was a very terrible thing. It should never, ever have happened. But I'm just wondering; you used to get really anxious inside when you thought about it, and now it looks like you're able to stay calmer inside when you think about it. What do you think? There's no right or wrong answer."

Some children hate the rating questions, both because they find them difficult and also because the questions may remind them of being quizzed at school. In some cases, it's more helpful for the therapist to observe the child's body language and facial expression as a way to judge any change in SUD.

I worked with a teenager who was resistant to EMDR because of her prior experience with EMDR in another city. She said, "I can't stand those number ratings—they pressure me." She was willing to participate in EMDR when it was agreed that the SUD would not be utilized. She was then able to successfully reprocess memories of sexual abuse. The lesson here is to attune and adapt to the individual needs of the child or teen.

The following vignette illustrates the importance of the presence of the adoptive mother to provide emotional support and the use of cognitive interweaves for time orientation, reassurance of the younger part of self, and empowerment to resolve feelings of fear and helplessness.

Vignette With 13-Year-Old Joan: Memory of Court-Ordered Visits to Biological Mother at Age 2

Joan was adopted at age 4, but she had lived with her adoptive parents since she was removed from her biological parents for abuse and neglect at age 2. Joan's symptoms included arguing and violent anger explosions. Joan and her parents had been participating in IATP-C for approximately 4 months when she spontaneously shared a distressing memory in which her present parents were dropping her off to have a visit with her biological mother when she was 2 years of age.

Joan knew, intellectually, that the visits had been ordered by the judge. However, Joan could not get past the stuck 2-year-old feeling that her present parents didn't want her.

- Target = Adoptive mother (who was her foster mother at the time) placing Joan into the arms of her biological father.
- NC = "My *[adoptive]* parents don't want me."
- PC = "My *[adoptive]* parents had to leave me there, but they didn't want to."
- VOC = 3
- Feelings = rejection, fear, anger
- Body = sensations in chest
- SUD = 8

This is the second session targeting the memory. Joan's adoptive mother is sitting with Joan to provide support. Fast BLS is applied with bilateral lights and buzzies attached to an eye scan machine. The vignette begins partway into the session.

Therapist: What's there now?
Joan: Scared . . .
Therapist: Okay . . . where do you notice that in your body?
Joan: Ummm . . . in my hands.
Therapist: Go with that. *(BLS.)* What's there now?
Joan: Confused.
Therapist: Anything in your body?
Joan: Confused why we had to go back and forth.
Therapist: Go with that. *(BLS.)* What are you getting now?
Joan: When I was with Mom and Dad, it was all good, and then I went back to the place, it wasn't very good.
Therapist: Go with that. *(BLS.)* (*Joan is crying through the eye movements.*) Okay, let me ask Mom a question. Mom, when Joan was visiting her biological mother, and you were at home, how were you feeling and how was Dad feeling?

Mom: We were worried about you, and we missed you.
Therapist: So while she was over there, you were thinking about her . . .
Mom: All the time.
Therapist: She was in your heart and mind the whole time she was there.
Mom: All the time. For both Dad and me. (*Joan nods.*)
Therapist: Is it okay if Mom puts her arm around you?
Joan: Yeah.
Therapist: Okay. All those feelings are okay, Joan. (*Slightly later in the session.*) (*BLS.*) What are you noticing?
Joan: I'm sad in my heart.
Therapist: Okay. Yes. Just let yourself feel it. Joan, what would you say to that little girl, that little Joan?
Joan: Sorry.
Therapist: Mom, what would you say to littler Joan?
Mom: It wasn't fair. I'm sorry you went through that. (*Joan looks at Mom with tears in her eyes.*)
Therapist: Go with that. (*BLS.*) What's there now?
Joan: Sad.
Therapist: Can you picture the smaller child you in your mind, Joan? (*Joan nods.*) What do you want to do for her?
Joan: Love her.
Therapist: Love her? Can you give her a big hug? (*Joan nods.*) Mom, what can you do for her?
Mom: I want to give love to the little Joan and the big Joan. I love you.
Therapist: (*Joan is crying more.*) Just let those feelings out, Joan. Can you follow the lights now? (*BLS.*) What are you noticing now?
Joan: I feel sad in my heart and happy in my head at the same time.
Therapist: Go with that. (*BLS.*) What are you getting now?
Joan: I feel happy.
Therapist: Okay. Why don't you scooch over close to Mom a little more, get comfy and then watch the lights again?
Joan: (*Begins watching the lights while getting a big hug from Mom.*)
Therapist: What's there?
Joan: Relieved.
Therapist: Ah, yeah . . . what do you notice in your body?
Joan: That I'm relaxed.

Therapist: Oh, good, yes, just notice that relaxed feeling and follow the lights. *(BLS.)* What are you getting?

Joan: That I'm in a safe and happy place now.

By the end of the session, Joan's SUD was 0 and her VOC was 7. This work was a turning point for Joan in letting go of her anger and opening her heart to trusting her adoptive parents.

ADDRESSING PREVERBAL TRAUMA

Some kids report high disturbance related to the preverbal events in their therapeutic story. There was a time when it was commonly believed that trauma prior to age 2½ was not consciously remembered and therefore had no long-term impact. Research into the implicit memory system and the storage of preverbal trauma within the limbic brain (e.g., van der Kolk & Fisler, 1992) changed all of that. Our observations are consistent with the research: Children who are placed in permanent, safe homes prior to age 2½ frequently exhibit the same intense emotional and behavioral dysregulation as children who are placed later. The question then becomes: How do we reprocess trauma that is not consciously remembered?

As stated in Chapter 8 regarding writing of the therapeutic story, it's important to avoid generating what could be false memories. We should always stay with what we know to be factual. We should never fabricate events based on guesswork, nor should we fabricate details to an event or situation, even if we know the situation to be generally true. We also should never ask children or teens to "try to remember" or to "search for memories" related to their past. However, some children will bring up what seem to be fragments of preverbal trauma during EMDR processing or outside of EMDR processing. It can be helpful to the child or teen to process their images and their feelings related to the images, as long as the therapist stays curious and present and avoids making interpretations for the child.

Target a Memory Fragment Related to Preverbal Trauma

Five-year-old Danielle had been removed from a situation of abuse and neglect by drug-abusing biological parents just before she turned 2. The therapist had initiated EMDR with Danielle to help calm her fears related to bedtime. In the middle of reprocessing, Danielle stated, "I woke up and I was all by myself in my crib. I could see out the window. Mommy and Daddy were at a party across the street." The EMDR therapist continued the bilateral stimulation to reprocess this very early traumatic memory. Through EMDR Danielle was able to separate her current situation from her early life, and the therapist was able to install the PC, "My forever mommy and daddy will keep me safe through the night."

Targeting Imagined Pictures Related to Preverbal Trauma

Eleven-year-old Lori had an intellectual disability. She was adopted from overseas at 9 months of age. She'd been placed in an orphanage by her birth mother when she was just 2 days old. When discussing her history in a family therapy session, she said, "I can see my birth mother's face when she left me at the orphanage. It is a mad face, because she didn't like me. I think I must have been bad, and that is why she left me there."

This information was brought to the EMDR therapist for reprocessing. It is unlikely that Lori actually remembered the birth mother's face. However, the picture in her imagination was disturbing Lori and represented her negative beliefs related to her known history. The EMDR therapist targeted the imagined face of the birth mother and the NC, "She left me because I was bad."

Between sets of BLS, the EMDR therapist prompted the adoptive mother to provide an informational interweave by asking the mother, "What do you know about Lori's birth mother?" The adoptive mother replied, "I was told that she loved Lori very much, but she was too poor to take care of Lori herself." The BLS was resumed immediately, allowing Lori to integrate the adaptive information, desensitize the picture, and install the PC: "She left me because she loved me and wanted me to have a mother who could take care of me."

GRIEF

Children or teens with a history of attachment trauma are often suffering from traumatic grief related to the loss of attachment figures in their life. They may be grieving deeply for the loss of extended family members, friends, homes, pets, and more. Adopted and foster kids may also be grieving for the loss of their previous community or ethnic or cultural group.

Grief related to loss of biological parents, whether the child or teen can remember them or not, is often complicated by the knowledge that their family-of-origin is still in the world but out-of-reach to them. Kids may feel helpless and heartsick due to the lack of knowledge as to the whereabouts and well-being of their biological parents or other family members. They may grieve for the lack of knowledge regarding their origin story.

Common NCs related to grief are "I'm unimportant," "It's all my fault," "My sad feelings are not okay" or "I can't ever be happy." Common PCs are "I'm important," "I did nothing wrong," "I can have these feelings and be okay," or "I have room inside for my sad feelings and my happy feelings all at the same time."

The parent should be coached to provide warm, sensitive attunement to their child's grief. In the case of kids who are grieving for biological parents, it's important that both the therapist and parent convey a compassionate attitude toward the family-of-origin. EMDR reprocessing of the traumatic grief is a wonderful window of opportunity for bonding between the current parent and the child or teen if parents can adequately convey their empathy and compassion for their child's situation. Emotional support from the parents along with the bilateral stimulation can remove the child's protective defenses to feeling and expressing their grief during EMDR, allowing the traumatic grief to integrate with adaptive information, including the sense that they are not all alone with their feelings. Sometimes the best interweave is to simply say, "I'm so sorry" between sets of BLS. EMDR doesn't magically remove appropriate feelings of grief related to significant loss, but the release of emotions during EMDR can bring relief. The therapist should avoid focusing too much on the SUD when processing children's grief. Kids may believe reporting a SUD as 0 invalidates the significance of their first attachments and the enormity of their losses. When taking the SUD it can help to say, "A zero doesn't mean you're not sad or that these relationships weren't important to you. It just means that you can think of your losses now and your body is able to stay calm."

Vignette With 10-Year-Old Boy Processing Grief

Carl, age 10, had been removed from his biological mother at age 2 due to neglect and lived with his grandmother until placement with the adoptive parents at age 3. His parents stated that he never appeared sad, but he was often controlling, oppositional, and aggressive. Although his behaviors had improved through ARD and family therapy, he was still guarded and became tearful when discussing the biological grandmother.

- Target = Picture of driving away from Grandma's house
- Feeling = Sad and scared (in Carl's heart)
- NC = "I'm unwanted."
- PC = "Grandma loved me, but she just couldn't take care of me."
- VOC = 2
- SUD = 9

Carl's adoptive parents sat closely on either side of him while he held a sheet of feelings faces as a reference to help him identify his emotions during the reprocessing.

> **Therapist:** Okay, Carl, just let yourself think of the picture of leaving Grandma's home along with that upset thought, "I'm unwanted," and where you feel the feelings in your heart. We'll all be quiet for a few moments while you watch my fingers and notice any other thoughts, feelings, or pictures that come up. (*BLS.*) Breathe, let it go, and what's there now?
>
> **Carl:** She wasn't able to take care of me, but she wanted the best for me. (*Repeating what he had been told.*)
>
> **Therapist:** Go with that. (*BLS.*) A breath, let it go, and what's there now?
>
> **Carl:** Worry. I think Grandma didn't really like me.
>
> **Therapist:** Go with that. (*BLS.*) What are you getting?
>
> **Carl:** Confused. I thought that she liked me, but then it seemed like she didn't.
>
> **Therapist:** Go with that. (*BLS.*) Breathe, let it go, and what's there?
>
> **Carl:** Hurt. Disappointed. (*Very tearful now.*)
>
> **Therapist:** Just notice your feelings. (*BLS.*) Breathe, and what are you getting?
>
> **Carl:** Sad. Hurt. In my heart.
>
> **Therapist:** Let's pretend little Carl is right here sitting next to me. (*Adaptive information is provided through an interweave.*) Let's take turns speaking to him. I'll start. "Little Carl, I want you to know that you are special and lovable. Your grandma loved you, but she was a much older lady. She didn't feel she could keep up with a little boy. She didn't feel she could do a good job."
>
> **Mom:** (*Pretending to take little Carl from the therapist.*) "Little Carl, your

grandma did a very hard thing. She loved you, but she knew she wasn't the best person to raise you. You are a wonderful boy." (*The therapist now taps on Carl's knees while Mom and Carl look in each other's eyes.*)

Dad: (*Taking his turn.*) "Little Carl, your grandma loved you so much that she wanted only the very best for you. She knew she couldn't give you what you needed." (*The therapist taps on Carl's knees while Dad speaks.*)

Therapist: Just notice those feelings, Carl, let them out; it's so healing for you. Feelings come and feelings go. These feelings are normal. (*Taps on Carl's knees.*) Mom? Could Carl come to you any time with his feelings?

Mom: (*Turning to Carl.*) I want you to come to me with your feelings. I want to help. When you cry, I feel sad because I love you. (*The therapist taps on Carl's knees.*)

Carl: (*With tears.*) I love you, Mom.

Mom: (*Through her tears.*) I love you, Carl.

Dad: I love you, Carl, you can always come to me.

Therapist: Carl, just think of what your parents said. (*BLS.*) Breathe, and what's there now?

Carl: Happy and sad at the same time. She had to give me away, but she wanted me. And happy I was able to be with her for a while.

Therapist: Go with that. (*BLS.*) Take a breath, let it go. What's there now?

Carl: Happy and sad.

Therapist: What would you say to her?

Carl: I miss you. (*Tearful.*)

Therapist: Just notice the missing feelings. Feeling your feelings is healing your feelings. (*BLS.*)

At the end of the session, Carl reported a SUD of 5. The session was closed by talking about the fun things they were going to do the rest of the day.

Carl's Follow-Up Session

The following week, the EMDR therapist asked Carl what he noticed when he brought up in his mind the picture of leaving Grandma's home. Carl's face immediately crumpled. He said he no longer believed that Grandma had abandoned him. He understood why Grandma couldn't keep him. "But," Carl said, "I just miss her." Mom and Dad snuggled on either side while the therapist commenced the EMDR.

Therapist: Just bring up that memory of leaving Grandma and notice the missing feeling . . . in your heart. (*BLS.*) Breathe, and what's there now?

Carl: Just sad. Just missing her. (*Tearful.*)

Therapist: Just notice that. (*BLS.*) And now?

Carl: Still the same. (*Tearful.*)

Therapist: (*Speaks to Mom and Dad.*) Let's each take turns looking at Carl and letting him know how truly sorry we feel. Carl, I am so, so sorry. I am so sorry that that happened to you. (*Tapping on Carl's hands while looking in Carl's eyes.*)

Mom: (*Tearful, and looking at Carl.*) Carl, I am so, so sorry that that happened to you. I feel so sad that you had to experience such a loss. (*The therapist is tapping on Carl's hands.*)

Dad: (*Looking at Carl.*) I am real sorry that you had to go through that, Carl.

Therapist: Why don't you snuggle with Mom, and let yourself feel whatever you are feeling right now, Carl. (*Switches to taps on Carl's knees, while Carl cries with Mom. Dad has a hand on his shoulder.*) What is there now, Carl?

Carl: I feel better, happier.

Therapist: And I hope you are remembering that what happened was not your fault. You didn't do anything to cause it. (*BLS.*) Breathe, and what's there?

Carl: (*Turning to smile at each of his parents.*) I feel happy.

The therapist proceeded to installation phase and Carl chose to install the PC "I miss Grandma, but I'm okay." Then the therapist asked Carl and his parents to practice sitting close every single day during the upcoming week, and they all agreed. The therapist asked to talk with Carl's parents alone and suggested to his parents that whenever they noticed Carl feeling mad or sad, they give him a hug and tell him how sorry they felt.

Prior to treatment, Carl had suppressed his grief and it caused him to be shut down and angry. His natural feelings of grief were now free to process naturally. Carl continued to experience sad feelings about his grandma from time to time but now he was open about his feelings and receptive to comfort.

CONTINUING THE IATP-C

1. Begin each EMDR session by asking the parent, "What did you appreciate about _____ this week?" Reinforce the parent's positive messages of love with slow bilateral stimulation.
2. Continue reinforcing positive experiences of connection and positive affect by periodically returning to ARD, RDI, and SRDI activities.
3. Continue creating future rehearsals for meeting challenges with new resources and skills.
4. Continue reprocessing triggers and develop future templates (utilizing the Detective Work of the family therapist).
5. Continue reprocessing any traumatic experiences the child or teen identifies during EMDR or family therapy.
6. Add to the therapeutic story as new insights are gained or important memories are identified. Reread the revised story with BLS. Reprocess any remaining emotional charge by asking, "What part of the story is most upsetting to you now?"

BRINGING CLOSURE TO TREATMENT

When parent reports and therapist observations indicate improved symptoms and an improved quality of parent–child interactions, the IATP-C therapist gradually decreases the frequency of meetings to ensure gains are maintained before treatment is brought to a close. The therapist reassures both parents and kids that therapeutic tune-ups are available following discharge. New stressors for kids or parents, hormonal changes, or new developmental tasks as the child or teen grows and matures may naturally require another round of therapeutic support, and the sooner the situation is addressed, the easier it is for the family to get back on track, preventing smaller crises from turning into bigger crises.

A special art activity can be a meaningful way to close treatment and provide kids with something they can take home as a visual reminder of the healing they've experienced. Here are a few ideas, but you may have many of your own.

With Children
1. Make two imprints of the child's hand from plaster of paris. Paint the hand imprints. The therapist can write affirmations on the imprint as well. The child leaves one with the therapist and takes one home.
2. The child and parent and therapist string bead necklaces or bracelets and exchange them with one another.
3. The therapist, child, and parent decorate cookies together.
4. The therapist and child pot a plant for the child to keep.
5. The therapist, child, and parent create a painting or collage with words and images representing the child's strengths, talents, and positive characteristics.
6. The therapist, child, and parent create a painting or collage illustrating the child's circle of love.
7. The therapist, child, and parent share snacks and play a favorite therapy game.

With Teens
1. Provide art supplies to create a poster illustrating their strengths and positive characteristics.
2. Share snacks and listen to some of the teen's favorite songs and play *The Ungame* or the *Chicken Soup for the Soul* game.
3. Create a collage together with images and words representing the teen's future hopes and dreams.

CONCLUSION

Children and teens with a history of attachment trauma often resist therapy due to the overwhelming nature of their traumatic memories, their mistrust, and their lack of regulation. EMDR therapy is uniquely appropriate for children and teens, as it can be applied with flexibility while still maintaining fidelity to the EMDR procedures (Civilotti et al., 2021). For children and teens who present with challenging behaviors and developmental deficits due to their early life experiences, EMDR therapy is a powerful tool. Through the IATP-C model and the supportive strategies provided throughout all 3 stages, children and teens can experience healing and look forward to a happier life.

Part IV

Addressing Additional Challenges With Kids and Parents

CHAPTER 10

Strategies for Problematic Dissociation

> Through reading this chapter, you'll gain skills for:
>
> – Making sense of symptoms of dissociation for kids and parents
> – EMDR resource activities for a healthier internal system and improved stability
> – Making sense of dissociative symptoms through a dissociation story
> – Grounding during processing of triggers and traumas

For kids suffering from attachment injuries, some level of dissociation, especially when traumatic memories are consciously or subconsciously activated, is to be expected. The IATP-C approach naturally minimizes symptoms of dissociation by improving emotional support and sense of belonging, increasing self-awareness and tolerance for triggers and emotions, strengthening of the biggest kid self and safety for younger parts of the self. This chapter includes additional strategies for children and teens who need further assistance for dissociative symptoms.

RECOGNIZING PROBLEMATIC DISSOCIATION IN KIDS

Symptoms of dissociation in children and teenagers are varied. Periods of regressed behaviors can be a symptom of dissociation. We have to be careful with our observations, however, for two reasons. First, all younger children show periods of developmental regression during times of stress. For example, a 6-year-old may regress to wetting the bed or talking in baby talk temporarily upon a move to a new neighborhood and starting at a new school, which resolves after a period of adjustment and reassurance from parents. Secondly, children and teens affected by prenatal alcohol exposure or on the autism spectrum or children with chronic maltreatment may be delayed in their development and regularly exhibit behaviors that resemble a younger child.

Sudden episodes of regression that are a striking change from the day-to-day presentation of the child or teen may indicate dissociation. When triggered by some reminder of the past that may or may not be obvious, they may baby talk, suck their thumb, or forget how to use the toilet properly before returning to age-appropriate functioning.

Another clue to problematic dissociation is excessive daydreaming and the creation of internal imaginary worlds beyond what is expected developmentally. The child or teen may refer to imaginary people or speak aloud to imaginary others.

Children with very high levels of dissociation may exhibit sudden episodes involving aggression and meltdowns, picking or scratching at their skin, extreme silliness and giddiness, or imitating an animal. They may at times have a pattern of shutting down or staring vacantly, with slowed movement and speech.

Older children and teens may exhibit sudden personality changes or mannerisms that are not typically considered regressive but are strikingly different from typical functioning. For example, a child or teen may suddenly exhibit overtly sexual behaviors, refer to themselves by a different name, or switch from a shy and withdrawn presentation to a loud and aggressive one. Co-occurring periods of memory loss may indicate a developing dissociative identity disorder.

See Appendix D for useful assessments that can assist with understanding the dissociative processes that may be present. It's important to be cautious, however, regarding the diagnosis of a dissociative disorder with teens who may dramatize symptoms of dissociation as a maladaptive way of gaining a sense of connection. The seeking of connection through gaining attention makes sense for kids with early unmet needs related to childhood neglect.

Conceptualizing Dissociation Through the Attachment Lens

The Strange Situation, an assessment developed by Mary Ainsworth (1967; 1982), identifies attachment patterns in infants and toddlers. During the Strange Situation assessment, the child plays while the parent and a stranger are moved in and out of the room. The attachment designation is determined by the child's response to the parent after being reunited. The youngster with a disorganized pattern exhibits odd behaviors such as twirling, covering their face or head, crawling backwards, or flapping their arms. Researchers discovered that the disorganized youngsters are caught in a double bind. They yearn to run to their parent for comfort, while their parent is also the source of their fear. The parent may have facial expressions or vocal tones that frighten the child or they may behave in other ways that are frightening. Attachment disorganization is an automatic response of the nervous system when all other defenses fail, and it's associated with dissociative disorders later on.

Conceptualizing Dissociation in Kids Through the Structural Dissociation Model

The Structural Dissociation model (van der Hart et al., 2006) conceptualizes the front self, or what we might refer to as the *biggest kid self*, as the apparently normal part (ANP) of the personality. The neural networks encapsulating traumas and associated emotions and perceptions are conceptualized as emotional parts (EPs), neural networks that are cut off from the rest of the self due to phobia for the memories and for the emotions they hold. The model suggests that dissociative individuals are also phobic regarding their EPs and their present attachment relationships. Our observations are consistent with the Structural Dissociation model. Kids who exhibit severe problems of dissociation are typically fearful and avoidant of feelings, thoughts, and memories and highly anxious regarding their attachment relationships. Due to lack of neural integration, without adequate preparation and stabilization they are at risk of losing present-day orientation during EMDR trauma work.

Dissociation may be rooted in early attachment trauma and reinforced by struggles with the present-day parent. Like the toddler in the Strange Situation assessment, the present-day teen or child yearns for closeness and connection, but they're afraid and push their parents away at the same time. They often seek to get their needs met through maladaptive means, such as meltdowns or arguments, because attention gives the illusion of connection.

WORKING WITH PARENTS OF HIGHLY DISSOCIATIVE KIDS

For parents, the mixed messages and ongoing symptoms can be confusing, frustrating, anxiety provoking, and hurtful. Parents may believe the child has an evil part or a bad side and become quite punitive, increasing the child's fear and dissociation. Parents need help understanding the cause of dissociation and how they can help stabilize their child. The therapist can utilize the parent guide, *Attachment Trauma in Kids: Integrative Strategies for Parents* (Wesselmann, 2025), as a curriculum for parents of highly dissociative children.

Introducing the Concept of Dissociation to Parents Script

Say to parents, "The behaviors and symptoms you've described are associated with problems of dissociation. There are lots of different kinds of behaviors and symptoms that we observe with dissociative kids, but all the symptoms began with frightening experiences in which they felt trapped and helpless. Dissociation, or mental separation from the memories and the feelings of fear, is a common, automatic response of the brain and nervous system. The fearful feelings are associated with adults, and therefore they're easily triggered by interactions with you. It's critical that we find ways to help your child develop trust and safe connection with you to reduce their symptoms."

Teaching Parents to Bring the Biggest Kid Part Forward at Home

For kids who have frequent symptoms of dissociation, parents need practical help with words and actions that help bring the biggest kid state forward at home. Parents often don't know what to say or how to reinforce the presence of the child's most mature state.

Speaking to Parents: Bringing the Biggest Kid Part Forward at Home Script

Say to parents, "We're going to work on stabilizing your child by enhancing the security of their relationship with you and by helping your child strengthen their most mature self. In their mature self, or what we call their biggest kid self, they're better able to access the executive functions such as problem solving, decision making, and impulse control. They're better able to recognize present safety. To help bring their biggest kid self forward at home, you can highlight their mature, positive moments. For example, you can say: *I just love being with you. It's so fun to spend time together, and I'm impressed by your biggest kid self right now.* When your child is in a regressed state or dissociating in another way, you can minimize symptoms by saying, *I love all parts of you, but I know all the parts of you feel better and we communicate better when you're in your biggest kid self. Can I have some time with your biggest kid self right now?"*

REINFORCING DISSOCIATIVE PATTERNS

When a child or teen has a pattern of periodic regression, there is likely a younger state seeking to get earlier unmet needs met in present day. It's not uncommon for parents to inadvertently reinforce the pattern because in the regressed state, the child or teen may actually behave in a more cuddly, funny, and playful manner than is typical for the child in a nonregressed state. Parents may give hugs and snuggle the child who is operating from a toddler-like part, for example, but feel much less comfortable hugging the teen who is acting like a teen. Unfortunately, for the dissociative child or teen, receiving attention and affection in the regressed state is rewarding.

Parents may also inadvertently reinforce the regressed state of the child or teen by responding with anger. The parent's anger may feel gratifying to the smaller, younger child part, who feels really seen and heard in that moment.

The therapist or parent may unintentionally reinforce the separateness of parts by giving names to dissociated states or asking to speak directly with them and treating them as separate individuals. A good rule of thumb is: When working with children and adolescents, never ask to speak directly to a part or name a part. Joyanna Silberg (2022) states:

> If the therapist asks for a different "identity" to emerge or for a voice to talk to the therapist, the therapist is unwittingly giving the client more opportunities to practice the brain habit that they [therapist/parents] are attempting to extinguish. By allowing clients additional opportunities to practice dissociation, clinicians may reinforce the neural pathways that support dissociative coping. In younger children, the brain is still growing, pruning, and selecting the neural networks that will become most utilized as they grow into adults. (p. 101)

If a child or teen has already created names for parts of their self, the therapist should make it clear that the part is not a separate individual, and that a name is for convenience only. For example, the therapist might say, "Let's help create safety on the inside for that part of you that you refer to as _____." If a part comes forward and speaks of the youth in the third person, the therapist should avoid reinforcing the part with special attention, assure the part that work will be done to create safety on the inside and encourage the biggest kid self to come forward to do the work.

EMDR RESOURCE ACTIVITIES FOR DISSOCIATIVE CHILDREN

The following are EMDR preparation activities to increase stabilization during Stage 2 for severely dissociative kids. Ideally, the parent participates in the activities, as the development of healthy connection is an antidote to dissociation in children and teens. However, the therapist uses clinical judgment regarding involvement of parents, taking into account the preferences of the child and the capacity of the parents to remain compassionate and emotionally present. Of course, some children have no permanent placement. If parents are not present, therapeutic trust (with appropriate boundaries) is paramount.

Repeated Future Rehearsals for Strengthening the Biggest Kid Self

Kids with frequent symptoms of dissociation or regression need extra assistance to strengthen and operate from their biggest kid self. As described in Chapter 6, the EMDR resource activity for finding and strengthening the biggest kid self can be followed by future rehearsals (mental movies or role-plays with slow BLS) for managing present-day challenges while functioning in their most mature state. For kids with a tendency to dissociate or regress, repeated future rehearsals with their biggest kid self can further strengthen their present-day state and improve present-day functioning.

Enhanced Safe Places for the Smaller Child Parts on the Inside

The creation of a Safe Place for a smaller child part is a standard part of IATP-C preparation Stage 2 as described in Chapter 6. The activity helps stabilize dissociative children and teens. Dissociative kids hold a felt sense on the inside that danger is in the present day. Smaller parts stay vigilant and also look for ways to get their needs met. During the activity, it's important to reinforce the following perspectives:

- Smaller parts of the self *do not* have to be vigilant to danger in the child's present life.

- Smaller parts of the self are safe and cared for *on the inside*.
- Smaller parts of the self are part of the child or teen in the *present time*. They are *not* residing in the past.

To further enhance the safe place for the smaller part(s) of the self for highly dissociative kids, it's helpful to conduct the work of providing an additional caregiver figure or figures to nurture and protect the smaller part(s) in the safe environment on the inside as recommended by Potter and Wesselmann (2023) in working with adults with attachment injuries. The procedure for providing additional caregivers within the safe place is described in Chapter 6 of this book in the section, "Creating Internal Safety and Nurturing for Kids With Unstable Environments or Problematic Dissociation." As described in Chapter 6, the additional caregiver(s) can come from history books, fiction books, or movies or can be from the child's real life if the therapist can make clear that the figure represents only the very best parts of the person. The section also describes the option of bringing in the Circle of Caring or the power animal to provide extra nurturing and protection for the smaller part(s) of self. For kids who need something concrete to vivify the imagery, offer art supplies or the sand tray to create safe places and protective and nurturing figures for the smaller part(s).

Vignette: 14-Year-Old Franklyn and a Safe Place for the 4-Year-Old

Franklyn had been in and out of foster care for the past 10 years as his biological mother struggled with drug addiction relapses. His current foster home was supportive, but there was no plan for permanency at this time. Franklyn had created a drawing of a magical tree house for his 4-year-old younger self on the inside. The therapist had created a circle of caring for the smaller child part since there were no permanent adults in Franklyn's life.

> **Therapist:** Franklyn, this is such a wonderful place for a 4-year-old. And your Circle of Caring includes teachers and social workers and pets and even me! But that 4-year-old part is still getting triggered sometimes. How about we add a special caregiver figure to watch over the 4-year-old and help him feel safe?
> **Franklyn:** Sure. But who?
> **Therapist:** Can you think of a figure from your imagination, from a book

or movie or TV show? Or some kids use animals or angels. So, any ideas come to you? You could use your resource figure representing wisdom, Obi-Wan Kenobi. He's so powerful that he could have more than one purpose.

Franklyn: Naw, my 4-year-old needs Chewbacca, because he's all furry and soft but big and tough at the same time.

Therapist: I love that! (*Franklyn draws Chewbacca into the picture.*) How do you feel as you look at your new picture?

Franklyn: Happy. Good.

Therapist: Do you want to hold the buzzies for a second while you look at this? (*Turns on buzzies, slow speed.*) What do you imagine Chewbacca is doing with your 4-year-old today?

Franklyn: Oh, I know what he's doing. Chewbacca's in the hammock over here, and the 4-year-old is lying on top of him taking a nap.

Therapist: (*Turning on slow buzzies again.*) That sounds so cozy and nice. Chewbacca has special powers for both protection and love, so your 4-year-old self feels especially safe and loved now. Would you be willing to give your 4-year-old self some good messages today? I have some ideas and you can add any other messages you want.

Franklyn: Sure.

Therapist: (*Turning on slow buzzies again.*) Can you imagine stepping into the tree house and reminding 4-year-old Franklyn that he can stay there and play and just be a kid? He doesn't have to worry about a thing in his tree house. You might remind him that he's lovable and good and safe. The past is over, and he'll never be alone.

Make a Cord of Love on the Inside

The Magical Cord of Love or Cord of Love is a standard part of ARD with kids and parents as described in Chapter 6. An additional enhancement of the Safe Place for the younger child part involves a sand tray, drawing, or visualization of a Magical Cord of Love connecting the heart of the smaller child part to any protective and nurturing figures and also to the heart of the biggest kid self. The Cord of Love adds emphasis to the sense of ongoing, unconditional love and connection and the sense that the younger part of self is never alone. The image and associated feelings of security and connection can be deepened with one or two slow, short sets of BLS.

Magical Cord of Love on the Inside Script

Say to the child or teen, "Picture that wonderful Safe Place for the smaller child part of you and the loving and safe figure(s) protecting that smaller child part of you there, now. Remember the (Magical) Cord of Love? _____ There's a (Magical) Cord of Love on the inside too. What color do you see this loving cord to be? _____ See this beautiful, colored light, shimmery and shiny cord, running from the heart of that littler you to the hearts of the loving figure(s) and also to the heart inside of the biggest kid self you. This smaller child part of you will always and forever be nurtured, loved, and safe, connected heart to heart to the loving figure(s) on the inside and always connected to you. This is where this littler one belongs, safe and sound, surrounded by love and care." (*If observable response is positive, add slow ongoing taps or buzzies at any point during the visualization.*)

Tucking Child Parts Back Inside as Needed

Any time the therapist notices the child or teen is operating from a younger state, the therapist can intervene to bring the present-day self forward and provide safety for the smaller child parts on the inside by tucking them back into safe places as advised in the adult parts model of Potter and Wesselmann (2023). Strengthening of the biggest kid self and tucking in of smaller parts allows more access to adaptive information and present-day orientation. Operating from the biggest kid self allows for healthy integration of the system over time.

The following script demonstrates language for bringing the biggest kid self forward and tucking in the child part to use with a child or teen who is showing behaviors associated with regression/dissociation.

Bringing the Biggest Kid Part Forward While Tucking in the Smaller Parts Script

Say to the child or teen, "I think a younger kid part of you is activated today. I'd really like to have your biggest kid self here with me. Can you find your big kid body posture? _____ (*Models shifting of posture.*) That's great. How about taking a look at your hands. Look at how big they are. (*Holds out hands and demonstrates.*) And look at your older kid feet and how big they are. (*Demonstrates.*) Can you shift your body posture to help you step into your biggest kid self? (*Demonstrates.*) That's great. And now, let's look at this picture of the safe place for that smaller child part. See if you can remind the smaller child part(s) that your big kid life is fine and you're safe and all your younger parts are safe on the inside, in present day. The child part(s) of you can play and have fun and be cozy inside their special place. And remember the cord of love that's always there no matter what. Now, with your younger self tucked in, you can be in your present life with your biggest kid self. (*If parent is present . . .*) Mom/Dad, what are the things you enjoy about watching your child/teen grow and mature?" _____

Following this work, it's always beneficial to conduct future rehearsals using mental movies or role-plays to help the child or teen practice handling day-to-day tasks and challenges from their biggest kid self. Through this work, over time, we're rewiring the child's brain, in a sense, allowing more mature functioning and access to adaptive information for managing triggers and tolerating emotions.

In the following vignette, 13-year-old Eli has exhibited some regressive behavior. Eli has a tendency to regress, and the therapist intervenes to orient him to his present-day 13-year-old self and tuck the smaller self in the safe place.

Vignette: Creating a Safe Place for a Younger Part With 13-Year-Old Eli and His Mom

Mom: We've had a tough morning. It started out tough when Eli wet himself right after he'd gotten dressed.

Eli: I went pee-pee. (*Eli puts his thumb in his mouth.*)

Mom: Eli, stop that. (*Mom pulls Eli's thumb out of his mouth.*)

Therapist: Eli, it sounds like you've had a tough morning. I think you'll feel a lot better when your most 13-year-old self is more present. Can you show me how you hold your body when you're in your most 13-year-old self? (*Eli takes his thumb out of his mouth and sits up straight.*) I'll bet that feels a lot better. Can we look at your hands for a moment? (*Eli holds his hands out in front of him.*) Wow, just notice your hands, Eli. These are 13-year-old hands! They've gotten big! And notice your 13-year-old feet, Eli. (*Eli lifts his foot and examines it.*) Mom, don't you just love having a 13-year-old boy?

Mom: Yes, I do. I love watching him learn 13-year-old things.

Therapist: Eli, can you take a big breath with me and feel the floor under your feet? (*Eli nods.*) Now, I'm going to pull out the wonderful drawing you made of your 4-year-old self in the gingerbread house with Mom and Dad and the giant panda. Can 13-year-old you remind the 4-year-old part of you that there's no need to worry about your 13-year-old life anymore? The 4-year-old part of you can snuggle with the panda in the gingerbread house so the 13-year-old you can enjoy your life here. We can help the 4-year-old feel safe and sound here anytime.

Eli: I want to put a swing set inside the gingerbread house.

Therapist: Great idea! Can you draw it there?

Eli: Yep, I can.

Later, the therapist conducted a future rehearsal accessing Eli's biggest kid self to role-play getting up in the morning and going through his morning routine in his 13-year-old state. The therapist placed buzzies in his pocket and ran them at a slow speed throughout the role-play.

More Time Orientation Through Past and Present Activity

If it seems the child or teen has difficulty recognizing the difference between past conditions of danger and present conditions, the therapist can repeat the Past and Present" activity from Chapter 8. The therapist asks the child or teen to stand by the paper representing the present and says, "Let all parts of you on the inside know that we are in the present. The present is safe. The past will not happen again. The memories and even the feelings cannot hurt you. The memories and the feelings are not dangerous." If the response is positive, add some slow taps or buzzies to deepen the positive effect.

PARTS OF THE SELF WITH MISGUIDED BEHAVIORS

Difficult, very stuck behaviors are often driven by smaller child parts that learned the behavior as a way to self-protect. The activated parts lead to automatic behaviors with little capacity to pause and think things through before acting. Common misguided behaviors associated with self-protective mode are aggressive outbursts, hoarding food, stealing, making up false stories, self-harming, and sexually reactive behaviors.

The therapist ensures the presence of the biggest kid self and then invites exploration of the origin and purpose of the misguided behavior when the child or teen was a smaller child. The therapist then invites a collaborative exploration of desired new, skillful behaviors to substitute for the old ones.

Once the child or teen has gained insight, the therapist invites gratitude to the younger child part of self for the efforts to self-protect and guides the child or teen in dialogue with the younger part to let go of the efforts at this time. Future rehearsals with slow BLS are conducted to practice new skills and behaviors to replace the old patterns.

The IATP-C therapist uses clinical judgment regarding the inclusion of parents. Involvement of the parent can increase the parent's attunement and support, but in some cases it can activate defensiveness in the child or teen.

Working With the Misguided Part Script

"Let's make sure you're in your biggest kid self here with me today. What was a recent situation where you felt confident about the way you handled something? _____ Can you think about that good feeling and remember how that felt in your body? _____ Do you think you're operating from your biggest kid self right now? _____ (*If not, add some grounding messages such as "look at your hands and how big they are, and look at the size of your feet." If response is positive, continue.*) That's great. Now I know this behavior we've discussed bothers you as much as it bothers others, and I know without a doubt that you're a good kid. I believe that a younger part of you may be stuck in some mixed-up ways that seemed somehow necessary for self-protection. This isn't a bad part of you; we just have to help this part get unstuck. Would it be okay with you if we work on this together? _____ Okay, we know that things were really hard when you were little. A lot of times, you must have felt alone/unsafe/powerless. Keeping your biggest kid self here with me, does it make sense why your younger self may have learned this behavior as a way to keep yourself feeling seen/connected/safe/in control as a way to protect yourself? (*Pause.*) _____ (*Therapist and youth may have further discussion about the purpose of the misguided behavior.*) Can we put our heads together and think about situations in which you struggle with those old feelings and this mixed-up behavior today? _____ (*Discuss the situations that leave the youth feeling vulnerable or unsafe in some way.*) Can we think together to figure out some better ways to feel seen/connected/safe/in control today? _____ (*Collaborate on ideas such as asking for help from a parent, taking a pause to use some self-calming strategies, journaling, drawing, or using other fun activities to distract.*) Can you see that this part of you is not bad? Just mixed-up? _____ Let's look at this picture of the safe place for this younger part again. (*Holds up drawing.*) Let's think about how understandable it is that this smaller child part may have gotten stuck in this mixed-up behavior. (*Pause.*) But things are different today from in the past, and also you have new skills today. Perhaps, in your mind, you can let this smaller child part know that you have new ways to handle things today. (*Pause.*) How do you think this smaller part of you is feeling about that? (*Collaboratively problem solve any worries or concerns.*) Let's do a practice. Let's pretend you're in a situation, _____ (*Name the situation.*) that often leads to the behavior. Let's act it out and let you try some new skills, staying in your biggest kid self. (*The therapist, child or teen, and possibly the parent role-play the situation together. If the response is positive, the EMDR therapist may use one or two slow, short sets of taps or buzzies while directing the child or teen to notice the good feelings of safety on the inside and the good feelings with the biggest kid self in charge.*)

Thirteen-year-old Nan was a generally reserved girl who worked hard at her studies. She was adopted at age 9, after 3 years in foster care. She was removed from her biological home at age 4 for neglect and there was also suspicion of sexual abuse. Nan had begun engaging in sexual talk with adult males over the internet. The IATP-C preparation-phase activities were implemented along with enhancement of her Safe Places, followed by work with the part of her that was activated when she was engaging in risky internet activity:

Vignette With Nina Involving Dialogue With a Younger Part About Misguided Behaviors

(The therapist chose to implement this activity without the parent in the room to reduce Nina's feelings of shame and embarrassment.)

> **Therapist:** Nina, I know this is something you don't want to do anymore, is that right? But you haven't known how to stop doing it? I think there's a part of you, maybe a younger part of you, who's stuck in doing this. It's not a bad part of you. It's a part that thinks it's necessary. We just have to help this part get unstuck. Would it be okay with you if we work on this together?
>
> **Nina:** I suppose so.
>
> **Therapist:** Okay, here's what I'm wondering. I know that you were alone a lot when you were little. Keeping your biggest kid self here with me, can you consider that you may have learned that you had to get someone

to pay attention somehow, some way, to make sure you were seen or felt connected as a way to protect yourself? (*Nina nods.*) Can we put our heads together and think about when you struggle with this behavior in present time?

Nina: I think it's when I'm in my room by myself at night.

Therapist: That makes sense, Nina. Can we think together to figure out some better ways to feel seen and connected when you're struggling with that alone feeling?

(*The therapist and Nina talk about going to her mom or dad or asking her sister to play a game together.*)

Therapist: Can you see where this part of you is not bad? Just mixed-up?

Nina: I guess so.

Therapist: I know you feel bad about it, but you're not bad, Nina. You're a good kid that's been stuck in some mixed-up ways to protect yourself. Let's look at this picture of the safe place for this smaller part of you again. (*Holds up drawing.*) Let's think again about how understandable it is that this smaller child part of you has been trying to be seen and connected. You were alone a lot when you were little, and you learned to get others to pay attention in any way you could. That helped you survive. Perhaps, in your mind, you can let this smaller child part know that you have new ways to handle the alone feeling now. (*Pauses.*) Were you able to do that? (*Nina nods.*) So let's pretend you're alone in your room, and it's evening time. Let's act it out and let you try the new way you'd like to handle it. Is it okay if we place the buzzies in your pocket while we role-play?

THERAPEUTIC STORY FOR DISSOCIATION

The Therapeutic Story method described in Chapter 8 can be effective for helping kids and parents find compassion and understanding for what the child or teen needs in order to improve the dissociative symptoms. The IATP-C therapist may utilize a therapeutic story for dissociation at any point in therapy, once therapeutic trust has been established.

The following therapeutic story was written to help Alex and his grandmother make sense of the dissociation. It's also designed to motivate Alex to step into his most 14-year-old state while keeping smaller child parts tucked in.

Alex's Dissociation Story

The 14-year-old boy named Alex is a wonderful artist and reader of science fiction books. He lives with his grandmother and siblings. Alex has a good friend, Ana, and his older sister, Shey, is like a friend, too.

Alex had some really hard things happen when he was younger, and his brain did something amazing to try to help him manage his upset feelings. His 6-year-old self held onto his hard memories and his hard feelings in a separate place in his brain so Alex could go to school and play with friends and do things he enjoyed. The hard thing was that as a 14-year-old, Alex wanted to do 14-year-old things and enjoy relationships, but sometimes the 6-year-old part of him got triggered and became aggressive to protect himself. When that happened, 14-year-old Alex didn't remember what he did and that was upsetting. He often felt like he must be a very bad kid.

The truth was, Alex was a very good kid. His 6-year-old part was good, too. The 6-year-old just didn't understand.

Alex and his grandma are starting to understand about the 6-year-old part of him. Alex is working on making his 14-year-old self stronger, and he's working on keeping his 6-year-old tucked into his Safe Place. His grandma is working on listening more and helping him when he's stressed or triggered, and Alex is working on trusting his grandma more and letting her help. Alex is good and he's strong and he has support from his grandma and sister and friend and he has what he needs on the inside to heal.

EMDR REPROCESSING WITH HIGHLY DISSOCIATIVE CHILDREN

The IATP-C sequence of starting with reprocessing of present triggers (Chapter 7) and then transitioning to the past through therapeutic stories (see Chapter 8) are extremely helpful with highly dissociative children and teens. The therapist uses their clinical judgment to determine when the child is ready for EMDR reprocessing of specific traumatic memories.

All of the strategies provided in Chapters 7 through 9 for reprocessing triggers and traumas are helpful for keeping dissociative kids grounded and stable during the work. The EMDR therapist must stay consistently present and attuned throughout the work with highly dissociative kids. The presence of a safe parent or other safe adult can provide additional reassurance and coregulation. Bringing out a sand tray and art supplies allows the youth to show instead of tell and provides extra grounding and distance from the memory. Using playful BLS such as stomping and hand-clapping games also helps keep the child or teen present.

Cognitive interweaves as described in Chapters 7 and 9 assist with grounding and accessing of adaptive information. Optionally, the therapist may apply some version of EMD (see Appendix G) to help keep the child or teen within their window of tolerance throughout the processing if they're not ready for associations to other memories. Very simple methods also can be used to ground the child or teen between sets. For example, between sets the child or teen can be invited to notice the floor, notice the parent's arm around their shoulder, or notice the size of their hands. A pillow or a beanbag can be tossed back and forth between sets (Knipe, 2015, p. 13). Kids also do well with periodic checks through Knipe's "Back of the Head" scale (Knipe, 2015, p. 99). This method involves asking the child or teen to use their hand to demonstrate whether they're more present in the room or more immersed in the memory. The hand in front of the head shows "I'm very present," the hand more toward the ear means "I'm partially present," and the hand all the way in back of the head says, "I'm struggling and not really present right now."

The therapist and child or teen may also negotiate a short session of just 10 to 20 minutes of processing followed by a playful activity. The therapist can close an incomplete session down safely by asking, "What's the most helpful thought or idea you want to hold onto for today?" The therapist then invites the child or teen to place everything else into a container. The therapist says, "I'll keep it right here for you, and if anything comes up during the week, you can mentally send it back to me."

CONCLUSION

Dissociation is an automatic nervous system response when young children find themselves in frightening situations in which there is no one to turn to for safety and comfort, frequently because their attachment figures are the source of their fear. When the phenomenon is experienced repeatedly, it can become a well-learned pattern in their young brain.

Dissociative symptoms fall on a continuum from mild, occasional symptoms to severe symptoms such as frequent episodes of regressing to a younger state or retreating to imaginary worlds. The IATP-C therapist makes sense of the symptoms for the child or teen and their families, avoids inadvertent reinforcement of symptoms, and helps the child or teen strengthen their most mature state and develop a nurturing and safe internal space for younger parts.

CHAPTER 11

Adaptations for Fetal Alcohol Exposure, Autism, and Other Brain-Based Conditions

> Through reading this chapter, you'll gain skills for:
>
> – Recognizing the impact of prenatal substance abuse on the brain
> – Recognizing characteristics that can be associated with other common brain-based conditions
> – Making referrals to appropriate adjunctive diagnostic and treatment services
> – Applying accommodations and modifications for IATP-C Stages 1, 2, and 3

Brain-based conditions related to alcohol or drug exposure in utero or other neurodivergent conditions can't be eliminated with treatment. Brain-based challenges have lifelong impact. However, children and teens with brain-based conditions can have secondary symptoms caused by deficits in their environment as well as struggles directly related to attachment trauma. They deserve the most effective treatment we can provide, which means becoming familiar with *all* their conditions, attuning to their strengths and challenges, and appropriately modifying the IATP-C methods as needed.

PRENATAL ALCOHOL AND/OR DRUG EXPOSURE

Approximately 11% of infants in this country have been exposed to alcohol prenatally and about 8% have been exposed to illicit drugs, according to a recent Casey Family Programs Brief developed in partnership with Children and Family Futures (Casey Family Programs Brief, 2023). Children and teens with a history of early childhood neglect or abuse related to actions of parents impaired by substance abuse frequently have been exposed to the substance abuse in utero.

Data indicate fetal alcohol spectrum disorder (FASD) affects 1 to 5% of the population, but kids in out-of-home placements have a much higher occurrence of FASD when they are diagnosed properly (May et al., 2018). In a study of 547 children from foster and adoptive care, 156 met criteria for a fetal alcohol exposure diagnosis. A full 80% of those children had not been diagnosed previously by the professional community. The children in the study also had high rates of missed diagnoses for mental health disorders, learning disorders, communication disorders, intellectual disability, and signs of neurocognitive damage (Chasnoff, 2015).

Fetal Alcohol Spectrum Disorder (FASD) and Fetal Alcohol Syndrome (FAS) Diagnoses

Alcohol exposure in utero has the greatest impact of all substances used prenatally. The term fetal alcohol spectrum disorder (FASD) encompasses the range of effects that can occur from fetal alcohol exposure. Specific effects are largely dependent upon the timing and extent of alcohol exposure in utero. Even a small amount of alcohol used at critical points in fetal development can have devastating impact.

Fetal alcohol syndrome (FAS) is typically identified through what are termed sentinel facial features including a small head and flat face, a thin upper lip and small eye openings, an upturned nose and lack of the groove between the nose and mouth. In a recent study of 8 children with FAS and 69 children with FASD, the FAS children had an average IQ of 69.5, and the FASD children has an average IQ of 79.5, although IQ varied widely in the latter group (Fadeeva & Nenasteva, 2022). However, the lifelong impact from prenatal alcohol exposure can be just as severe in the case of FASD as with FAS (Clarke & Gibbard, 2003).

The neurological impact of fetal alcohol exposure in general includes an underdeveloped frontal brain and a brain that is smaller than the brain of nonexposed children. Several vital structures in the brain are impacted by fetal alcohol exposure, including the corpus callosum, which facilitates communication between the right and left brain; the subcortical basal ganglia, involved in learning and motor control; the hippocampus, involved in memory and processing emotions; and the cerebellum, involved in motor control. Babies exposed in utero are frequently born with low birth weight, feeding problems, intense irritability, high-pitched cries, below average muscle tone, and even seizures. Twenty percent of individuals impacted by prenatal alcohol exposure live with a seizure disorder (Sumner et al., 2013).

Adults and kids with FASD are typically dysregulated with small frustrations. They perseverate because they're unable to make shifts from one topic to another. They struggle with social skills because they're unable to read others' cues or understand the nuances of interpersonal relationships. They may repeat things they hear verbatim and read pretty well, but with no real understanding of what they're saying, hearing, or reading. Mood and sensory processing problems are very common due to underdevelopment in the regulatory regions of the brain. The poorly developed frontal regions leave them unable to manage impulses or anticipate consequences. Kids with FASD also confabulate stories with no intent to be deceitful. The symptom is an inherent part of their neurological differences. Standard characteristics of FASD are behaviors that resemble a much younger child and asynchronous development—varying capacities in different areas of development such as expressive language, comprehension, emotion regulation, social skills, and self-care skills (Drew & Kane, 2014; FASCETS, 2018; Gibbard et al., 2003; Malbin, 2017). It's also important to recognize that kids with FASD and other substance exposures can exhibit strengths as well as challenges. For example, they may be musical, creative, artistic, or athletic. They often can become adept at skills such as woodworking or auto mechanics through hands-on learning.

Life is extremely frustrating for any child or teen whose brain functions differently from most others. When others around them respond to their behaviors as if they were intentional, they naturally feel inadequate and alone, with little capacity to ask for help. As a result, they're at risk for a wide range of secondary mental health disorders. In addition, they frequently reside in out-of-home placements and suffer from traumatic stress and attachment problems, with little capacity to make sense of their feelings and experiences (Clarke & Gibbard, 2003).

Prenatal Illicit Drug Exposure

Alcohol is considered the most harmful teratogen for the developing fetus; other types of drug exposure have serious impact as well, mediated by the timing and extent of the maternal substance use. Fetal tobacco exposure is associated with restricted growth in utero; abnormalities in the neurobehavior of the newborn; and impulsivity, attention, and behavior problems later on. Opiate, cocaine, and methamphetamine exposure are all associated with low birth weight and abnormal neurobehavior in newborns. Marijuana exposure is associated with problems with attention, hyperactivity, and problem solving later on. Opiates exposure is associated with problems with attention, hyperactivity, and memory as well as perceptual difficulties. Studies indicate exposure to cocaine leads to problems of attention, behavior, visual-motor ability, and working memory. More studies are needed, but amphetamine exposure appears to be linked to later behavioral problems and problems with peers. Polysubstance exposure is extremely common as well, and the impact on the brain becomes more severe with use of multiple substances (Behnke, & Smith, 2013; Richardson et al., 2008).

OTHER BRAIN-BASED CONDITIONS

Neurodivergence is not a pathology, but a description. The term neurodiversity reflects the wide variation in neurological makeup found among individuals within any population. The term neurodivergent indicates there is a difference in the neurological makeup of an individual from the majority of individuals. The struggles of those with some form of neurodivergence are now recognized to be primarily related to the lack of capacity to conform to society's expectations, replacing the old view that brain-based differences represent pathology. Indeed, those who are born with some form of neurodivergence may have wonderful strengths, such as artistic talent, a sense of humor, playfulness, athleticism, and the capacity for expertise in areas that interest them. Their struggles are primarily related to fitting in with society's expectations. As with conditions of prenatal substance exposure, treatment can't eliminate the brain-based differences. Kids and adults with brain-based problems struggle with frustration and self-doubt because they're trying to navigate life with their brain differences and because they're coping with negative reactions from others. The more neurodivergence is understood and accommodated, the more individuals with brain differences will feel accepted as valuable members of their families and communities and the better they will feel about themselves.

Neurodivergent conditions we're all most familiar with include autism spectrum disorder (ASD), attention-deficit hyperactivity disorder (ADHD, ADD), dyslexia (related to reading), dyscalculia (related to math), dysgraphia (related to writing), and other learning conditions. Some experts include mental health conditions with a heritable component as under the umbrella of neurodivergence including bipolar disorder, Tourette's, and obsessive-compulsive disorder (Baumer & Frueh, 2021). About 20% of the world's population are believed to have some form of neurodivergence (Doyle, 2020). Some consider FASD also to be a form of neurodivergence, even though it is acquired in utero.

Autism Spectrum

Autism may be experienced as a few mild symptoms that cause some functional challenges or multiple symptoms that lead to more global struggles, depending upon the combination and severity of autism characteristics. Some autistic individuals are highly intelligent and some suffer from intellectual disability. Concrete thinking is a common characteristic, reducing the ability to visualize or understand nuances in spoken and unspoken communication. Communicating with others effectively may be challenging, and some autistic individuals don't speak at all. Changes in routine or sensory experiences may be overwhelming. Even too much eye contact may be overwhelming. Emotions may be experienced intensely, leading to frequent dysregulation by some individuals with autism but experienced only minimally by others. Stimming, or self-stimulation through repetitive movements or sounds such as hand-flapping, rocking, scratching the skin, or repeating a word or phrase over and over may be used to self-regulate. Hyper-focus may cause perseveration and difficulty switching topics or tasks. Individuals may struggle with social cues and social interactions (Bishop et al., 2007; NIH, 2022).

On the other hand, autistic individuals have many strengths. They may follow structure and rules very well. Their ability to hyper-focus in areas that capture their attention may help them develop strong talents in those areas. They can be intuitive, creative, and passionate about things they enjoy. Stimming behaviors are calming and self-regulating and not harmful. When autistic characteristics are accepted by others around them, secondary symptoms and functioning improve.

ADHD or ADD

ADHD or ADD is now understood by many experts as a form of neurodivergence associated with both challenges and strengths. Challenges may include a high-energy level, difficulty sitting still, or trouble focusing. Individuals struggle with staying with a task and often feel things intensely. However, they can be highly creative, passionate, able to think outside the box, and good at multitasking. They may miss details, but they see the big picture and when something grabs them they can hyper-focus and accomplish great things. (See Children and Adults with Attention-Deficit/Hyperactivity Disorder at CHADD.org for more information regarding ADHD or ADD.)

Dyscalculia, Dysgraphia, Dyslexia, and Dyspraxia

Kids with other forms of neurodivergence also have both challenges and strengths. Those with dyscalculia have trouble making sense of numbers, even though they may excel in other areas. Naturally, they avoid tasks involving numbers and are often perceived as unmotivated or lazy, which is not true. Kids with dysgraphia have a hard time writing or typing their thoughts. They struggle with proper punctuation, grammar, spelling, or handwriting. Kids with dyslexia have difficulty making sense of letters and words on a page. Kids with dyspraxia have trouble judging where their body is in space, catching a ball, or navigating around a physical space. Kids with these types of learning issues may also be intuitive, creative, and passionate about the things they enjoy. (See National Center for Learning Disabilities at NCLD.org for more information regarding learning disabilities.)

ADJUNCTIVE DIAGNOSTIC AND TREATMENT SERVICES

It's important to provide families with appropriate referrals for diagnostic and treatment adjunctive services. A speech and language assessment and an evaluation with a neuropsychologist who has experience and expertise in brain-based conditions can provide insight into how the child's brain is functioning. Assessment by an occupational therapist is critical for identifying whether the child's nervous system is managing input from the environment. Occupational therapy can help the child or teen with sensory issues (See SPD Foundation, spdfoundation.net, for more information.)

Appropriate diagnosis for FASD can be difficult and frustrating, especially when sentinel facial features are absent and there is no maternal history. Researchers continue to work on accurate methods for obtaining an FASD diagnosis without the typical sentinel physical characteristics or a prenatal history. Some gains have been made, however. BRAIN-online (2023) is a new web-based screening tool that uses all observable cognitive and behavioral features as a first step when considering a fetal alcohol exposure diagnosis. BRAIN-online can be found at fasdunited.org/brain-online/. The screening tool was developed at San Diego University through research by Mattson and colleagues (2023). Finding the right medication or medication combination for kids with FASD can be very challenging for prescribers. After extensive research concerning medication use with affected children, the Canada FASD Research Network offers an official FASD medication algorithm to assist medication providers (https://canfasd.ca/algorithm/).

For up-to-date research and information about a wide range of topics related to FASD, see the United States organization, FASD United (fasdunited.org), the United Kingdom organization, National FASD (nationalfasd.org.uk), and the Canada FASD Research Network (canfasd.ca).

In the case of kids with ASD, early diagnosis along with the proper accommodations and services are critical. Adjunct professionals providing assessment services or prescribing medications should have appropriate training and expertise with both ASD and traumatic stress.

Applied behavior analysis (ABA) is an evidence-based approach widely used to address behavioral challenges associated with ASD (Slocum et al., 2014) that can be applied simultaneously with IATP-C therapy. ABA treatment providers closely analyze the reinforcers for the child's behaviors and develop a detailed plan for each individual child and their parent. It's an intensive, long-term treatment approach. ABA does not treat traumatic stress and attachment in the autistic child, as it focuses strictly on behaviors. If ABA is chosen as an adjunct therapy, it's critical to make referrals to providers who are attuned and respectful of neurodivergent traits, who highlight strengths, and who show sensitivity to the child's emotions and needs. In the early days of ABA, it was common for ABA providers to force eye contact and refuse to allow stimming behaviors, and now many autistic adults are recalling their childhood ABA experiences as traumatic.

Floor Time is another approach being used to help autistic youngsters (Pajareya & Nopmaneejumruslers, 2011; Wieder & Greenspan, 2003) as an alternative to or in conjunction with ABA. For 2 to 5 hours per day the child and parent engage in floor play. There is early evidence that the therapy enhances and deepens the relationship, builds positive emotions, and increases the child's stability.

Neurofeedback therapy involves sensors that are placed strategically on the head, impacting brain waves through feedback from an electroencephalograph. There are numerous studies to date demonstrating the effectiveness of neurofeedback therapy for positive effects on executive functioning in individuals with ADHD, although more standards for training and clinical practice are recommended (Enriquez-Geppert et al., 2019). Neurofeedback therapy has been shown to improve some cognitive functions for autistic children in the majority of studies published thus far, although there is a need for larger randomized controlled studies (van Hoogdalem, 2020). There is little research involving neurofeedback with FASD at this time. When referring children for neurofeedback it's important to make sure the provider has experience and expertise with the child's brain-based condition. (See International Society for Neuroregulation and Research, isnr.org, for more information.)

APPLICATION OF IATP-C WHEN KIDS HAVE BRAIN-BASED CONDITIONS

Kids with brain-based conditions have reduced capacity to make sense of traumatic events or tolerate their confusing emotions, yet they are at greater risk for experiencing trauma than kids who are neurotypical (Biederman et al., 2013; Kautz-Turnbull et al., 2023; Kerns et al., 2015). Attachment trauma naturally impacts their capacity to trust the adults who care for them. They need effective assistance to build trust and address their traumas with appropriate modifications of the IATP-C, within an attuned and emotionally supportive environment.

Parent Psychoeducation

Raising a child with prenatal substance exposure, autism, or other forms of neurodivergence in addition to a traumatic past can be confusing, frustrating, and stressful for parents. IATP-C parent psychoeducation should begin with compassionate understanding for the parent's emotions. The therapist should help the parent develop a support system and a self-care plan. Parents may benefit from their own EMDR to process their feelings of powerlessness and grief regarding their child's struggles, the collateral impact, the loss of the easy relationship they'd hoped for, and the loss of time for themselves, for other children in the family, or for their partner relationship. They may need to process situations that were overwhelming or frightening such as situations in which the child was aggressive toward them or toward other family members (Wollin, 2023). If the present mother is a biological mother who exposed the child to substances in utero, the mother may benefit from EMDR therapy to process shame and grief, find self-forgiveness, and help maintain sobriety if needed. The biological mother may also benefit from a support group or supportive network. (See the University of Washington Fetal Alcohol and Drug Unit for a listing of family resources for each state at fadu.psychiatry.uw.edu/resources/.)

Consider inviting siblings, extended family members, and even nannies to one or more psychoeducation sessions. Increasing the sensitivity of the entire support system will help stabilize the child. Psychoeducation should include an in-depth look at the child's behaviors through the lens of the brain-based condition in addition to the lens of trauma and attachment, separating the behaviors and symptoms that are trauma-based or caused by stress from those that are just part of the brain-based condition. Impulsivity and low tolerance for distress, for example, are frequent problems related to traumatic stress but may also be an ongoing part of the child's brain-based challenges. Parents need to understand that even with improved traumatic stress symptoms and increased trust, their child will continue to need their parents' assistance with emotion regulation, problem solving, and managing impulses due to their brain-based condition. The therapist should also provide for parents a respectful perspective regarding the child's brain differences and a focus on what the child needs from their environment to accommodate and support their functioning. Parents should have a clear understanding that adjusting expectations to match their child's capacities can reduce the child's secondary symptoms and related behaviors (Malbin, 2017). The more the adults' expectations are out of sync with their child's capacities, the more the child will struggle and dysregulate.

Ironically, some attachment-based parenting strategies such as negotiating and offering compromises, offering choices, mirroring of the child's emotions, and discussing the "why" behind the rules can be dysregulating for kids affected by prenatal substance exposure and other brain-based conditions (Wollin, 2019). Because they are slow processors and easily overwhelmed by too much input or too many choices, and by changes in routine or structure, they typically require very straightforward, consistent rules and routines. They have difficulty generalizing or managing gray areas, so they don't understand how to adapt to rules that change. Negotiating about rules may feel unsafe and confusing. Many kids with executive functioning issues can become dysregulated by a strict, authoritarian tone or by discussions about rules when parents use too many words (Wollin, 2019).

Every child with a brain-based condition has a unique neurological makeup and requires an individualized approach. Many autistic children and teens with autism respond well to a behavioral approach, but the manner in which the adult applies the method makes all the difference. Any behavioral strategies should involve positive reinforcers, not punishments, and a sensitive, supportive, attuned, and calm demeanor is critical.

Kids with FASD or prenatal drug exposure may not respond as well as other kids to behavioral methods due to their inability to connect the action with the consequences. If a reward system is used, the adult must remain encouraging and remind them of the coming reward, and the reward must be consistent, immediate, and dependable. Any behavioral system should be created by considering what works with each child individually. If a reward system is successful, it's important to make the system ongoing to maintain stable behaviors and not assume that permanent learning has occurred. Expectations should be realistic, and if a system isn't working, it should be reevaluated and changed accordingly.

Many parents need guidance for creating connection with kids who are overwhelmed by closeness or eye contact due to sensory issues. For example, many kids converse and connect best if they're sitting side-by-side or engaging in an activity with the parent. Many parents need help advocating for appropriate accommodations in the school and providing appropriate accommodations at home (Malbin, 2017). Accommodations at home, for example, may include ongoing help with organizing their child's schoolwork, their backpack, and their bedroom. Their child may need ongoing supervision during play with siblings and assistance with simple chores. They may need calm, positive, assistance with managing their emotions. The key for parents is recognizing their child's limitations and remaining supportive.

(For more assistance with psychoeducation for parents of kids with FASD, ASD, or other forms of neurodivergence in addition to attachment trauma, see the parent guide, *Attachment Trauma in Kids: Integrative Strategies for Parents*, Second Edition [Wesselmann, 2025].)

Vignette With 7-Year-Old Micha: Exposed to Drugs in Utero
Micha's parents had adopted their son as a toddler 7 years earlier. They were distressed and frustrated by his oppositional and aggressive behaviors and negative moods. The mother had left her job to manage the younger boy's behaviors for several years. Their older son was angry and felt deprived of attention from his parents. The younger boy was on Ritalin for ADHD, which had not improved his mood or behaviors. During history taking, the therapist learned the boy had significant prenatal methamphetamine exposure. The boy and his family became more regulated and stable during Stage 1 through appropriate referrals and psychoeducation. The therapist educated the boy's parents and older brother about the younger boy's brain-based challenges, coached them regarding more effective strategies, and provided guidance for managing stress related to the younger boy's symptoms. A psychiatrist with expertise in prenatal drug exposure removed the Ritalin and prescribed Abilify for the boy, and an occupational therapist assisted with sensory issues. The parents began attending a support group, and the older brother began EMDR therapy to help him process his feelings about his younger brother. The mother returned to work, something she'd always wanted to do, after years of staying home to care for the son.

Accommodations and Modifications for the IATP-C Family Therapy Activities

During family therapy activities for widening their window, navigating their inside world, and strengthening their relationships as part of IATP-C Stage 2 (Chapter 5), the therapist should keep language brief, simple, and concrete and maintain a calm, playful, and accepting demeanor.

Many kids with brain-based challenges are relieved of shame through learning about their condition and understanding that other kids share similar brain-based challenges. For kids with FASD or other prenatal substance exposure, it's important to emphasize that most parents don't drink or use substances with the intention to hurt their babies. It's helpful for children and teens to understand what it means when someone suffers from an addiction through clear and simple language (FASCETS, 2018). Develop a collaborative problem-solving approach with kids and parents regarding how their brain learns best and how adults can best assist with learning and completing tasks in daily life.

Often, children and teens with brain-based conditions can repeat statements the therapist makes without truly understanding the meaning of the

Adaptations for Fetal Alcohol Exposure, Autism, and Other Conditions   239

statements. Children and teens with FASD, especially, may clearly understand something one day and have no memory for the same information the next day. For example, a role-play to practice asking permission for a bag of chips may not translate to asking for a cookie tomorrow. Repetition can help information integrate into long-term memory. Expectations should be modified and small achievements celebrated.

To provide the child with language for emotions, the therapist should avoid talking too much and instead show picture cards, posters, emotion faces cards and books and act out emotions with facial expressions and body movements. The therapist can coach the child or teen in noticing sensations in the body as they tense and relax, hold an ice cube, run in place, or hold their breath and exhale.

During skills work, the therapist minimizes words and focuses on role-plays in which child, therapist, and parent act out situations and how best to respond with their biggest kid self. Big stuffed animals and little stuffed animals can be used to role-play their biggest kid self and smaller child self or their thinking brain and feeling brain.

It may be beneficial to include siblings in some family sessions and to offer individual sibling sessions during which siblings can share their frustrations openly. Within the family sessions, role-plays involving siblings encourage a collaborative effort to get along at home.

The therapist should highlight the strengths of the child or teen as frequently as possible. Because many kids with FASD, ADHD, or other brain-based conditions are artistic or good with their hands, they may stay more engaged if art tools are part of the activities. It's also helpful to provide wiggly kids with sensory seating such as wiggle seats, wobble cushions, or sensory chairs. Some kids enjoy computers and stay engaged if given the opportunity to look up information or YouTube videos related to a needed social skill or self-calming activity. Encouraging them to see something, touch something, or do something helps them more successfully remember and integrate what they learn.

Accommodations and Modifications Within IATP-C EMDR Therapy

The EMDR therapist's keys for success include observing the child's responses, attuning to their developmental and learning needs, attuning to their sensory sensitivities, and making appropriate accommodations.

Finding BLS the Child Enjoys

Due to sensory sensitivities, finding a method of BLS the child or teen enjoys is critical. Some enjoy the buzzies, but some don't at all. Some kids allow the parent to sit with their arm around them, applying gentle pressure on their upper arms while they suck on a lollipop, play with a fidget, or draw. Younger kids may sit on the parent's lap and allow the parent to sway them gently from side to side. Some kids avoid touch altogether and prefer participating in active BLS such as bilateral hand-clapping games, stomping their feet, shaking maracas, marching, or moving the rings of a big, old-fashioned metal Slinky rhythmically from one hand to the other. For kids with ADHD, Darker-Smith (2023) suggests incorporating BLS through wobble boards or balance boards. Some kids with brain-based conditions prefer bilateral audio tones. Some kids enjoy watching the lights on an eye scan machine or a light-up sword in a darkened room.

EMDR Resource Activities

Many children and teens with brain-based conditions are artistic and enjoy creating their Safe Place (Chapter 6) using art tools or a sand tray. The most concrete method for creating a Safe Place is by creating a little cozy safe space in the office before adding the slow BLS. For example, a younger child may enjoy a nest with pillows, blankets, and stuffed animals. A teen may wish to play a favorite peaceful song wrapped up in a soft blanket and hugging a pillow.

For EMDR resource work (Chapter 6) and processing of triggers and memories (Chapters 7 and 9), role-plays or acting out scenes with puppets or stuffed animals are much more effective than directions to imagine something. For the Biggest Kid Self activity, the therapist invites the child or teen to draw or role-play a recent situation in which they felt proud of themselves. Slow BLS is added to strengthen the good feelings. Then, while the child or teen is still connected to their positive feelings and sensations, the therapist initiates a role-play future rehearsal, encouraging the child to practice responding to a triggering situation with their thinking brain and their biggest kid self. Their positive affect is again strengthened with a little bit of slow BLS.

During ARD activities that require closeness with the parent (Chapter 6), the therapist stays attuned to the child's attention span and tolerance for physical closeness and eye contact. Some kids respond better to the Messages of Love activity if they're sitting on a wobble cushion for regulation, for example, instead of sitting with the parent. It's easier for some kids to remain regulated if they look at family photo albums during the activity.

The Cord of Love may be made more concrete by running a long piece of yarn from the parent to the child. The child and therapist can leave the office while the child holds onto their end of the cord of yarn to help the child grasp the idea of ongoing connection along with application of the slow BLS.

For some kids with brain-based conditions, the concept of creating a safe place for the smaller child on the inside is too abstract. It can be helpful to ask the foster or adoptive parent to bring in a photo of the child at a young age (or make a drawing if there are no photos) and glue the photo to paper or canvas encircled by pictures or drawings of everything the parent would have wished for the younger child to have. Slow BLS is applied as the parent talks about the pictures.

S-RDI involves coregulation for small moments of dysregulation (Chapter 6). The therapist avoids excessive talking and sits with the child using a calm demeanor, modeling slow, deep breaths or providing short, reassuring phrases such as "Your feelings are okay." If the child or teen is cooperating, a short set of slow BLS can be applied while stating something like, "I'm amazed at how you're calming your body."

The parents should be reminded that strengthening the parent–child connection will enhance trust and stability but won't remove the need for academic, social, or emotional assistance at home and school. Removing accommodations at home or school because their behaviors have improved may cause the child or teen to regress. If parents learn to advocate for their child at school, it will have a positive impact on the child's trust for the parent (Wollin, 2023).

Assessment Phase

Kids with brain-based conditions usually do better with a container that is concrete such as a drawer in the office or a container made from a box or jar. Before going home after addressing hard things, the child or teen can be invited to place drawings of difficult events or NC cards in the container.

When assessing the components of a triggering event (Chapter 7) or traumatic memory (Chapter 9), the therapist can invite the child or teen to role-play, draw, or make a sand tray about it to help them access their feelings for EMDR processing. Identification of cognitions can be difficult for the child due to neurological differences (Darker-Smith, 2023). The therapist can offer a few NC (and later PC) options orally or on index cards, but it's important to emphasize that it's okay to reject the therapist-chosen NCs and PCs, as some kids with brain differences are too eager to please the therapist (Wollin, 2019). Sometimes it's helpful to obtain the emotion first and then the thought that goes with the emotion (e.g., "What is the mad thought?" or "What is the thought connected to feeling hurt?"). The NC may simply be "I don't like this" or "I can't handle it" and the PC may be simply "I can handle it" (Wollin, 2019).

It's important not to overlook any experiences of being bullied. NCs may be along the lines of "I'm not good enough," "I'm weird," or "No one likes me." PC possibilities may include, "Lots of people like me as I am" or "I'm good as I am, some people just don't understand autism/FASD/ADHD."

It's best to keep the VOC and SUD directions simple, asking the child or teen to demonstrate with their hands close together or a distance apart or by pointing to numbers on a number line. If they're triggered by the ratings, forgo the ratings for therapist observations.

Identification of emotions and sensations can be especially difficult due to neurological differences. Pointing to feelings faces or making faces or pointing to places on their body or a doll's body may help. The therapist can make facial expressions to show possible feelings the child can choose from as well.

Reprocessing Phases

For kids with ADHD, the therapist should be prepared to move around the room as needed in addition to playfully changing BLS modalities to keep the child engaged during reprocessing (Adler-Tapia & Settle, 2023). I successfully applied eye movements on one occasion with a boy who was hanging upside-down from the sofa!

Although kids with ADHD often require short sets of BLS with plenty of opportunity to share thoughts and feelings to keep them engaged, autistic children and teens or kids with FASD may be slow processors and require very long sets. Rather than guess at the length of the set that is needed, the therapist can invite the child or teen to look up or hold up a hand when they have a thought or feeling to share.

Some kids with brain differences need a cognitive interweave after every set of BLS and that's okay. The therapist should keep in mind that kids with brain differences who have had no power in many situations in their lives often need empowering interweaves, such as "If you could bring anyone with you back to

Adaptations for Fetal Alcohol Exposure, Autism, and Other Conditions   243

that situation, who would you bring? _____ What would *they* say or do? _____ What would *you* say or do?" Alternatively, they can show you on paper or in a sand tray. (See Chapters 7 and 9 for more cognitive interweave examples.)

Reprocessing of triggers should be followed by future templates to help them integrate the new learning. Acting out the future template is often best, perhaps with a variety of situations over multiple sessions (Wollin, 2019).

Reprocessing of either triggers or traumas may be best through the shortened, more contained EMD approach. (See Appendix G.) For the child or teen who likes to draw during processing, provide small pieces of paper and suggest stick figures to avoid hyper-focusing on details or trying to get it right. Keep the language very simple throughout the session.

With kids who feel things very intensely, the EMDR therapist should stay attuned to signs of overwhelm, confusion, shutting down, or tuning out. If the child or teen is showing signs of overwhelm, the EMDR therapist should help them process the event with short pieces of work lasting anywhere from 10 to 20 minutes. To close, the therapist can invite them to identify the most helpful thought so far. To help with integration of the positive shift, the child or teen writes the positive thought or draws a picture about it to take home. The session is continued with a playful activity to ensure a positive state and create connection.

Timeline and Therapeutic Story

The therapist can assist kids who have concrete thinking by using butcher paper and illustrating the Timeline with drawings or photographs showing where they lived or went to school at different points or with the Candy Land method, as described in Chapter 8. It's best to begin with neutral and positive events and then place the difficult events on the Timeline with neutral labels and no details. The Timeline activity is a good time to explore the possibility of bullying events (Lievegoed et al., 2013).

When beginning the Therapeutic Story (as described in Chapter 8), ample positive events can help balance the inclusion of traumatic events. Concrete thinkers can benefit from a collaborative project in which the therapist and child make an illustrated story or a short book together.

Use of third person or an animal character can provide needed distance for many kids but may prevent some concrete thinkers from identifying with the story as theirs. For some kids and teens, the use of second person may be more concrete and effective. For example, the therapist can begin a second person story by saying, "I'm going to tell you a story about what happened to you to help you make sense of things. Here's your story . . . "

As stated in Chapter 8, the EMDR Therapeutic Story method has been shown effective in case studies with children and adults with autism and/or intellectual disability (Lobregt-van Buuren et al., 2019; Wesselmann et al., 2025b). The reading of the story while applying BLS with neurodivergent kids appears to be effective for accessing the memory network and integrating the adaptive information needed to help bring the trauma to adaptive resolution. For kids with autism and other brain-based issues, separate stories may need to be provided for different traumatic events to avoid overloading the child or teen.

In can be helpful to provide the child or teen with a fidget or a lollipop to help keep them regulated and engaged during the reading of the story. Allowing kids to choose the method of BLS and the speed they prefer can give them a sense of control and increase their cooperation. It can be helpful for kids with learning issues to hear the story during multiple sessions.

CONCLUSION

Kids with brain-based challenges have a decreased capacity to make sense of the traumatic events of their lives and manage their complicated emotions. Kids with brain-based challenges have inherent difficulties and also innate strengths. Our intention is not to conduct therapy with the aim of making neurodivergent or substance-exposed kids function like kids who are neurotypical. Our intention is to conceptualize symptoms and behaviors with as much accuracy as possible, educate parents, engage outside resources, create helpful accommodations at home, and apply therapy modifications for optimal positive impact. Promoting an attitude of acceptance for the child's neurodivergence and demonstrating compassion for the challenges faced by all family members improves therapeutic outcomes and quality of life for the whole family.

CHAPTER 12

Enhancing Reflective Functioning (RF) for Parents Through EMDR Therapy

Parents who bring their kids for IATP-C carry their own networks of memories, both good and bad, as we all do. For any of us, challenging interactions with our kids can automatically light up old feelings of rejection or fear stored within our memory networks. A strong capacity to reason and reflect is needed to cope with our vulnerable feelings and respond to our kids from a place of attunement. This capacity, called Reflective Functioning (RF), is directly related to our early attachment experiences.

REFLECTIVE FUNCTIONING

Reflective Functioning is the capacity to understand our own and others' internal state. This means we can mentalize and reflect upon our own thoughts, feelings, intentions, and motivations as well as the thoughts, feelings, intentions, and motivations of others without making assumptions. If we're naturally reflective, we think about the impact of our words and actions on others with humility and honesty, and we initiate repairs when we make mistakes.

To be reflective, we need to be able to stay present in difficult moments and tolerate our feelings. We notice our feelings and our thoughts without assuming there is only one right way to think or feel. High RF doesn't mean we stay in a highly reflective, mentalizing state 100% of the time. We all have emotion-driven thoughts and behaviors that aren't helpful at times. However, high RF allows us to more easily recognize when our perceptions and actions have been hurtful or unhelpful so we can change course and initiate repair.

Low RF may show up as believing there's only one way to feel in any given situation. Our window of tolerance for distress is low, which leads to quick dysregulation. Without capacity for reflection, we're unable to correct our missteps, change course, or initiate an emotional repair.

Carried Beliefs, Themes of Childhood

Low RF is associated with nonsecure and/or disorganized attachment patterns and a store of negative attachment memories and beliefs. (See Chapter 3 and Appendix C for more information regarding attachment patterns.)

Parents with a (nonsecure) dismissive pattern learned to suppress their feelings and needs during childhood experiences in which a primary parent was uncomfortable with expressed emotions. They show the same avoidance in the presence of their children's feelings and needs. The following are examples of possible negative perceptions of parents with dismissive attachment patterns and unmet childhood needs:

1. *My child is invading me/overwhelming me/suffocating me.*
2. *My child is too needy/babyish/spoiled.*
3. *My child's feelings and needs are unacceptable.*
4. *I should have absolute authority over my child.*
5. *My child just needs to suck it up.*

Parents with a (nonsecure) preoccupied pattern learned to express their needs and feelings with great intensity during childhood experiences in which they had to be demanding in order to have their feelings or needs acknowledged. During interactions with their children, they remain preoccupied with being seen and heard and therefore may often fail to pick up on the needs and feelings of their child. The following are examples of possible negative perceptions of parents with preoccupied attachment patterns with unmet childhood needs:

1. *My child doesn't love me enough.*
2. *My child doesn't care about me.*
3. *I need my child to make me worthwhile.*

Enhancing Reflective Functioning (RF) for Parents Through EMDR Therapy

   4. *I need my child's comfort.*
   5. *My child is pushing me around.*

Parents with an unresolved/disorganized attachment pattern have a store of inadequately processed traumatic memories related to maltreatment or significant loss. The following are examples of possible negative perceptions of parent who has an unresolved/disorganized attachment pattern and a trauma history that might be triggered by interactions with their child:

   1. *My child is mistreating me.*
   2. *My child is out of control.*
   3. *My child is shameful/bad/dangerous.*
   4. *My child wants to hurt me.*
   5. *Something bad is going to happen.*

ENGAGING PARENTS

Parents with characteristics consistent with a preoccupied pattern may be motivated to address their early memories, especially if the therapist remains attuned and sensitive to the parent's distress. Parents may feel more connected if the therapist leans in and retains a voice tone and facial expression that demonstrates empathy and concern.

Parents with characteristics of a dismissive pattern may believe accepting help is unacceptable. For dismissive parents, the invitation to participate in therapy should emphasize the external challenges they face. Parents with dismissive tendencies are more comfortable with a matter-of-fact demeanor. Physically, the therapist might lean back in the chair, keeping an open facial expression. Too much intensity in body posture or emotions could trigger the dismissive parent to pull back.

Addressing stored memories through EMDR therapy naturally enhances RF over time. EMDR jump-starts processing and the therapist's repeated question of "What's there now?" invites reflection regarding internal thoughts and feelings. The ability to reason takes a leap as new associations are made. Furthermore, as we integrate adaptive information with childhood memories, we develop empathy for ourselves as young children and old self-judgments and defenses gradually are reduced. As we gain compassion for our younger selves, we naturally feel increased empathy for children in our care. Even dismissive parents will reconnect with cutoff emotions from their childhood during EMDR reprocessing, leading to increased capacity to reflect and attune to the emotions of their children. Preoccupied parents gain a stronger sense of themselves as worthy and lovable, reducing their preoccupation and calming their nervous system and increasing their capacity to reflect and attune. Unresolved/disorganized parents have multiple networks storing disturbing memories, but over time, EMDR therapy can move their memories into adaptive resolution, regulating and organizing their nervous system. In all of these situations, parents' window of tolerance for challenging situations with their children slowly expands as they reprocess maladaptively stored memories.

EMDR therapy is a three-pronged protocol. Present triggers naturally include challenges with their child. Reprocessing triggers and developing future templates allow the new beliefs and perceptions to integrate into new, more attuned and reflective parenting.

STARTING INDIVIDUAL WORK WITH PARENTS

History taking and EMDR treatment planning with a parent can be a first step toward increased mentalization and improved RF. To build therapeutic trust with the parent, the therapist accesses their own mentalizing state, letting go of judgments, staying curious, and attuning to the parent's internal state.

The first step in Phase 1 EMDR history taking and treatment planning is identifying the present-day priority issue. The therapist can ask, "What problematic situation with your child is creating the most distress for you?"

The parent may say something like "My biggest problem is my adolescent's defiance," or "My child won't stop having those meltdowns." Even though the parent's focus is on the child, it's a good place to start, and it feels validating for the parent.

Next, the therapist invites the parent to elaborate and talk about how they felt, thought, and responded in various situations. For EMDR treatment planning, the therapist keeps in mind the four major themes: responsibility/defectiveness/action; safety/vulnerability; control/choices; and connection/belonging. However, with the parent, the therapist avoids an expert attitude and maintains a nonjudgmental, curious demeanor to develop therapeutic trust.

Once specific triggering events are identified, the therapist can invite the parent to connect the dots between the present triggers and childhood events. One method is direct questioning: "When you think back to earlier in your life, perhaps all the way to childhood, were there early experiences that gave you this same kind of feeling?"

The affect scan can be especially helpful for finding the most relevant early memories as it tends to sneak through internal defenses. To initiate the affect scan, the therapist invites the parent to think of the present-day triggering situation and then says, "Notice the feelings and sensations inside of you and scan back to childhood if you can. Just be curious, let your mind float back, and see where it goes. You might go to a specific memory, to thoughts of a person, or to a certain period of time." Once a memory has been activated, the parent is invited to think of any similar memories including the *worst memory* and the *first memory*. The therapist is careful to keep discussion of memories superficial to avoid activating emotions or sensations.

Next, the therapist invites the parent to think about the triggering present situation again and the response they'd rather have. If it's too difficult for the parent to even imagine a more effective response, it's okay to let that go for now.

It's not necessary to complete all of the exploration for a full Phase 1 history taking and treatment planning in the beginning of therapy. Like their children, parents can become dysregulated by a full history-taking session and show more tolerance for it after some preparation and stabilization work has been completed.

History-Taking and Treatment-Planning Sample Cases

Sam described his teenage son's refusal to ride in the passenger seat while he drove him to school each day: "Clay won't sit in the front. Instead, he slumps down in the back seat. I tell you, he's ashamed to be seen with me. What did I do to deserve this?" Sam was suffering from feelings of rejection related to the theme of connection/belonging. With some direct questioning and an affect scan related to the feelings of rejection, he identified memories related to rejection from his stepfather and older stepbrother when he was growing up.

Kalia described attending the parent–teacher conference at her daughter's elementary school: "The teacher said Colette won't do her homework. She won't stay in her seat. She won't listen. I felt the teacher was judging me and trying to figure out why I can't make my daughter behave. I was mortified." Kalia's reactions of shame and embarrassment were related to the theme of responsibility/defectiveness/action and a sense that her daughter's behaviors were a reflection of her inadequacy. With some direct questioning related to the feelings of shame and embarrassment, Kalia remembered feelings of shame related to criticism by parents and teachers when she was a child due to behaviors related to her own ADHD.

Donna described her adolescent son's meltdowns and her overwhelming anxiety: "Gus screams and bangs the walls. I have an urge to run away and hide, but I know I can't do that." Her desire to flee is related to the theme of safety/vulnerability. Through the affect scan, Donna remembered wanting to run and hide when her dad was angry.

Harrison described his 6-year-old's compulsion around taking food from the kitchen and hiding it in her bedroom: "Mia's so sneaky. I don't have any idea when she takes this stuff. I don't know until I see the candy and chip wrappers stuffed in her dresser drawer. I've been trying to catch her in the act, but I can't. It's so frustrating I want to pull my hair out." Harrison's frustration was related to the theme of control/choices and the sense that he had no control. With some direct questioning he was able to identify memories of having no control in a very authoritarian but chaotic home while growing up.

PHASE 2 PREPARATION AND STABILIZATION

To prepare the parent for reprocessing, the therapist develops a safe/calm place or state, a standard step for all EMDR therapists, and provides any additional skills the parent needs for affect tolerance and self-regulation. If the parent has been attending family therapy sessions with the child and therapist, they have developed brainwork and bodywork strategies right along with their child. Additionally, the therapist may consider utilizing the resource development and installation (RDI) procedures to help the parent access needed resources for increasing effective responses to their child and for addressing their past.

Resource Development and Installation (RDI) With Future Rehearsals for Parents

RDI has become a standard part of the basic EMDR training program and is considered an optional preparation phase activity, but it's a good way to enhance stability and improve behavioral patterns prior to addressing the past. The first step of RDI is to identify the needed resource. The therapist asks, "What quality would help you respond to your child's most upsetting behaviors using the methods we discussed?" For example, Donna said she wanted to feel strong in order to stay calm and ride out her son's meltdowns without getting activated.

The second step of RDI is to identify a memory of a time in which they exhibited the quality or, alternatively, a figure or symbol that inspires the quality. Donna identified a beloved teacher from nursing school who inspired strength.

The third step of RDI is to describe a picture of the memory, the figure, or the symbol. Donna pictured the teacher by her side with a hand on her shoulder, bracing her and encouraging her to be strong and calm.

When the client reports positive affect associated with the picture, just four to six passes of slow BLS are used to deepen the positive connection. (We find slow tactile BLS helps avoid associations and encourages a relaxed state.) This can be repeated as needed.

Optionally, the parent can pair the positive resource image with a cue word that can later be used to help access the image. The cue word, along with the image, is deepened with another slow, short set of BLS.

Finally, future rehearsal helps integrate the new quality into present-day actions. The parent is asked to imagine bringing their resource along to enhance their response to the challenge situation. The parent may need to talk it through a bit in terms of how they will use their resource and how they wish to imagine responding. Once they have it in mind, the therapist adds a slow, short set of BLS to deepen positive affect associated with the response. If it goes well, the therapist suggests the parent run a movie of the imagined response in their mind, and then pair the movie with slow BLS.

Donna imagined the nursing instructor standing next to her, sharing her strength and reminding her to breathe and stay calm throughout one of her son's meltdowns. The slow BLS deepened her sense of confidence and strength in her ability to follow through.

Harrison decided he needed more acceptance of his daughter's struggles with FASD and food hoarding. He remembered practicing acceptance when he learned that he was suffering from atrial fibrillation. He got in touch with how the sense of acceptance felt in his body. The felt sense of acceptance was deepened with slow BLS. Finally, he brought his felt sense of acceptance from the memory into an imagined scenario in which he discovered food hidden in his daughter's room. This scene was strengthened with slow BLS. He played it in his mind again as a movie from the beginning to the end, and the positive movie was deepened with slow BLS.

HELPING PARENTS CREATE SAFETY ON THE INSIDE

Parents who've witnessed attachment resource development (ARD) with their kids are already familiar with the concept of younger hurt parts of the self. For parents, settling *kid parts* into safe places with nurturing and safety can help them separate out child parts of the self and operate from an adult state in present time (Potter & Wesselmann, 2023). The internal work also helps them develop empathy for their younger parts of the self and view the child in their care through the same compassionate lens.

Safety and Nurturing for the Parent's Younger Parts Intro Script

Say to the parent, "Remember how we talked about younger parts on the inside with your child? (*Pulling apart a nesting doll to make a line of smaller dolls.*) We all have these younger parts of us, made up of the thoughts and feelings we carry from childhood. When childhood feelings are triggered, even subconsciously, it's hard to operate from our most adult part of self. It can be helpful for all of us to take care of our younger parts. When younger parts of us are settled and safe on the inside, we have more capacity to operate from our most adult part of our self. But that's not easy when our kids are struggling and we're stressed. In addition, our children are always a subconscious reminder of our own childhood years. Can you think back to a moment recently when you were triggered during an interaction? _____ How old did you feel in that interaction?_____ This might mean that particular child part of you needs some internal safety and care. Just as we developed a safe place and resources for your adult self, we can develop a safe place for that child part of you to create an internal sense of safety and calm."

The therapist talks with the parent to brainstorm a Safe Place that is protective and nurturing for the child part of self. The therapist reminds the parent they're not visiting past memories—they're creating internal safety in the present time. If the therapist senses activated memories, the memories are placed in a container for later work. Next, the therapist invites the parent to think of a protective and nurturing caregiver figure to enhance the Safe Place for the child self (Potter & Wesselmann, 2023). The figure may be a spiritual figure, a famous figure, an historical figure, a figure from movies or books, or someone who cared for them in real life. If they choose a real figure, the therapist explains they will bring in the *spiritual essence*, only the best parts of the individual. The parent is guided in a visualization of the protective and nurturing place, with imagery involving the care and protection of the figure toward the child. If the parent's response is positive, the warm affect is deepened with a couple of slow, short sets of tactile BLS. After creating the enhanced Safe Place for the child part, the parent can be guided to step into the Safe Place, to reach out in some way, and to dialogue with love and compassion for the child part.

Safety and Nuturing for Parent's Younger Parts Script

Say to the parent, "Can you imagine a place in your mind's eye where your child part can settle in and feel protected and comfortable? It can be a place totally out of your imagination—a place the child part of you would love to be. _____ (*Brainstorm together as needed.*) Now that you've visualized the place, I'd like you to think of a loving and protective caregiver figure for that child part of you. It can be a spiritual figure, a famous figure, an historical figure, or a figure from movies or books, or it can be the spiritual essence of a real person you had in your life. _____ (*Brainstorm together as needed.*) I'd like to have you bring up this place in your mind, invite or guide the child part of you there, and invite your caregiver figure to be there with the smaller you, providing loving care and protection. (*Elaborate with some details.*) How does that feel? _____ (*If response is positive, deepen positive affect with a slow, short set of BLS.*) If you're willing, I can guide you in reaching out to the child part in some way with affirming and reassuring messages. Would you be willing to give it a try?" _____ (*If the response is negative, reassure the parent that it's okay to leave the child part of the self in the care of the loving figure for now and deepen positive affect with another slow, short set of BLS to close. If response is positive, continue with the script.*) Imagine your adult self stepping into the safe place and sitting near the child part of you or reaching out in any way you would like. How does that feel to you? _____ (*If the response is positive, apply slow tactile BLS and continue the BLS throughout the rest of the dialogue.*) Let this child part know that this is a special safe place where they can stay, where they can let go of worries or concerns, and just be a kid. The events of childhood are in the past. They have everything they need and they will always be protected and nurtured there. Tell the child part of you that adult you will handle adult life and parenting. Let the child know they are worthy and lovable. Let them know they belong and will always be a part of you. Add anything else you want to say. (*Pause the BLS.*) How did that go? (*If the response is positive, add another slow, short set of tactile BLS to deepen the associated positive affect.*)

If the parent senses activation of other ages of self, the activity can be repeated with multiple safe places for multiple younger parts of the self. If the parent struggles with any part of the visualization, the therapist can suggest the parent invite the help of their resource figure for assistance (Potter & Wesselmann, 2023).

Following the activity, the therapist can encourage the parent to pay attention to when the child part of themselves is triggered and to respond with a quick visualization of the younger self in the safe place. Placing their hand over their heart and repeating some of the reassuring dialogue may also help settle the child part of the self.

EMDR REPROCESSING WITH PARENTS' MOST RELEVANT TARGETS

The ideal order for reprocessing of memories is past-present-future because memory work leads to insights regarding triggers. However, some parents may be avoidant or too overwhelmed by the thought of addressing their memories early on. In this case, place the memories in a container and initiate reprocessing with triggers and future templates. Processing can be restricted through some version of EMD (see Appendix G) to increase safety if needed.

Sam agreed to reprocess the triggering situation involving his teenage son's refusal to ride in the front seat with him. He preferred to set aside the memories involving his stepdad and stepbrother until a later date. Target assessment identified the worst image, the NC, PC, VOC, emotions, SUD, and body sensation.

Vignette: Phase 3 Target Assessment With Sam, Clay's Father

Therapist: Sam, when you think of Clay refusing to sit in the front passenger seat on the way to school, what is the picture that represents the worst part of that for you?

Sam: His scowly face glaring back at me when I suggest he sit in the front.

Therapist: What words go best with that picture that express your negative belief about yourself now?
Sam: He's ashamed of me. He's embarrassed to be seen with me.
Therapist: (*Therapist intervenes to find a self-referencing NC.*) And as you say those things, is there a negative thought about yourself that comes up?
Sam: I suppose just that I'm not good enough for Clay.
Therapist: (*Therapist intervenes to find a more generalizable NC.*) When you think about that situation does it give you a general feeling of "I'm not good enough"?
Sam: Yep, I would say so.
Therapist: And when you think of that picture again, what would you rather think instead?
Sam: Probably just that I'm good enough. It sure doesn't feel that way though.

The therapist completed the Phase 3 Target Assessment by checking the VOC and helping Sam identify the emotion, SUD, and body sensations. When reprocessing with BLS commenced, Sam associated to a memory of his stepdad shoving him out of the room and telling him to shut up and be quiet. Sam wasn't ready to address his past, so the therapist inserted a cognitive interweave that separated the past from the present: "And how is this situation with Clay different?" Sam responded, "Well, my dad was a grown-up and was supposed to behave like one. Clay's a teenager, and all teenagers get moody, I suppose." Reprocessing continued until Sam achieved a SUD of 1 and a VOC of 7.

Following the reprocessing of the present trigger, the therapist helped Sam develop a future template in which he saw himself staying calm, centered, and positive while driving Sam to school.

Later, Sam was able to reprocess the memory of his stepdad shoving him and other memories related to feelings of unworthiness. He then reprocessed other present triggers. Following the work, Sam was able to respond to Clay from a place of security, knowing that Clay's behaviors were driven by Clay's past and had nothing to do with Sam.

Harrison, Kalia, Donna, and Sam all reprocessed past memories and present triggers with future templates, allowing them to attune to their kids from their best selves in the present time with more reasonable perceptions and more attuned responses.

PARENTAL GRIEF

Many parents struggle with underlying grief related to disappointments or losses in their lives. Many suffer from unresolved grief related to the death of loved ones. Divorced parents may be grieving the loss of their partner. Parents who stepped up to care for a grandchild, niece, or nephew may grieve for their previous lifestyle. Adoptive parents may struggle with grief related to infertility or miscarriages. Parents may grieve for the ideal family they'd imagined.

The EMDR therapist holds a safe, nonjudgmental space for parents to speak openly about their complicated feelings. When proposing EMDR to assist with processing grief, the therapist avoids conveying an intention that the feelings will be eradicated or that the parents' emotions are unacceptable. The therapist emphasizes that EMDR reprocessing of the sadness, loss, or disappointments can remove internal blocks to allow a healthy processing of emotions.

An EMDR therapist can address negative beliefs such as "I'm not good enough," "I'm bad for feeling what I'm feeling," "I'm defective," "I have a bad child," or "My family is defective." The EMDR can shift parents to more helpful cognitions such as "My life has meaning," "My feelings are just feelings," "I can help my child heal," "I'm a good person," "My child has a good heart," or "My family is a good family." When measuring the SUD, the therapist can suggest that 0 is not the absence of emotion or the presence of good feelings related to the target. Zero means the parent can bring up the situation and their body is calm.

When therapists recognize unresolved grief in parents who are stuck in anger, resentment, or despair, it's vital to give the parents every opportunity to work through their stuck emotions and find healing for themselves. Without such healing, the parent's stuck emotions and perceptions can impact the entire family.

CONCLUSION

EMDR therapy with parents can be a game changer for parents with low RF. The experience of noticing and naming their thoughts and feelings throughout the reprocessing phases increases their capacity to mentalize. Increasing sensitivity for their younger self through reprocessing of memories increases their sensitivity to the traumas driving their child's behaviors. As parents gain insights regarding their memories and their triggers, they gradually become free of their automatic negative assumptions and beliefs about themselves and their child.

This opens up space for reflective functioning—sensitive, attuned reflection upon their child's inner state and their own inner state, with greater capacity for compassion and understanding.

Closing Thoughts

The world is not getting any easier for kids and families. Generational trauma, social and cultural trauma, socioeconomic pressures, mental health disorders, and substance addiction continue to plague families and put children at risk for maltreatment. The U.S. Centers for Disease Control and Prevention (2023) estimates that 1 in 7 children in this country experience some sort of maltreatment. Many other children and teens experience adversity caused by chaotic homes, unsafe neighborhoods, and unsafe school environments. It's not fair. But the statistics are not changing anytime soon. Every one of those hurt kids deserves a chance to find belonging, self-worth, safety, health, and healing and a chance for a new life course for themselves and for their future children. The need for effective mental health care is dire, but the road to healing can be complicated, especially when children and teenagers are held hostage by maladaptive memory networks and self-protective defenses. I know that if you're reading this book, you're a dedicated mental health therapist who is making a difference in the lives of kids and families. It's my hope that the integrative EMDR and family therapy model will help you feel even more effective and empowered in your work. Thank you for the work you're doing to bring new light into the world's darkest places.

APPENDIX A

IATP-C Checklist

STAGE 1 PARENT PSYCHOEDUCATION & CASE CONCEPTUALIZATION	
☐ History-Taking Checklist ☐ Parent Psychoeducation	
STAGE 2 BUILDING GOOD FEELINGS & LEARNING TO TRUST	
FAMILY THERAPY ACTIVITIES *Widening Their Window* ☐ The Language of the Window ☐ The Pause ☐ Breathwork and Bodywork ☐ Brainwork Activities ☐ High-Alert/Low-Alert Language ☐ Facts About Feelings ☐ Recognizing their Biggest Kid Self *Navigating Their Inside World* ☐ What Babies Need ☐ Recognizing and Appreciating the Smaller Child on the Inside *Strengthening Their Relationships* ☐ Relational Games ☐ The Jobs of Moms and Dads ☐ Who Has the Floor? Communication Game ☐ Skills Practice	**EMDR THERAPY ACTIVITIES** *Building a Resourced State* ☐ Introducing EMDR ☐ Safe Place Activity ☐ Strengthening Their Biggest Kid Self ☐ Finding Their Power Animal ☐ Optional Butterfly Hug *Attachment Resource Development (ARD)* ☐ Messages of Love (with Optional Games) ☐ Magical Cord of Love ☐ Circle of Love ☐ Safe Place for the Smaller Child on the Inside ☐ (Optional) Songs and Playful Activities *Self-Regulation Development & Installation* ☐ Coaching With Slow BLS ☐ (Optional) Coaching With Photographs and Games *Future Rehearsals* ☐ Role-Plays and Mental Movies

STAGE 3 HEALING TRIGGERS & TRAUMAS	
Gaining Insight ☐ The Dominoes Activity ☐ Detective Work	**EMDR Reprocessing** ☐ Trigger Tolerance Work ☐ Future Templates ☐ (Optional) Processing Unhealthy Compulsive Behaviors ☐ Therapeutic Story ☐ Trauma Work

APPENDIX B

History-Taking Checklist

Name _____
DOB _____
ID _____
Parents/Guardians _____

Current or Recent Behaviors
- ☐ Indiscriminate affection with strangers and others
- ☐ Clingy and attention-seeking with parent
- ☐ Arguing
- ☐ Defiance
- ☐ Destruction of property
- ☐ Quick to anger
- ☐ Meltdowns
- ☐ Aggression toward people or animals
- ☐ Acute jealousy toward siblings
- ☐ Stealing
- ☐ Lying
- ☐ Running away
- ☐ Whining
- ☐ Difficulty concentrating
- ☐ Hyperactivity
- ☐ Excessive masturbation
- ☐ Sexualized behaviors toward others
- ☐ Defiance/opposition
- ☐ Difficulty falling asleep

- ☐ Difficulty staying asleep
- ☐ Nightmares
- ☐ Toileting problems
- ☐ Highly abnormal bathroom behaviors such as urinating in odd places or smearing feces
- ☐ Controlling/bossy toward others
- ☐ Does not go to parents for comfort
- ☐ Will not accept closeness or comfort
- ☐ Other: _____

Current Triggers (Situations That Seem to Lead to Acting Out Behaviors)

- ☐ Mom/Dad/Teacher saying no
- ☐ Mom/Dad giving attention to a sibling
- ☐ Playing with siblings or peers
- ☐ Direction or correction from a parent
- ☐ Mom/Dad/Teacher with an angry face
- ☐ Mom/Dad sick, sad, preoccupied
- ☐ Receiving a consequence
- ☐ A family holiday or birthday
- ☐ An experience of closeness and connection with a parent
- ☐ Bedtime
- ☐ Time to get up
- ☐ Messages of love from a parent
- ☐ A compliment
- ☐ A criticism
- ☐ A transition from one activity to another
- ☐ Time to go to school
- ☐ Direction or correction from a teacher
- ☐ A good grade
- ☐ A bad grade
- ☐ Peers having fun together
- ☐ Something exciting coming up
- ☐ Frustrating or confusing job or homework
- ☐ A negative expression on someone's face
- ☐ Awareness of some difference between themselves and others

Appendix B

- ☐ Being left out or rejected in some way
- ☐ Other: _____

Traumatic Past Events
- ☐ Loss of and/or changes in primary caregivers
- ☐ Temporary placement such as foster care or orphanage care
- ☐ Early experiences of abuse of any kind, neglect, or rejection by caregivers
- ☐ Early medical interventions
- ☐ Early experiences of pain that may have interfered with the child's ability to relax and bond, such as ear pain or colic
- ☐ Early separations from primary caregivers due to hospitalizations or any other reasons
- ☐ Frequent changes in day care providers
- ☐ A frightening or chaotic environment, such as domestic violence, which may have interfered with the child's ability to relax and bond
- ☐ Parental addictions that may have removed the safe emotional presence of the parent
- ☐ Parental stressors such as illness in the family, death in the family, job loss, etc., that may have removed the safe emotional presence of the parent
- ☐ Parental emotional problems such as PTSD that may have removed the safe emotional presence of the parent
- ☐ The child's overhearing of information that interfered with feelings of safety and trust in parents
- ☐ Ridicule or rejection from classmates or teachers
- ☐ Discrimination or marginalization experiences in the community, the school, or the family
- ☐ Other: _____

Negative Cognitions (NCs)
(Think about the child's history and their current behaviors. Hypothesize which upsetting thoughts and beliefs may be driving the child's actions.)

- ☐ "I'm not safe."
- ☐ "I cannot trust Mom/Dad."

- ☐ "I cannot trust or depend on anyone."
- ☐ "I have to get what I need/want for myself."
- ☐ "It's not safe to be close."
- ☐ "It's not safe to be vulnerable."
- ☐ "It's not safe to care about others."
- ☐ "I'm powerless."
- ☐ "I'm bad/evil."
- ☐ "If I make a mistake, I am a mistake."
- ☐ "I need food/stuff to be okay."
- ☐ "She/he is out to hurt me."
- ☐ "She/he is against me."
- ☐ "Moms/Dads are mean."
- ☐ "Moms/Dads will leave."
- ☐ "She/He deserves to be punished."
- ☐ "I have to be in control."
- ☐ "I should have done something."
- ☐ "I'm not good enough."
- ☐ "I don't belong."
- ☐ "I don't fit in."
- ☐ "I'm not important to others."
- ☐ "Something is wrong with me."
- ☐ "My feelings are bad/unsafe/scary."
- ☐ "It's not safe to share my feelings."
- ☐ "It's not safe to love or accept love."
- ☐ "I don't deserve love."
- ☐ "I don't deserve to be complimented."
- ☐ "A compliment is unsafe."
- ☐ "Bad things always happen."
- ☐ "Good things are not safe."
- ☐ "I'll disappear if you don't see me and hear me."
- ☐ "I don't deserve to be here."
- ☐ "Biological kids are more special than adopted kids."
- ☐ Other: _____

Appendix B

Desired Positive Cognitions (PCs)

(Hypothesize the thoughts/beliefs the child may need to adopt or strengthen in order to feel and behave better.)

- ☐ "I'm safe."
- ☐ "I can trust my mom/dad."
- ☐ "I can relax and depend upon my mom/dad to give me what I need."
- ☐ "It's safe to be close."
- ☐ "It's okay to be vulnerable."
- ☐ "I have choices."
- ☐ "I have a good heart."
- ☐ "My mom/dad wants the best for me."
- ☐ "My mom/dad is on my side."
- ☐ "My mom/dad will always be here for me."
- ☐ "I'm loved and lovable."
- ☐ "There are other people who are similar to me."
- ☐ "There are others who want to include me/kids like me."
- ☐ "There are people who want to help."
- ☐ "I can give others a chance."
- ☐ "I'm important to others."
- ☐ "I did the best I could."
- ☐ "I don't have to be perfect."
- ☐ "I belong."
- ☐ "I'm fine as I am."
- ☐ "My feelings are normal and okay."
- ☐ "It's safe to share my feelings."
- ☐ "It's safe to love and be loved."
- ☐ "I deserve love."
- ☐ "I deserve compliments."
- ☐ "Compliments are safe."
- ☐ "Mostly good things happen."
- ☐ "Good things are safe."
- ☐ "I'm important even when others aren't paying attention to me."
- ☐ "I deserve to be here."
- ☐ Other: _____

Future Templates (Behaviors You Would Like the Child to Adopt)
- ☐ Cooperating while getting ready for bed
- ☐ Cooperating about getting ready in the morning
- ☐ Saying "Okay" when Mom/Dad says "no" or makes a request
- ☐ Sharing, taking turns
- ☐ Finding something else to do when Mom/Dad pays attention to a sibling
- ☐ Coping with homework frustration
- ☐ Accepting a compliment
- ☐ Expressing hurt or angry feelings appropriately
- ☐ Coping when Mom/Dad is sick, sad, preoccupied, or angry
- ☐ Joining in the fun on a family holiday or birthday
- ☐ Handling criticism skillfully
- ☐ Handling a consequence
- ☐ Saying "I'm sorry" and correcting the situation
- ☐ Coping skillfully with a bad grade
- ☐ Coping skillfully with a good grade
- ☐ Asking for something appropriately
- ☐ Seeking help or comfort
- ☐ Other: _____
- ☐ List any strengths/positive behaviors: _____

APPENDIX C

Transmission of Attachment Patterns, Parent to Child

PARENT PATTERNS	CHILD PATTERNS
Secure The parent enjoys closeness in relationships and is able to reflect upon their own inner state as well as the inner states of others. The parent enjoys closeness with the child and is sensitive and responsive to the child's feelings. The parent mirrors the child's feelings and responds with reassurance and sensitivity.	**Secure** The child's secure parent is well-attuned and the child feels seen and heard. The mirroring by the parent allows the child to understand their own inner state, which allows the child to self-reflect and reflect upon the inner state of the parent. The child is comforted by the attachment relationship and learns to view relationships as a source of security. The relationship becomes a secure base from which the child explores the world. The child learns to trust the intentions of others.
Nonsecure/dismissive The parent manages anxiety by avoiding vulnerability and emotional closeness in relationships. The parent is uncomfortable and withdraws from the child when the child exhibits emotional needs. The parent is unable to reflect upon the child's inner state	**Nonsecure/avoidant** The child learns that the parent draws away from them when the child expresses feelings or needs. The child learns to suppress their feelings and needs. The child does not experience adequate mirroring from the parent and therefore lacks awareness of their inner state.
Nonsecure/preoccupied The parent lacks a sense of security or trust in relationships. The parent manages their mistrust and insecurity by taking charge of getting their needs met in their relationships. The parent can be affectionate with the child but is not attuned to the child's feelings and what they need due to the parent's own emotional struggles.	**Nonsecure/ambivalent-resistant** The child manages the anxiety caused by the parent's inconsistent responsiveness by increasing the intensity of their demands. The child does not learn to reflect upon their inner state due to inconsistent mirroring. Due to lack of trust and security, the child is not easily comforted by their parent.

Unresolved/disorganized The parent's stored trauma is easily triggered by the child, leading to feelings of fear or anger. As a result, the child sees signs of either fear or anger, although either is frightening to the child. The disorganized parent is unable to attune, mirror, or respond with sensitivity or comfort in response to the child's anxiety.	Disorganized The child yearns to go to the parent for comfort, but the parent's facial expression, posture, or tone of voice causes the child to be afraid and want to pull away at the same time. This double bind is disorganizing to the child's nervous system, and there is no way to manage the subsequent anxiety. The child is at high risk for later dissociative disorders and other major mental disorders by the time they reach adolescence.

The above chart provides a summary for each of the attachment patterns as described within seminal contributions to attachment research and theory. These citations represent some of the most important early works: Ainsworth, 1967, 1982; Liotti, 1999; Main & Hesse, 1990; Main & Solomon, 1990; and van IJzendoorn, 1992.

NOTES

1. The Attachment Continuum

Dismissive or preoccupied attachment patterns may look different from one individual to the next and may range from mild underlying tendencies to rigid, more challenging patterns of behavior.

Adults with a strong characteristics of both dismissive and preoccupied characteristics, designated as the Cannot Classify attachment pattern, are at risk for personality disorders. Strong characteristics of an unresolved/disorganized pattern leave adolescents and adults at risk for a dissociative disorder.

2. Attachment-Related Diagnoses in the *DSM-5*

Attachment-related diagnoses may be over diagnosed, but children who have been born into or placed into settings that have not allowed them to form significant attachment relationships may meet criteria for:

- *Reactive attachment disorder of early childhood:* Appears detached and uninterested in genuine relationships. (Could be viewed as an extreme version of the childhood avoidant attachment pattern.)
- *Disinhibited social engagement disorder of early childhood:* Attempts

to gain affection and closeness with multiple adults. Superficial engagement in relationships. (Could be viewed as an extreme version of the childhood ambivalent-resistant attachment pattern.)

The above diagnoses in childhood are associated with a heightened risk for mental health disorders, personality disorders, addictions, and dissociative disorders in adulthood.

3. Earned Secure Attachment Pattern

Although attachment patterns may be lasting, they can also change. Adults may move down the continuum toward more severe patterns with adulthood trauma, or they move down the continuum to milder patterns or even security with corrective emotional experiences such as relationships with secure individuals and effective therapy. Adults who experienced attachment injury in childhood but achieved a secure attachment pattern in adulthood are capable of raising securely attached children and are categorized as *earned secure*.

APPENDIX D

Useful Child Assessments

Adolescent Dissociative Experiences Scale
- (Armstrong, Putnam, Carlson, Libero, & Smith, 1997)
  - A 30-item self report screening tool for children ages 11 to 18 that assesses a range of dissociative symptoms. Online source: https://www.carepatron.com/files/ades-self-report-questionnaire.pdf

Beery-Buktenica Developmental Test of Visual-Motor Integration, Sixth Edition
- (Beery, Buktenica, & Beery, 2005)
  - Screens for visual-motor problems, ages 2 and up. Online source: https://www.pearsonassessments.com/store/usassessments/en/Store/Professional-Assessments/Motor-Sensory/Beery-Buktenica-Developmental-Test-of-Visual-Motor-Integration-%7C-Sixth-Edition/p/100000663.html

Behavior Assessment System for Children, Third Edition
- (Reynolds & Kamphaus, 2015)
  - A comprehensive set of rating scales and forms for understanding the behaviors and emotions of children and adolescents ages 2 to 21. Online source: https://www.pearsonassessments.com/store/usassessments/en/Store/Professional-Assessments/Behavior/Behavior-Assessment-System-for-Children-%7C-Third-Edition-/p/100001402.html

Child Behavior Checklist for Ages 6–18
- (Achenbach, 1991)
  - A 113-item assessment completed by parents to assess children's level of competency and overall emotional and behavioral symptoms. Can be ordered online from ASEBA at www.ASEBA.org.

Child Dissociative Checklist
- (Putnam & Peterson, 1994)
  - A 20-item screening tool for children ages 5 to 11 that is completed by the parent. Online source: https://www.carepatron.com/files/child-dissociative-checklist.pdf

Kaufman Brief Intelligence Test, Second Edition
- (Kaufman & Kaufman, 2022)
  - Measures verbal and nonverbal intelligence, ages 4 and up. Online source: https://www.pearsonassessments.com/store/usassessments/en/Store/Professional-Assessments/Cognition-%26-Neuro/Kaufman-Brief-Intelligence-Test%2C-Second-Edition-Revised-/p/P100013000.html

Kaufman Test of Educational Achievement, Third Edition Brief Form
- (Kaufman & Kaufman, 2015)
  - Academic screener for very young children. Online source: https://www.pearsonassessments.com/store/usassessments/en/Store/Professional-Assessments/Academic-Learning/Kaufman-Test-of-Educational-Achievement-%7C-Third-Edition-Brief-Form/p/100001342.html

Multidimensional Inventory of Dissociation (Version for Adolescents)
- (Dell, 2006)
  - A 218-item, clinician-administered, client self-report screening for symptoms of dissociation. Online source: https://www.mid-assessment.com/

Trauma Symptom Checklist for Children/Trauma Symptom Checklist for Young Children
- (Briere, 1996)
  - An assessment of trauma symptoms for children ages 3 to 12, completed by the parents. Includes scales for sexualized behaviors and dissociation. Online source: https://www.parinc.com/Products/Pkey/461

UCLA PTSD Reaction Index for *DSM-5*
- (Pynoos & Steinberg, 2015)
  - An assessment of traumatic stress and dissociative symptoms in school-age children and adolescents. Online source: https://www.reactionindex.com/measures/

Wide Range Achievement Test, Fifth Edition
- (Wilkinson & Robertson, 2017)
  - Academic assessment for ages 5 and up; identifies learning disabilities. Online source: https://www.pearsonassessments.com/store/usassessments/en/Store/Professional-Assessments/Academic-Learning/Wide-Range-Achievement-Test-%7C-Fifth-Edition/p/100001954.html

APPENDIX E

The Tale of the Hamster and the Porcupine Coat*

Once upon a time, there were a great many hamsters who lived in the forest near the Inky Black Lagoon. All the hamsters had been told from as early as they could remember: never EVER drink from the Inky Black Lagoon. Any hamsters who drank from the Inky Black Lagoon could NEVER stop, because it tasted SO great. But the great-tasting black water from the Inky Black Lagoon caused hamsters to get mixed-up thoughts and do strange things, so it was very dangerous.

Once upon a time there was a mommy hamster and a daddy hamster who drank from the Inky Black Lagoon. It was a very sad thing, because they had a baby hamster who needed them and depended upon them. But when the mommy and daddy hamster drank the great-tasting black water, they became mixed-up and confused. They soon stopped taking care of their baby hamster, and sometimes they left him/her all alone.

The baby hamster became hungry, and he/she was afraid of all the other animals who lived around the Inky Black Lagoon because he had no one to keep him safe. He had to do something to protect himself. One day, he was rooting around in the yard looking for something to eat, when he found a funny-looking coat covered with sharp pointy quills. A porcupine coat! This was just what he needed! He put it on, and suddenly he didn't feel so scared anymore. This will stab and hurt anyone who comes near me, he thought.

One day, a group of very nice hamster supervisors came to the yard where the baby hamster was looking for something to eat. They were shocked that no

---

* Originally presented by Debra Wesselmann at the 2006 EMDRIA conference, Philadelphia, PA

one was taking care of the baby hamster! They said, "You come with us, little one! We will find you a forever mom and dad to take care of you."

The supervisor hamsters searched for a new hamster family for the little hamster. The little hamster was moved to one family and then another, but they had not yet found just the right family. The supervisors noticed that the little hamster was wearing a very uncomfortable-looking coat covered with sharp quills, and they knew they needed to find just the right mommy and daddy hamster who knew how to take care of a baby hamster wearing such a coat. One day a mommy and daddy hamster saw the little hamster playing outside, and they fell in love with the baby hamster. They said, "We want to raise this baby hamster as our own, forever!" The supervisors looked at each other, and then they looked at the mommy and daddy and they said, "You are the ones we have been looking for!"

The mommy and daddy hamster noticed that the little hamster was wearing a porcupine coat. The mommy hamster knew just what she needed to do to take care of the little hamster. She knew she had to find a porcupine coat that she could wear, so that she could love and hug and care for the little hamster without getting pricked. She went into the forest and gathered porcupine quills from the ground, and then she went home and found an old coat, and then she started sewing on one quill at a time until it was nicely covered.

The new mommy hamster loved her new child more than anything. At first, she had to wear her own porcupine coat every day. It gave her protection so that and the little hamster's quills didn't bother her one bit. But some days, the little hamster's coat fell away, and the hamster fur beneath the prickly coat was smooth and soft. On those days, the mommy hamster smiled and threw off her own porcupine coat, and she relaxed with her new child. They both enjoyed the closeness and the love they shared on those special days.

One day the mommy hamster felt sad for the little hamster. She noticed that the other hamsters playing outside avoided her little hamster when he was wearing the porcupine coat, because they didn't want to get poked. She looked in her little hamster's eyes and said, "Honey, why don't you take your coat off to play? Then the other hamsters will stick around because they won't be afraid of getting poked! And you will have a lot more fun."

There are two endings to this story. You get to pick.

Ending #1. They continued the rest of their days together, mommy hamster and little hamster. The little hamster continued to take his porcupine coat off on some days, and those were the days they both enjoyed the best. They laughed together, played games, and had a great time. On some days, the little hamster wore the prickly coat all day long. Sometimes he wore the coat for several days in a row. Those were not the most enjoyable days for either of them, but the mommy hamster loved her child no matter what, and all she had to do was wear her own porcupine coat. The protection assisted her, so she could handle her prickly little hamster child just fine, caring for him, teaching him, and helping him grow. But she still felt sad for him, because on the days he wore his prickly coat, the other little hamsters stayed away and he was lonely. He didn't have as much fun as he could have had.

Ending #2. They continued the rest of their days together, and soon, the little hamster's porcupine coat was left in the bottom of the closet and forgotten. The mommy threw her porcupine coat in the bottom of the closet, too, and before long, birds were flying off with the discarded quills to use in their nests. The mommy hamster and her child had lots of good times together. Once in a while the little hamster got grumpy, but never so grumpy that the porcupine coats came out of the closet. The mommy and child liked to relax, play, and talk. And the little hamster had lots and lots of friends, too, and they all enjoyed playing together each day.

APPENDIX F

A Quick Review of the EMDR Phases With Tips for Working With Kids

Before getting into reprocessing strategies specific to kids with attachment trauma, let's do a speedy review of the reprocessing phases that are geared to kids in general. If you feel you have the basics down pat and don't need the review, skip this section.

REVIEW FOR PHASE 3: TARGET ASSESSMENT

The target may be a present-day triggering situation or a past trauma. The therapist and child or teen should have agreed upon a neutral label for the event. Remember, with traumatic memories, it's not necessary to probe for details—how much they share is completely up to them. This is one of the reasons EMDR is a gentle approach to trauma.

To begin the target assessment, the EMDR therapist asks the child or teen "What's the worst picture (*Or worst part for kids who aren't visual.*) when you think about what happened?" Many kids have difficulty with using their words and do better with showing.

Showing Versus Telling

At the beginning of the assessment phase, have a sand tray or drawing supplies handy for kids who want to show the triggering event or the traumatic memory. For drawings, I like to provide small-size sheets of paper and some colored pencils or markers to discourage kids from getting caught up in drawing unnecessary details that slow things down.

Later, during the reprocessing phases, they can be invited to continue showing thoughts, feelings, or pictures when they want to, between sets of bilateral stimulation (BLS).

Identifying the NC, PC, and VOC

The therapist helps the child or teen identify the negative cognition (NC) and desired positive cognition (PC) and measures the validity of the positive cognition (VOC) as simply as possible. The therapist may say:

- "What is the upset/yucky thought that goes with this worst part/picture as you think about it right now?" (*The therapist may suggest some possible NCs or write some possible NCs on index cards and lay them out on the table for them to consider. Kids' NCs may not always be self-referencing. For example, many attachment-injured kids will say "Parents are mean." The therapist can keep in mind the likely underlying self-referencing beliefs: "I can't trust" and "I don't belong."*)
- "What's a good thought that would be more helpful—even if it doesn't really feel completely true right now?" (*The therapist may suggest some possible PCs or write some possible PCs on index cards and lay them out on the table for them to consider.*)
- "As you think about that worst part/picture, how true does that good thought feel right now?" (*Show a 1 to 7 number line, explaining the meaning of the numbers or ask the child to show how true it feels by moving their hands close together or far apart.*)

Identification of PCs and NCs is too complex for many children age five and younger (Tinker & Wilson, 1999, p. 87). However, the EMDR therapist may be able to offer the young child a very simple *upsetting thought or yucky thought* and a very simple *good thought* or *helpful thought* while observing the child's response to determine whether the thoughts resonate for the child. For example, the therapist may say, "When you remember what happened, does your brain say, I'm a bad kid? _____ Would you like your brain to say, I'm a good kid?"

Identifying Emotions and Subjective Units of Disturbance (SUD)

To identify an emotion, the therapist can simply say,

- "As you think about that worst part/picture, what do you feel now?"

Kids who struggle to put words to feelings can often point to feelings faces on cards or a poster. The therapist can help by wondering aloud, for example, "I wonder if you might feel either sad or mad or a little of both." The therapist can offer, "Gee, if it were me, I think I might feel _____ or _____ . But you might have a different feeling, and that's okay." The therapist should stay attuned to the child's reactions and notice what seems to resonate. It may help to ask, "What do you suppose you did feel when you were in that situation?" Then ask, "Do you suppose you have a little bit of those feelings inside you now?" or "Do you suppose the littler you inside your heart still has some of the feelings?"

To identify the SUD, the therapist can say,

- "When you think about what happened, how upsetting is it to you right now _____?" (*Show a 0 to 10 number line, explaining the meaning of the numbers, or ask the child to show the size of their upset feelings right now when they think about the trigger by moving their hands closer together or farther apart.*)

Identifying Disturbance in the Body

To identify the disturbance in the body, the therapist can say, "Where do you feel the upset in your body?" _____ If the child or teen is unsure, it may be helpful to add, "Some kids feel things in their head, some feel things in their neck or shoulders, some in their chest or tummy, and some in their arms or legs. Take your time and just notice where you might feel it." If the child or teen still struggles, the therapist can explore the sensation in some other way. For example, the therapist can ask, "If that feeling had a color, what color would it be?" _____ "If you could see that color in your body, where do you think it would be?" _____ Alternatively, the therapist can offer an outline of a body or trace the child's body on butcher paper and say, "Do you think you could use the marker to color where you might have this feeling in your body?"

If the child has chosen a picture of an animal or human face to match what they're feeling, it may be helpful to suggest the child think about what the person or animal in the picture is feeling in their body. For example, the therapist may say, "I wonder what the dog in this picture might be feeling inside of his body?" _____ "Do you suppose your body might feel like that, too?" _____

REVIEW FOR PHASE 4: DESENSITIZATION

Once the assessment phase is complete, Phase 4 desensitization commences by directing the child or teen to "Think of the picture and the upsetting/yucky thought _____ (the NC) and the feelings in your body and then let's do the _____ (*Agreed-upon BLS*)." After a set of fast BLS, ask, "And what are you noticing? Thoughts? Feelings? Pictures?" (Later, you may only need to say, "What's there now?") After they respond, continue with sets of fast BLS. If you think the child is just having trouble articulating, suggest, "Show me your thoughts or feelings on this paper with colors or a very simple drawing." After the child is done, say, "Think of those thoughts and feelings and let's do some more (*Agreed-upon BLS*)."

When the child or teen reports nothing new for two or more sets, ask them to think of the (*neutral name*) target, however it comes to them now, and then continue sets of BLS. If it appears they may have a very low SUD, check the SUD (or observe their response if they're unwilling or unable to give a SUD). Target where they feel any remaining emotion in their body and if it doesn't reduce further, ask "What is keeping it from being a 0?" and then reprocess whatever comes to them. When the SUD is 0 or a level that is ecological (understandable in the context of the child's situation), move on to the installation of the PC.

REVIEW FOR PHASE 5: INSTALLATION

The first step of installation of the PC is to ask, "Do you still like the helpful thought _____ or is there a better thought you want to use?" After checking the VOC, the therapist asks the child to hold the PC and the target memory together and applies sets of BLS until the VOC equals 7. If the strength of the PC appears to be stuck at a VOC less than 7, the therapist can check on whether the child feels anything in the body and say "Notice that" with the next set. Or an apparent block can be identified by asking "What keeps the good thought _____ from feeling completely true?" The therapist may also consider whether the PC may be too unreachable at this point, in which case the therapist suggests a more achievable PC. For example, "I am lovable" could be nuanced to be more achievable with, "I am learning I am lovable." The therapist can also notice whether the present VOC is ecological, considering that other early memories may also be feeding the negative view, or that the child or teen may need time to try out the good thought.

REVIEW FOR PHASE 6: BODY SCAN

The last step in the reprocessing session is scanning the body for any remaining disturbance. Often, kids feel impatient with the body scan because they're ready to close and move on to other things, in which case it's best to rely on the observation of the child's body and get to closure quickly.

REVIEW FOR PHASE 7: CLOSURE

If time has run out and the session is incomplete, the therapist asks, "What's the most helpful thought or idea that has come to you today?" Their perspective has likely begun shifting, and most children and teens can identify a helpful thought that has occurred to them such as "It's all over now," "My new parents/foster parents/grandparents will keep me safe," "I do have people in my life now who care about me," "It wasn't my fault," or "I'm good in my heart." The therapist responds by saying "That's awesome. I'd love it if you could take that thought home with you this week."

Whether reprocessing is complete or incomplete, the therapist may wish to invite the child or teen to place other worries and bothers in the container before they leave.

The therapist reminds parents that processing may continue, and that temporarily their child may be more sensitive and need extra attunement and support between sessions. Ask the parents to note anything unusual in their child's words or behaviors and to call if there is a serious escalation in behaviors or symptoms.

REVIEW FOR PHASE 8: REEVALUATION

At the beginning of the following session, the therapist checks with the parent first to ask about behaviors or problems following the EMDR work and to interpret the behaviors in terms of the issues with which their child is dealing. When the child or teen joins the session, the therapist asks about any thoughts, feelings, or dreams after the session and then asks "When you think about what we worked on last time, what thoughts or feelings do you notice?"

If the memory still has emotional charge, the child or teen is prompted to think of the memory, the emotion, and where they still feel it and continue the BLS. If only installation of the PC or the body scan are left, the therapist begins where they left off.

APPENDIX G

The EMD to EMDR Continuum

The earliest version of Francine Shapiro's work was called "EMD" for Eye Movement Desensitization (Shapiro, 2018, pp. 7–11). The "R" was not there originally, because Shapiro was using short sets and returning to the target after each set. She wasn't aware that bilateral stimulation with longer sets and more freedom to make associations could help people gain new insights and make new meaning around past memories or triggers. Later, with more experimentation, Shapiro began to recognize the deeper effects from application of the full standard procedures. However, EMD or some version of EMD in terms of shorter sets and more frequent returns to the target is still useful for many situations. For example, EMD is used frequently by EMDR therapists working in emergency room settings or working with first responders after a disaster because it's safe and relieves immediate distress in a short time (Shapiro, 2018, pp. 226, 315). EMD or some version of it is also very useful for kids who have a short attention span and low tolerance for staying with the material for long, and for kids who aren't ready to address memory associations that may come up through standard procedures.

To implement EMD or some version of EMD with a child or teen, the therapist suggests the child place all other upsetting things in their container and choose just the one present trigger/ difficult memory to work on. The NC is identified, but with kids, the PC may be skipped. The VOC may also be skipped.

During Phase 4 desensitization, the therapist applies shorter sets of fast BLS, for example 11 to 15, along with frequent returns to the target. ("As you think of the _____ trigger/memory however you think of it now, what feelings or thoughts do you have?") The shortened sets and frequent returns

Appendix G

to the target help avoid the possibility of becoming overwhelmed by too many associations. The EMD *continuum* means that the sets can be shortened just a little or a lot, and the returns to the target trigger or memory may be frequent or less frequent, depending upon the tolerance of the child or teen.

If the therapist observes that shortened sets and frequent returns to the target are restricting the child's processing so much that nothing is happening, the sets can be made longer and the returns to the target trigger can be less frequent.

With EMD or processing that's close to EMD, the goal is not a SUD of 0 or 1 because kids aren't experiencing the full reprocessing procedures. Continue the sets until it seems the SUD is as low as it can go and then ask, "What's the most helpful thought or idea you've had today?" This becomes the PC that is installed with short, fast sets. Repeat until the VOC is as high as it can go or skip the VOC and observe the child or teen to judge their response. Always skip the Phase 6 body scan when applying EMD to avoid activating new material. These adaptations are all consistent with EMD protocol.

The therapist can move back and forth on the EMD continuum, removing restrictions if the child or teen needs more freedom to process or adding restrictions to avoid associations. The EMD continuum leaves room for the IATP-C therapist to use clinical judgment and intuition to make adjustments that match the needs of the child or teen.

APPENDIX H

Suggested Books for Young Children

Feelings, Feelings, Feelings by Teresa Brown
The Rabbit Listened by Cori Doerrfeld
Island Hopper by Cara Fairfax
Listening to My Body by Gabi Garcia
Listening with My Heart by Gabi Garcia
A Terrible Thing Happened by Margaret M. Holmes
Heart String by Brooke Boynton Hughes
The Bad Seed by Jory John
The Invisible String by Patrice Karst
There's No Such Thing as a Dragon by Jack Kent
Grumpy Monkey by Suzanne Lang
The Kissing Hand by Audrey Penn
Poppy and the Overactive Amygdala by Holly Rae Provan
Riley the Brave by Jess Sinarski (a series)
How Hattie Hated Kindness by Margot Sunderland
Saying Goodbye by Katelyn Tsukamaki & Lora Groppetti

REFERENCES

Achenbach, T. M. (1991). Manual for the Child Behavior Checklist/4–18 and 1991 Profile. University of Vermont Department of Psychiatry.

Adler-Tapia R., & Settle, C. (2009). Evidence of the efficacy of EMDR with children and adolescents in individual psychotherapy: A review of the research published in peer-reviewed journals. *Journal of EMDR Practice and Research*, Supplemental Special Issue on the 20th Anniversary of EMDR, 3, 232–247.

Adler-Tapia, R., & Settle, C. (2023). *EMDR and the art of psychotherapy with children: Guidebook and treatment manual.* (3rd ed.). Springer.

Ainsworth, M. D. S. (1967). *Infancy in Uganda: Infant care and the growth of love.* Johns Hopkins Press.

Ainsworth, M. D. S. (1982). Attachment: Retrospect and prospect. In C. M. Parkes & J. Stevenson-Hinde (Eds.), *The place of attachment in human behavior* (pp. 3–29). Tavistock.

Allen, J. G., & Fonagy, P. (Eds.). (2006). *The handbook of mentalization-based treatment.* John Wiley & Sons.

American Psychiatric Association. (2013). Diagnostic and statistical manual of mental disorders (DSM-5). Armstrong, J., Putnam, F. W., Carlson, E., Libero, D., & Smith, S. (1997). The adolescent dissociative experiences scale. *Journal of Nervous and Mental Disorders, 185*(8), 491–497.

Baumer, N. & Frueh, J. (November 23, 2021) What is neurodiversity? Harvard Health Publishing. https://www.health.harvard.edu/blog/what-is-neurodiversity-202111232645

Beckley-Forest, A., & Monaco, A. (2020). *EMDR with children in the play therapy room: an integrated approach.* Springer Publishing Company.

Beer, R. (2018). Efficacy of EMDR therapy for children with PTSD: A review of the literature. *Journal of EMDR Practice and Research, 12,* 177–195.

Beery, K. E., Buktenica, N. A., & Beery, N. A. (2005). *Beery-Buktenica Developmental Test of Visual-Motor Integration, Sixth Edition*. Pearson Assessments.

Behnke, M., & Smith, V. C. (2013). Prenatal substance abuse: Short- and long-term effects on the exposed fetus. *American Academy of Pediatrics, 131*(3), 1009–1024.

Biederman, J., Petty, C. R., Spencer, T. J., Woodworth, K. Y., Bhide, P., Zhu, J., & Faraone, S. V. (2013). Examining the nature of the comorbidity between pediatric attention deficit/hyperactivity disorder and post-traumatic stress disorder. *Acta Psychiatrica Scandinavica, 128*(1), 78–87.

Bishop, S., Gahagan, S., & Lord, C. (2007). Re-examining the core features of autism: A comparison of autism spectrum disorder and fetal alcohol spectrum disorder. *Journal of Child Psychology and Psychiatry, 48*(11), 1111–1121.

Bowlby, J. (1973). *Attachment and loss: Vol. 2. Separation: Anxiety and anger*. Basic Books.

Bowlby, J. (1989). The role of attachment in personality development and psychopathology. In S. I. Greenspan & G. H. Pollack (Eds.), *The course of life: Vol. 1. Infancy* (pp. 119–136). International Universities Press.

Briere, J. (1996). *Trauma Symptom Checklist for Children (TSCC) professional manual*. Psychological Assessment Resources.

California Evidence-Based Clearinghouse for Child Welfare. (2010). https://www.cebc4cw.org/program/eye-movement-desensitization-and-reprocessing/

Casey Family Programs Brief. (2023). https://www.casey.org/prenatal-substance-exposure-prevention/

Centers for Disease Control. (2023). https://www.cdc.gov/violenceprevention/childabuseandneglect/fastfact.html

Chasnoff, I. J., Wells, A. M., & King, L. (2015). Misdiagnosis and missed diagnosis in foster and adopted children with prenatal alcohol exposure. *Pediatrics, 135*(2), 264–270.

Civilotti, C., Margola, D., Zaccagnino, M., Cussino, M., Callerame, C., Vicini, A., & Fernandez, I. (2021). Eye movement desensitization and reprocessing in child and adolescent psychology: A narrative review. *Current Treatment Options in Psychology, 8*, 110.

Clarke, M. E., Gibbard, W. B. (2003). Overview of fetal alcohol spectrum disorders for mental health professionals. *Canadian Child Adolescent Psychiatry Review, 12*(3), 57–63. PMID: 19030526; PMCID: PMC2582751.

Cronholm, P. F., Forke, C. M., Wade, R., Bair-Merritt, M. H., Davis, M., Harkins-Schwarz, M., Pachter, L. M., & Fein, J. A. (2015). Adverse childhood experiences: Expanding the concept of adversity. *American Journal of Preventive Medicine, 49*(3) 354–361. doi: 10.1016/j.amepre.2015.02.001. PMID: 26296440.

Darker-Smith, S. M. (August 2023). *Neurodiverse affirming EMDR therapy.* EMDRIA conference, Arlington, VA.

de Arellano, M. A. R., Lyman, D. R., Jobe-Shields, L., George, P., Dougherty, R. H., Daniels, A. S., Ghose, S. S., Huang, L., & Delphin-Rittmon, M. E. (2014). Trauma-focused cognitive-behavioral therapy for children and adolescents: Assessing the evidence. *Psychiatric Services, 65*(5), 591–602. https://doi.org/10.1176/appi.ps.201300255

Dell, P. F. (2006). The Multidimensional Inventory of Dissociation (MID): A comprehensive measure of pathological dissociation. *Journal of Trauma & Dissociation, 7*(2), 77–106.

Doyle, N. (2020) Neurodiversity at work: A biopsychosocial model and the impact on working adults. *British Medical Bulletin.* Oxford University Press. doi: 10.1093/bmb/ldaa021.

Dreckmeier-Meiring, M. (2024, April). Integrative eye movement desensitization and reprocessing and family therapy model for treating attachment trauma: Possibilities in the New Zealand context. *Journal of the New Zealand College of Clinical Psychologists, 34*(1), 4–13. doi: 10.5281/zenodo.10939122

Drew, P. D., & Kane, C. J. (2014). Fetal alcohol spectrum disorders and neuroimmune changes. *International Review of Neurobiology, 118,* 114–180.

Enriquez-Geppert, S., Smit, D., Pimenta, M. G., & Arns, M. (2019). Neurofeedback as a treatment intervention in ADHD: Current evidence and practice. *Current Psychiatry Reports, 21*(6), 46. https://doi.org/10.1007/s11920-019-1021-4

Fadeeva, E., & Nenasteva, A. (2022). Diagnostic results of IQ-test in school-aged children with fetal alcohol syndrome and fetal alcohol spectrum of disorders. *European Psychiatry,* S421.

FASCETS. (2018). Fetal Alcohol Spectrum Consultation Education and Training Services. Resources page. https://fascets.org/resources/

Felitti, V. J., Anda, R. F., Nordenberg, D., Williamson, D. F., Spitz, A. M., Edwards, V., Koss, M. P., & Marks, J. S. (1998). Relationship of childhood abuse and household dysfunction to many of the leading causes of death in adults: The Adverse Childhood Experiences (ACE) study. *American Journal of Preventive Medicine, 14*(4), 749–379.

Fonagy, P., Target, M., Steele, M., Steele, H., Leigh, T., Levinson, A., & Kennedy, R. (1997). Morality, disruptive behavior, borderline personality disorder, crime, and their relationships to security of attachment. In L. Atkinson & K. Zucker (Eds.), *Attachment and psychopathology* (pp. 223–274). Guilford Press.

Forbes, D., Bisson, J. I., Monson, C. M. & Berliner, L. (2020). *Effective treatment for PTSD: Practice guidelines from the International Society for Traumatic Stress Studies* (3rd ed.). Guilford Press.

Gibbard, W. B., Wass, P., & Clarke, M. E. (2003). The neuropsychological implications of prenatal alcohol exposure. *Child Adolescent Psychiatry Review, 12*(3), 72–76.

Guild, D. J., Alto, M. E., Handley, E. D., Rogosch, F., Cichetti, D., & Toth, S. L. (2021). Attachment and affect between mothers with depression and their children: Longitudinal outcomes of child parent psychotherapy. *Research on Child and Adolescent Psychopathology, 49,* 563–577.

Hesse, E. (1999). The Adult Attachment Interview: Historical and current perspectives. In J. Cassidy & P. R. Shaver (Eds.), *Handbook of attachment: Theory, research and clinical applications* (pp. 395–433). Guilford Press.

Hughes, D. A. (2017). *Building the bonds of attachment: Awakening love in deeply traumatized children* (3rd ed.). Rowman & Littlefield.

International Society for Neuroregulation and Research. https://isnr.org/

Kaufman, A. S., & Kaufman, N. L. (2022). *Kaufman Brief Intelligence Test, Second Edition*. Pearson Assessments.

Kaufman, A. S., & Kaufman, N. L. (2015). *Kaufman Test of Educational Achievement, Third Edition Brief Form*. Pearson Assessments.

Kautz-Turnbull, C., Rockhold, M., Handley, E. D., Olson, H. C., Petrenko, C. (2023). Adverse childhood experiences in children with fetal alcohol spectrum disorders and their effects on behavior. *Alcohol, Clinical, & Experimental Research, 47*(3), 577–588.

Kerns, C. M., Newschaffer, C. J. & Berkowitz, S. J. (2015). Traumatic childhood events and autism spectrum disorder. *Journal of Autism and Developmental Disorders, 45,* 3475–3486. https://doi.org/10.1007/s10803-015-2392-y

Knipe, J. (2005). Targeting positive affect to clear the pain of unrequited love, codependence, avoidance, and procrastination. In R. Shapiro (Ed.), *EMDR solutions: Pathways to healing* (pp. 189–212). W. W. Norton.

Knipe, J. (2015). *EMDR toolbox: Theory and treatment of complex PTSD and dissociation*. Springer.

Korn, D. L., & Leeds, A. M. (2002). Preliminary evidence of efficacy for EMDR resource development and installation in the stabilization phase of treatment of complex post-traumatic stress disorder. *Journal of Clinical Psychology, 58*, 1465–1487.

Lievegoed, R., Mevissen, L., Leuning, E., van Ommeren, T. B., Hopster, M., Teeken, V., van den Bert, W., Spuijbroek, P., Schipper, B., Westra, J., & Hagen, H. (2013). *Guidelines and tips for EMDR treatment for Autism Spectrum Disorders* (Retrieved from https://psycho-trauma.nl/wp-content/uploads/2014/01/GuidelinesEMDRASD-1.pdf)

Linehan, M. M. (1993). *Skills training manual for treating borderline personality disorder*. Guilford Press.

Liotti, G. (1999). Disorganization of attachment as a model for understanding dissociative psychopathology. In J. Solomon & C. George (Eds.), *Attachment disorganization* (pp. 291–317). Guilford Press.

Lobregt-van Buuren, E., Sizoo, B., Mevissen, L., & de Jongh, A. (2019). Eye Movement Desensitization and Reprocessing (EMDR) Therapy as a Feasible and Potential Effective Treatment for Adults with Autism Spectrum Disorder (ASD) and a History of Adverse Events. *Journal of Autism and Developmental Disorders, 49*(1), 151–164. doi: 10.1007/s10803-018-3687-6. PMID: 30047096.

Lovett, J. (1999). *Small wonders: Healing childhood trauma with EMDR*. Free Press.

Lovett, J. (2009, October). Using EMDR to treat trauma and attachment in children and adults. Paper presented at the Attachment and Trauma Center of Nebraska, EMDR Specialty Workshop, Omaha, NE.

Lovett, J. (2015) *Trauma-Attachment tangle: Modifying EMDR to help children resolve trauma and develop loving relationships*. Routledge.

Lyons-Ruth, K., Alpern, L., & Repacholi, L. (1993). Disorganized infant attachment classification and maternal psychosocial problems as predictors of hostile-aggressive behavior in the preschool classroom. *Child Development, 64*, 572–585.

Lyons-Ruth, K., & Jacobvitz, D. (1999). Attachment disorganization: Unresolved loss, relational violence, and lapses in behavioral and attentional strategies. In J. Cassidy & P. R. Shaver (Eds.), *Handbook of attachment: Theory, research and clinical applications* (pp. 520–554). Guilford Press.

Main, M., & Hesse, E. (1990). Parents' unresolved traumatic experiences are related to infant disorganized attachment status: Is frightened and/or frightening parental behavior the linking mechanism? In M. Greenberg, D. Cicchetti, & E. M. Cummings (Eds.), *Attachment in the pre-school years: Theory, research, and intervention* (pp. 161–182). University of Chicago Press.

Main, M., & Solomon, J. (1990). Procedures for identifying infants as disorganized/disoriented during the Ainsworth Strange Situation. In M. Greenberg, D. Cichetti, & M. Cummings (Eds.), *Attachment in the pre-school years: Theory, research, and intervention* (pp. 121–149). University of Chicago Press.

Malbin, D. (2017). *Trying differently rather than harder* (3rd ed.). FASCETS.

Manzoni, M., Fernandez, I., Bertella, S., Tizzoni, F., Gazzola, E., Molteni, M., & Nobile, M. (2021). Eye movement desensitization and reprocessing: The state of the art of efficacy in children and adolescent with post traumatic stress disorder. *Journal of Affective Disorders, 282*, 340–347.

Mattson, S. N., Jones, K. L., Chockalingam, G., Wozniak, J. R., Hyland, M. T., Courchesne-Krak, N. S., Del Campo, M., Riley, E. P., & CIFASD (2023). Validation of the FASD-Tree as a screening tool for fetal alcohol spectrum disorders. *Alcohol, Clinical & Experimental Research, 47*(2), 263–272. https://doi.org/10.1111/acer.14987

May, P. A., Chambers, C. D., Kalberg, W. O., Zellner, J., Feldman, H., Buckley, D., Kopald, D., Hasken, J. M., Xu, R., Honerkampy-Smith, G., Taras, H., Manning, M. A., Robinson, L. K., Adam, M. P., Abdul-Rahman, O., Vaux, K., Jewett, T., Elliott, A. J., . . . Hoyme, H. E. (2018). Prevalence of fetal alcohol spectrum disorders in 4 US communities. *Journal of the American Medical Association, 319*(5), 474–482. doi:10.1001/jama.2017.21896

Mevissen, L., Lievegoed, R., & De Jongh, A. (2011a). EMDR treatment in people with mild ID and PTSD: 4 cases. *Psychiatric Quarterly, 82*, 43–57.

Mevissen, L., Lievegoed, R., Seubert, A., & De Jongh, A. (2011b). Do persons with intellectual disability and limited verbal capacities respond to trauma treatment? *Journal of Intellectual and Developmental Disability, 36*, 278–283.

Mevissen, L., Lievegoed, R., Seubert, A., & De Jongh, A. (2012). PTSD treatment in people with severe intellectual disabilities: A case series. *Developmental Neurorehabilitation, 15*, 223–232.

Mevissen, L., Didden, R., Korzilius, H., & De Jongh, A. (2017). EMDR therapy for PTSD in children and adolescents with mild to borderline intellectual disability: A multiple baseline across subjects study. *Journal of Applied Research in Intellectual Disabilities, 30*(Suppl. 1), 34–41.

Miller, R. (2019). *The Feeling-State theory and protocol for behavioral and substance addictions: A breakthrough in the treatment of addictions, compulsions, obsessions, co-dependence, and anger.* ImTT Press.

National Institute for Health and Clinical Excellence (2018). Guidelines for Posttraumatic Stress Disorder.

National Institutes of Health. (2022). NIH Publication no. 22-MH-8084. U.S. Department of Health and Human Services. https://www.nimh.nih.gov/health/publications/autism-spectrum-disorder.

Ogden, P., Minton, K., & Pain, C. (2006). *Trauma and the body: A sensorimotor approach to psychotherapy.* W. W. Norton.

Pajareya, K., & Nopmaneejumruslers, K. (2011). A pilot randomized controlled trial of DIR/Floortime™ parent training intervention for pre-school children with autistic spectrum disorders. *Autism, 15*(5), 563–577. https://doi.org/10.1177/1362361310386502Perry, B. D. (2002). Childhood experience and the expression of genetic potential: What childhood neglect tells us about nature and nurture. *Brain & Mind, 3*(1), 79–100.

Popky, A. J. (2005). DeTur, an urge reduction protocol for addictions and dysfunctional behaviors. The desensitization of triggers and urge reprocessing (DeTUR) protocol. In R. Shapiro (Ed.), *EMDR solutions: Pathways to healing* (pp. 167–188). W. W. Norton.

Porges, S. W. (2009). The polyvagal theory: new insights into adaptive reactions of the autonomic nervous system. *The Cleveland Clinic Journal of Medicine, 76* (Supplement 2), 86–90. doi: 10.3949/ccjm.76.s2.17

Potter, A. (2011). The domino effect. Unpublished paper.

Potter, A., & Wesselmann, D. (2023). *EMDR and attachment-focused trauma therapy for adults (AFTT-A): Reclaiming authentic self and healthy attachments.* Springer.

Pynoos, R., & Steinberg, A. (2015). UCLA PTSD Reaction Index for DSM-5. Behavioral Health Innovations.

Putnam, F., & Peterson, G. (1994). Further validation of the child dissociative checklist. *Dissociation, 7*(4), 204–211.

Reynolds, C. R., & Kamphaus, R. W. (2015). *Behavior Assessment System for Children, Third Edition* (BASC-3). Pearson Assessments.

Richardson, G. A., Goldschmidt, L., & Willford, J. (2008). *Neurotoxicol Teratol, 30*(2), 96–106.

Schlattmann, N., van der Hoeven, M., & Hein, I. (2023). *IGT-K, Integratieve gehechtheidsbevorderende traumabehandeling voor kinderen: gezinstherapie en*

EMDR. (Translation and adaptation of Integrative Team Treatment by D. Wesselmann, C. Schweitzer, & S. Armstrong). Bohn Stafleu van Loghum.

Schultz P. N., Remick-Barlow G. A., & Robbins, L. (2007). Equine-assisted psychotherapy: a mental health promotion/intervention modality for children who have experienced intra-family violence. *Health and Social Care in the Community, 15*(3), 265–271. doi: 10.1111/j.1365-2524.2006.00684.x.

Shapiro, F. (2012). *Getting past your past: Take control of your life with self-help techniques from EMDR therapy*. Rodale.

Shapiro, F. (2018). *Eye movement desensitization and reprocessing: Basic principles protocols, and procedures* (3rd ed.). Guilford Press.

Shapiro, R. (2005) The two-hand interweave. In R. Shapiro (Ed.), *EMDR solutions: Pathways to healing* (pp. 160–166). W. W. Norton.

Siegel, D. J. (1999). The developing mind: Toward a neurobiology of interpersonal experience. Guilford Press.

Siegel, D. J. (2001). Toward an interpersonal neurobiology of the developing mind: Attachment relationships, mindsight, and neural integration. *Infant Mental Health Journal, 22*(1–2), 67–94.

Siegel, D. J. (2007). *The mindful brain: Reflection and attunement in the cultivation of well-being*. W. W. Norton.

Siegel, D. J. (2010). *Mindsight: The new science of personal transformation*. Bantam.

Siegel, D. J., & Bryson, T. P. (2011). *The whole-brain child: 12 revolutionary strategies to nurture your child's developing mind*. Bantam.

Silberg, J. L. (2022) *The child survivor: Healing developmental trauma and dissociation* (2nd ed.). Routledge.

Slocum, T. A., Detrich, R., Wilczynski, S. M., Spencer, T. D., Lewis, T., & Wolfe, K. (2014). The evidence-based practice of applied behavior analysis. *The Behavior Analyst, 37*(1), 41–56. https://doi.org/10.1007/s40614-014-0005-2

Spinazzola, J., van der Kolk, B. A., & Ford, J. D. (2021). Developmental trauma disorder: A legacy of attachment trauma in victimized children. *Journal of Traumatic Stress, 34*(4) 711–720.

Sumner, M., Bell, S., & Hwang, P. A. (2013). Fetal alcohol spectrum disorder: Epilepsy and neuropsychiatric disorders. *Clinical Neurophysiology, 124*(7), e5. https://doi.org/10.1016/j.clinph.2012.08.030.

Swimm, L. L. (2018). EMDR intervention for a 17-month-old child to treat attachment trauma: Clinical case presentation. *Journal of EMDR Practice and Research, 12*, 269–281.

Teicher, M. H., & Parigger, A. (2015). The "Maltreatment and Abuse Chronology of Exposure" (MACE) scale for the retrospective assessment of abuse and neglect during development. *PloS one*, *10*(2), e0117423. https://doi.org/10.1371/journal.pone.0117423

Teicher, M. H., Samson, J. A., Anderson, C. M., & Ohashi, K. (2016). The effects of childhood maltreatment on brain structure, function and connectivity. *Nature Reviews. Neuroscience, 17*(10), 652–666. University of Washington Fetal Alcohol and Drug Unit National Resource Directory. https://fadu.psychiatry.uw.edu/resources/

van der Hoeven, M. L., Plukaard, S. C., Schlattmann, N. E. F., Lindauer, R. J. L., & Hein, I. M. (2023). An integrative treatment model of EMDR and family therapy for children after child abuse and neglect: A SCED study. *Children and Youth Services Review, 152*, 1–12.

van der Hart, O., Nijenhuis, E. R. S., & Steele, K. (2006). *The haunted self: Structural dissociation and the treatment of chronic traumatization.* W. W. Norton.

van der Kolk, B. A. (2005). Developmental trauma disorder: Toward a rational diagnosis for children with complex trauma histories. *Psychiatric Annals, 35*(5), 401–408.

van der Kolk, B. A., & Fisler, R. (1992). Dissociation and the fragmentary nature of traumatic memories: Overview and exploratory study. *Journal of Traumatic Stress, 8*(4), 505–525.

van Hoogdalem, L. E., Feijs, H. M. E., Bramer, W. M., Ismail, S. Y., & van Dongen, J. D. M. (2020). The effectiveness of neurofeedback therapy as an alternative treatment for autism spectrum disorders in children. A systematic review. *Journal of Psychophysiology, 35*, 2. https://doi.org/10.1027/0269-8803/a000265

van IJzendoorn, M. H. (1992). Intergenerational transmission of parenting: A review of studies in nonclinical populations. *Developmental Review, 12*, 76–99.

Veterans Affairs/Department of Defense (2023). *VA/DoD Clinical Practice Guideline for Management of Posttraumatic Stress Disorder and Acute Stress Disorder.*

Wesselmann, D. (2013). Healing trauma and creating secure attachment through EMDR. In M. Solomon & D. S. Siegel (Eds.), *Healing moments in psychotherapy: Mindful awareness, neural integration, and therapeutic presence* (pp. 115–128). W. W. Norton.

Wesselmann, D. (2025). *Attachment trauma in kids: Integrative strategies for parents.* (2nd ed.). W. W. Norton.

Wesselmann, D., Armstrong, S., & Schweitzer, C. (2017a). Interweaves for children with an attachment trauma in foster and adoptive families. In R. Beer & C. De Roos (Eds.), *Handbook EMDR: Children and adolescents* (pp. 399−413). LannooCampus.

Wesselmann, D., Armstrong, S., & Schweitzer, C. (2017b) Using an EMDR integrative model to treat attachment based difficulties. In K. D. Buckwalter & D. Reed (Eds.) *Attachment theory in action: Building connections between children and parents.* Roman & Littlefield.

Wesselmann, D., Armstrong, S., Schweitzer, C., Davidson, M., & Potter, A. (2018). An integrative EMDR and family therapy model for treating attachment trauma in children: A case series. *Journal of EMDR Practice and Research, 12*, 196−207.

Wesselmann, D., Davidson, M., Armstrong, S., Schweitzer, C., Bruckner, D., & Potter, A. (2012). EMDR as a treatment for improving attachment status in adults and children. *European Review of Applied Psychology, 62*(4), 223–230.

Wesselmann, D., Hein, I., & Schlattmann, N. (in press). *Integrative attachment trauma protocol for children.* In R. Beer & C. de Roos (Eds.), Handbook of EMDR for children and adolescents. Oxford University Press.

Wesselmann, D., Schweitzer, C., & Armstrong, S. (2015). Child attachment trauma protocol. In M. Luber (Ed.), *EMDR therapy: Scripted protocols and summary sheets* (pp. 9−44). Springer.

Wesselmann, D., Schweizer, C., & Armstrong, S. (2021). Integratief opvoeden, strategieën voor de opvoeding van kinderen met gehechtheidstrauma. (Translation by N. E. F. Schlattmann, M. L. van der Hoeven, & I. M. Hein). Bohn Stafleu van Loghum.

Wesselmann, D., Settle, C., Mevissen, L., & Shapiro, F. (2025). Eye movement desensitization and reprocessing therapy (EMDR) with children and adolescents. In M. A. Landolt, M. Cloitre, & U. Schnyder (Eds.), *Evidence-Based treatments for trauma-related disorders in children and adolescents* (2nd ed.). Springer.

Wesselmann, D., & Shapiro, F. (2013). EMDR and the treatment of complex trauma in children and adolescents. In J. Ford & C. Courtois (Eds.), *Treating complex traumatic stress disorders in children and adolescents* (pp. 203–224). Guilford Press.

Wieder, S., & Greenspan, S. I. (2003). Climbing the symbolic ladder in the DIR model through floor time/interactive play. *Autism, 7*(4), 425−435. https://doi.org/10.1177/1362361303007004008

Wilkinson, G. S., & Robertson, G. J. (2017). *Wide Range Achievement Test,* Fifth Edition. Pearson Assessments.

Wollin, E. L. (Feb. 2019). The impact of fetal alcohol exposure on children and the trauma work we do. Presentation sponsored by The Attachment and Trauma Center of Nebraska.

Wollin, E. L. (Sept. 2023). The impact of prenatal substance exposure to substances on children. Presentation sponsored by Mother's Choice and Adoptive Families of Hong Kong.

World Health Organization (2013). Guidelines for the management of conditions that are specifically related to stress.

Zeanah, C. H., & Boris, N. W. (2000). Disturbances and disorders of attachment in early childhood. In C. H. Zeanah (Ed.), *Handbook of infant mental health* (2nd ed., pp. 353–368). Guilford Press.

INDEX

ABA. *see* applied behavior analysis (ABA)
abuse
  CDC on, 12–13
  sexual. *see* sexual abuse
ACE study. *see* Adverse Childhood Experiences (ACE) study
adaptive information processing (AIP) model, 11–13
ADD. *see* attention-deficit disorder (ADD)
ADHD. *see* attention-deficit hyperactivity disorder (ADHD)
Adler-Tapia, R., 170
Adolescent Dissociative Experiences Scale, 270
adoptive parents
  Therapeutic Story for boy relinquished by, 178
Adverse Childhood Experiences (ACE) study, 10–11
age
  as factor in IATP-C, 18–19
Ainsworth, M. D. S., 212
AIP model. *see* adaptive information processing (AIP) model
alcohol
  prenatal exposure to, 229–31
"All You Need is Love," 5
ambivalent/resistant attachment pattern, 6–7
animal story, 176
ANP. *see* apparently normal part (ANP)
apparently normal part (ANP)
  of personality, 213

applied behavior analysis (ABA)
  for ASD, 234–35
ARD. *see* Attachment Resource Development (ARD)
ARD activities, 18f, 23
  in tapping into love, 102–19, 114f. *see also* ARD activities in tapping into love
ARD activities in tapping into love, 102–19, 114f
  Circle of Love, Circle of Caring activity, 110–11
  creating internal safety/nurturing for children with unstable environments/problematic dissociation, 118–19
  described, 102–3
  Lollipop Game, 122
  Magical Cord of Love activity. *see* Magical Cord of Love activity
  Messages of Love activity, 105–6
  parent preparation for, 103–4
  Playing Baby activity, 121–22
  resistant children/teens script, 104
  Safe Place for the Smaller Child on the Inside activity. *see* Safe Place for the Smaller Child on the Inside activity
  through movement, song, and rhythm for younger children, 119–22
Armstrong, S., 120, 128
ASD. *see* autism spectrum disorder (ASD)
assessment phase
  for brain-based conditions, 241–42
  case example, 186
  in EMDR therapy, 186–87

assessment phase (*continued*)
  for kids who report no thoughts during, 186
  of Trigger Tolerance Protocol, 144–46
attachment continuum, 268
attachment disorders
  attachment loss and, 8–9
attachment disorganization
  described, 7–8
attachment injuries
  EMDR therapy for, 140–43
attachment lens, 6–9
  conceptualizing dissociation through, 212–13
  secure attachment patterns in children, 6
attachment loss
  attachment disorders and, 8–9
attachment patterns
  Cannot Classify, 268
  in children. *see* attachment patterns in children
  in *DSM-5*, 268–69
  earned secure, 269
  transmission from parent to child, 267–69
attachment patterns in children, 6–9
  continuum of, 8
  nonsecure/disorganized, 6–8
  secure, 6
Attachment Resource Development (ARD) activities. *see under* ARD activities
attachment struggles
  parental, 35–38. *see* parental attachment struggles
attachment trauma
  brain-based conditions and, 235–44
  cognitive interweaves for, 189–200. *see also* cognitive interweaves
  EMDR therapy for, 182–207
  forms of, 12–13
  reprocessing of, 187–88
Attachment Trauma in Kids: Integrative Strategies for Parents, second ed., xviii–xix, 28, 35, 45, 214

attention-deficit disorder (ADD)
  described, 233
attention-deficit hyperactivity disorder (ADHD)
  accommodations/modifications for IATP-C family therapy activities for, 239
  described, 233
  neurofeedback therapy for, 235
  reprocessing phases, 242
autism
  described, 232–33
autism spectrum disorder (ASD)
  ABA for, 234–35
  adjunctive diagnosis/treatment for, 234–35
  described, 232–33
  Floor Time for, 234–35
avoidant attachment pattern, 7

baby(ies)
  activities for, 75–76
The Beatles, 5
Beery-Buktenica Developmental Test of Visual-Motor Integration, sixth ed., 270
behavior(s)
  critical points in helping parents make sense of child's, 29–32
  in History-Taking Checklist, 261–62
  misguided, 221–24. *see also* misguided behaviors
  unhealthy compulsive. *see* unhealthy compulsive behaviors
Behavior Assessment System for Children, third ed., 270
behavior chain analysis
  dialectical behavioral therapy in, 134
belief(s)
  carried. *see* carried beliefs
  negative, 29–30
biggest kid self, 213
  repeated future rehearsals for strengthening, 216
Biggest Kid Self activity, 73–74
  for brain-based conditions, 240
  case example, 73–74

Index

Biggest Kid Self activity script, 74
bilateral stimulation (BLS)
   for brain-based conditions, 240–41
   described, 141–42
   in EMDR therapy, 141–42
   in EMDR trauma work, 184
   foundational EMDR therapy activities and, 95–96
   reading story with, 172–74
   in RF for parents, 251–52
   slow. *see* slow BLS
biological parents
   providing information about, 76–77
BLS. *see* bilateral stimulation (BLS)
body(ies)
   disturbance in, 278
body coaching script, 125
body scan
   in EMDR therapy, 280
Bodywork activities
   the Cooked Noodle, 64–65
   in parents' script, 63
   teaching script for, 63–64
   What Do You Notice? activity, 65–66
   in widening the window of tolerance, 63–66
bodywork coaching script, 125
Boris, N.W., 9
Bowlby, J., 8
brain
   downstairs. *see* downstairs brain
   upstairs vs. downstairs, 138–40
brain-based conditions
   accommodations/modifications of IATP-C EMDR therapy for, 239–41
   accommodations/modifications of IATP-C family therapy activities for, 238–39
   adaptations for, 228–44. *see also* fetal alcohol syndrome (FAS); *specific types, e.g.,* autism
   ADD, 233
   ADHD, 233
   adjunctive diagnosis/treatment for, 233–35
   ASD, 232–33
   assessment phase, 241–42
   attachment trauma associated with, 235–44
   BLS for, 240–41
   dyscalculia, 233
   dysgraphia, 233
   dyslexia, 233
   dyspraxia, 233
   EMDR resource activities for, 240–41
   EMDR therapy for, 235–38
   IATP-C for, 235–44
   introduction, 228
   NCs in, 242
   neurodivergence, 231
   parent psychoeducation for, 235–38
   PCs in, 242
   promoting accommodations in home, 35
   reprocessing phases, 242–43
   S-RDI for, 241
   Therapeutic Story method for, 243–44
   Timeline activity, 243–44
brain coaching script, 125
brain development
   developmental trauma and, 9–10
BRAIN-online, 234
Brainwork activities
   Thinking Brain, Feeling Brain activity, 66–69, 67*f*
   stuck memories activity, 69–70
   in widening the window of tolerance, 66–70, 67*f*
Breathwork activities
   in parents' script, 63
   teaching script for, 63–64
   in widening the window of tolerance, 63–64
Breathwork coaching script, 125
Bringing the Biggest Kid Part Forward at Home script, 214–15
Brown, T., 72*n*, 154
bullying
   gender identity–related, 179–80
Butterfly Hug activity
   in building good feelings, 101–2
Butterfly Hug activity script, 102

Canada FASD Research Network, 234
Candy Land Timeline, 169
Cannot Classify attachment pattern, 268
carried beliefs
    RF for parents related to, 246–47
case conceptualization
    case examples, 46–51
    initiation of, 42–43
Casey Family Programs Brief, 229
CDC. *see* Centers for Disease Control and Prevention (CDC)
CEBC. *see* Clinical Evidence-Based Clearinghouse (CEBC)
Centers for Disease Control and Prevention (CDC)
    on abuse/neglect of children, 12–13
    on maltreatment, 257
characters
    in Therapeutic Story, 169–70
checklist(s)
    History-Taking, 261–66. *see also* History-Taking Checklist
    IATP-C, 259–60
Child Assessments, 270–72
Child Behavior Checklist for Ages 6–18, 271
Child Dissociative Checklist, 271
childhood abuse/neglect
    CDC on, 12–13
childhood themes
    RF for parents related to, 246–47
child populations
    as factor in IATP-C, 18–19
children
    attachment patterns in, 6–9. *see also specific patterns and* attachment patterns in children
    resistant. *see* resistant children
    younger. *see* younger children
Children and Family Futures, 229
children without permanency
    Magical Cord of Love activity for, 110
Circle of Love, Circle of Caring activity script, 110–11
Clinical Evidence-Based Clearinghouse (CEBC) for Child Welfare
    on EMDR therapy, 13

closure
    in EMDR therapy, 280
coaching during S-RDI
    case examples, 125–30
    reinforcing positive experiences from, 127
coaching during S-RDI scripts, 124–25
Coaching with Photographs activity, 127–28
Coaching with Photographs activity script, 128
cocaine
    prenatal exposure to, 231
cognition(s)
    negative. *see* negative cognitions (NCs)
    positive. *see* positive cognitions (PCs)
cognitive interweaves
    case examples, 148–50, 197–200
    in completion of EMDR phases, 197–200
    described, 147–50
    in EMDR therapy, 189–200
    excerpts from sessions reprocessing present-day triggers, 150–52
    goals for, 189
    in helping being stuck in helplessness, 193–94
    in helping being stuck in shame for things done, 196
    in helping connect to one's emotions, 194–95
    in helping manage intense emotions/stay grounded, 190–91
    in helping release emotions, 195
    in helping to mentalize thoughts/feelings, 192–93
    in helping with stuck sadness/loneliness, 193
    in helping zero in on obstacle/feeder memory/stuck point, 192
    methods of providing, 189–90
    in providing needed information, 191
    Trigger Tolerance Protocol–related, 147–50
compulsive behaviors
    unhealthy, 155–63. *see also* unhealthy compulsive behaviors

Container activity, 140–41
Container activity script, 141
the Cooked Noodle activity, 64–65
  case example, 64–65
Cord of Love activity, 218–19
  for brain-based conditions, 241
couples in crisis
  therapy for, 40
cultural trauma
  talking to parents about child's, 31–32
custody issues
  Therapeutic Story for, 176

Darker-Smith, S. M., 240
Department of Veterans Affairs and Department of Defense
  on EMDR therapy, 13
desensitization
  in EMDR therapy, 279
Detective Work activities
  case example, 139–40
  described, 134
  in exploring triggers, 138–40
  in Timeline of Therapeutic Story, 168–69
Detective Work activities script, 139–40
Detective Work activity, 18f, 23, 24
DeTUR model, 156–58
  case example, 157–58
  LOU in, 156–58
development
  brain. *see* brain development
developmental trauma
  brain development impact of, 9–10
  health impact of, 10–11
developmental trauma disorder (DTD)
  described, 11
developmental trauma lens, 9–15
  AIP model, 11–13
  brain development effects, 9–10
  DTD, 11
  EMDR therapy, 13
  health effects, 10–11
  IATP-C, 13–14
Diagnostic and Statistical Manual of Mental Disorders, fifth ed. (*DSM-5*)
  attachment-related diagnoses in, 268–69

on disinhibited social engagement disorder, 9
  on RAD, 9
dialectical behavioral therapy
  in behavior chain analysis, 134
difficult events
  Therapeutic Stories for, 174–80
disinhibited social engagement disorder
  DSM-5 on, 9
dismissive attachment pattern
  parental, 36
  subtypes of, 36
dismissive derogatory pattern, 36
dismissive idealizing pattern, 36
dismissive parent script
  in speaking to parents, 36
disorganization
  attachment, 7–8
  described, 7–8
  mental, 7–8
disorganized attachment patterns in children, 6–8
dissociation
  attachment lens in conceptualizing, 212–13
  defined, 226
  helping parents with children with, 34
  parents' script, 214
  problematic, 211–27. *see also* problematic dissociation
  reinforcing dissociative patterns, 215–16
  reprocessing with kids with, 187
  strategies for, 211–27. *see also* problematic dissociation
  Structural Dissociation model in conceptualizing, 213
  Therapeutic Story for, 224–25
dissociative patterns
  reinforcing, 215–16
dissociative symptoms
  described, 226–27
disturbance in the body
  identifying, 278
doll(s)
  in Messages of Love activity, 107–8
  in nurturing the Smaller Child on the Inside, 116

domino effect
  described, 134–38, 135f
Dominoes activity, 18f, 23, 24
  described, 134–38, 135f
downstairs brain
  defined, 30
  upstairs brain vs., 138–40
downstairs brain script
  in speaking to parents, 30
DSM-5. see Diagnostic and Statistical Manual of Mental Disorders, fifth ed. (*DSM-5*)
DTD. *see* developmental trauma disorder (DTD)
dyscalculia
  described, 233
dysgraphia
  described, 233
dyslexia
  described, 233
dyspraxia
  described, 233
dysregulation
  reprocessing for, 187

early maltreatment script, 77
early orphanage care
  Therapeutic Story for, 175–76
early trauma
  explaining causes for, 77–78
earned secure, 269
earned secure attachment pattern, 269
EMD. *see* eye movement desensitization (EMD)
EMD Continuum, 282–83
  containing associations with, 188
EMDR
  introduction, xvii–xix
  of triggers and traumas, 18f, 24–25
EMDR and family therapy integrative approach. *see also under* EMDR therapy; family therapy activities
  introduction, xvii–xix
EMDR Continuum
  EMD to, 282–83
  Trigger Tolerance Protocol and, 152
EMDR resource activities
  for brain-based conditions, 240–41

EMDR therapy
  accommodations/modifications for brain-based conditions, 239–41
  addressing hardest parts of, 182–207. *see also* EMDR trauma work
  adjusting to child's level of tolerance, 187–88
  assessment phase of, 186–87
  for attachment injuries, 140–43
  BLS in, 141–42
  body scan in, 280
  for brain-based conditions, 235–38
  bringing closure to, 206
  case example, 254–55
  choosing memory in, 185
  closure in, 280
  cognitive interweaves in, 189–200. *see also* cognitive interweaves
  Container activity, 140–41
  described, 13
  desensitization in, 279
  family therapy activities with, 133–63. *see also under* family therapy activities
  future templates, 152–54
  grief-related, 201–5. *see also* grief
  history taking in, 41–51. *see also under* history taking
  installation in, 279–80
  introduction, 96–97
  NICE on, 13
  organizations recommending, 13
  parent involvement in, 183–85
  parents' most relevant targets, 254–55
  parents' script, 96
  phases of, 94, 187–88, 276–81
  for problematic dissociation, 216–21, 225–26
  reevaluation in, 280–81
  RF for parents through, 245–57. *see also under* Reflective Functioning (RF) for parents
  songs in, 154–55
  strategies for attachment trauma reprocessing, 187–88
  target assessment in, 276–78

Index 303

Therapeutic Story in, 164–81. *see also under* Therapeutic Story
three-pronged approach to, 94
Trigger Tolerance Protocol, 143–52. *see also* Trigger Tolerance Protocol
for unhealthy compulsive behaviors, 155–63. *ee also* unhealthy compulsive behaviors
virtual therapy, 142–43
WHO on, 13
EMDR therapy activities
foundational, 93–130. *see also* foundational EMDR therapy activities
EMDR trauma work
addressing hardest parts of, 182–207. *see also* EMDR therapy
BLS in, 184
bringing closure to, 206
continuing IATP-C, 206
grief-related, 201–5. *see also* grief
Monster in the Closet metaphor script, 184
preverbal trauma, 200–1. *see also* preverbal trauma
video game metaphor script, 184–85
EMDR trauma work parent script, 183–84
emotion(s)
cognitive interweaves in managing, 190–91
connecting to, 194–95
identifying, 277–78
releasing of, 195
emotional parts (EPs), 213
environment(s)
unstable. *see* unstable environments
EPs. *see* emotional parts (EPs)
eye movement desensitization and reprocessing (EMDR). *see* EMDR
eye movement desensitization (EMD) described, 282
eye movement desensitization (EMD) continuum
containing associations with. *see under* EMD

Facts About Feelings activity, 71–72
case example, 71–72
family therapy activities
accommodations/modifications for brain-based conditions, 238–39
EMDR therapy with, 133–63. *see also under* EMDR therapy
foundational, 55–92. *see also specific types and* foundational family activities
in IATP-C, 18*f,* 23–24
in understanding triggers, 134–40, 135*f*
FAS. *see* fetal alcohol syndrome (FAS)
FASD. *see* fetal alcohol spectrum disorder (FASD)
fear
love-related, 5–16. *see also under* love
feeder memory
cognitive interweaves in helping kids zero in on, 192
feeling(s)
building good, 53–130
good. *see* good feelings
of helplessness, 193–94
maladaptive positive. *see* maladaptive positive feelings
Feelings, Feelings, Feelings, 72*n*
Thinking Brain, Feeling Brain activity, 66–69, 67*f*
case example, 66–69, 67*f*
Feelings Faces activity, 72–73
Feelings Faces activity scripts, 72–73
fetal alcohol exposure
neurological impact of, 229–30
fetal alcohol spectrum disorder (FASD)
accommodations/modifications for IATP-C family therapy activities for, 238–39
adjunctive diagnosis/treatment for, 234
described, 229
diagnosis of, 229–30, 234
prevalence of, 229
reprocessing phases, 242
up-to-date research/information on, 234
fetal alcohol syndrome (FAS)
diagnosis of, 229–30

Floor Time
  for ASD, 234–35
foundational EMDR therapy activities
  ARD activities in tapping into love, 102–19, 114f. see also ARD activities in tapping into love
  ARD through movement, song, and rhythm for younger children, 119–22
  BLS in, 95–96
  building good feelings–related, 97–102
  Butterfly Hug activity, 101–2
  engaging children/teens in, 94–96
  future rehearsals with new skills, 130
  introduction, 96–97
  safe place activity, 97–98
  S-RDI in, 122–30. see also under self-regulation development and installation (S-RDI)
  strengthening biggest kid self activity, 98–100
  strengthening one's power animal activity, 100–1
foundational family activities, 55–92
  attuning/nuancing language for individual, 82
  Biggest Kid Self activity, 73–74
  Bodywork activities, 63–66
  Brainwork activities, 66–70, 67f
  Breathwork activities, 63–64
  described, 18f, 22
  Facts About Feelings activity, 71–72
  Feelings Faces activity, 72–73
  High-Alert, Low-Alert Language activity, 70–71
  in IATP-C, 18f, 22
  initiating, 56–58
  Kintsugi activity, 57–58
  Language of the Window activity, 58–62, 60f, 61f
  navigating their inside world, 75–82
  parental involvement in, 56–57
  the pause in, 62
  providing information about biological parents, 76–77
  relationship strengthening activities, 82–91. see also specific activities and relationship strengthening activities
  Smaller Child on the Inside activity, 78–82
  What Babies Need activity, 75–76
  in widening window of tolerance, 58–74, 60f, 61f, 67f. see also specific activities
front self, 213
functional EMDR therapy activities, 93–130
  in IATP-C, 18f, 23
future templates
  in History-Taking Checklist, 266

gender identity
  Therapeutic Story for child bullied due to, 179–80
good feelings
  building, 53–130
grief, 201–5
  attunement to, 202
  case example, 202–5
  NCs related to, 202
  parental, 256
  processing of, 201–5
  talking to parents about child's, 31
  types of, 201–2
grief script
  in speaking to parents, 31
groundedness
  cognitive interweaves in, 190–91

health
  developmental trauma impact on, 10–11
helplessness
  cognitive interweaves in assisting kids stuck in, 193–94
High-Alert, Low-Alert Language activity, 70–71
  case example, 71
history taking, 41–51. see also initial information gathering
  beginning case conceptualization, 42–43

Index 305

case conceptualization examples, 46–51
History-Taking Checklist, 43–46, 261–66
IATP-C, 41–51
initial information gathering, 41–46
History-Taking Checklist, 43–46, 261–66
    case conceptualization examples, 46–51
    case example, 44–45
    current/recent behaviors, 261–62
    current triggers, 262–63
    future templates, 266
    NCs, 263–64
    PCs, 265
    traumatic past events, 263
home
    promoting accommodations in, 35

IATP-C
    age as factor in, 18–19
    for brain-based conditions, 235–44
    child populations in, 18–19
    components of, 14, 17–29, 18f
    continuing, 206
    described, 13–14
    EMDR of triggers and traumas in, 18f, 24–25
    EMDR therapy. *see under* EMDR therapy
    family therapy activities. *see* family therapy activities
    foundational EMDR therapy activities, 18f, 23, 93–130. *see also* foundational EMDR therapy activities
    foundational family activities, 18f, 22, 55–92. *see also* foundational family activities
    history taking, 41–51. *see also* history taking
    integration with other modalities, 21
    introduction, xvii–xix
    overview, 17–29
    parent psychoeducation and case conceptualization, 18f, 21–22
    parent psychoeducation sessions, 28–40. *see also under* parent psychoeducation sessions

peer consultation in, 25–26
research, 14–15
stage 1, 3–51, 259
stage 2, 14, 53–130, 259
stage 3, 14, 131–207, 260
team vs. solo application of, 20–21
therapist demeanor in, 26
treatment complications management in, 26–27
IATP-C Checklist, 259–60
IATP-C therapist
    demeanor of, 26
IATP-C treatment plan, 51
identity(ies)
    gender. *see* gender identity
imagined pictures
    preverbal trauma–related, 201
incomplete session script
    closing of, 188
information gathering
    in history taking, 41–46
initial information gathering
    beginning case conceptualization, 42–43
    in history taking, 41–46
    History-Taking Checklist, 43–46, 261–66
installation
    in EMDR therapy, 279–80
Integrative Attachment Trauma Protocol for Children (IATP-C). *see* IATP-C
integrative parenting strategies, 32–33
integrative parenting strategies script
    case example, 33
    in speaking to parents, 32–33
internal attachment repair
    Safe Place for the Smaller Child on the Inside activity in, 112–15, 114f
International Society for the Study of Trauma and Dissociation
    on EMDR therapy, 13

Jobs of Mom and Dads activity, 83–85
    case example, 85

Kaufman Brief Intelligence Test, second ed., 271
Kaufman Tests of Educational Achievements, third ed., brief form, 271
Kintsugi activity, 57–58
Knipe, J., 158
known events
　in Therapeutic Story, 165–66

lack of permanency
　Therapeutic Story for child with, 177
language
　attuning/nuancing of, 82
Language of the Window activity, 58–62, 60f, 61f
Language of the Window activity script, 59–62, 60f, 61f
　case example, 59–62, 60f, 61f
level of tolerance
　adjusting EMDR therapy to, 187–88
Level of Urge (LOU), 156–58
Liotti, G., 34
Lollipop Game, 122
Lollipop Game script, 122
loneliness
　cognitive interweaves in helping kids with, 193
loss
　attachment. see attachment loss
LOU. see Level of Urge (LOU)
love
　afraid to, 5–16
　ARD activities in tapping into, 102–19, 114f. see also ARD activities in tapping into love
　attachment lens and, 6–9. see also attachment lens
　developmental trauma lens and, 9–15. see also under developmental trauma; developmental trauma lens
　as foundational, 5
Lovett, J., 24, 122, 128, 169, 170, 173
loyalty script
　in speaking to parents, 31

Magical Cord of Love activity, 108–9, 218–19
　for brain-based conditions, 240–41
　for teens/resistant children/children without permanency, 110
　for younger children, 109–10
Magical Cord of Love activity script, 109
Magical Cord of Love on the Inside script, 219
maladaptive positive feelings
　case example, 160–61
　targeting of, 158–61
maladaptive positive feelings script, 159–60
maltreatment
　CDC on, 257
maltreatment script, 77
marijuana
　prenatal exposure to, 231
Mattson, S. N., 234
memory(ies)
　choosing, 185
　feeder. see feeder memory
　stuck. see stuck memories activity
　traumatic. see traumatic memories
memory fragment
　preverbal trauma–related, 200–1
memory script, 185
mental disorganization, 7–8
mentalization script
　in speaking to parents, 34
mentalizing state
　modeling/encouraging, 33–34
Messages of Love activity, 105–6
　for brain-based conditions, 240–41
　case examples, 105–8
　doll/stuffed animal for resistant children, 107–8
　optional games, 108
　parent prompts, 106–7
　for teens who lack permanency, 107
methamphetamines
　prenatal exposure to, 231
Miller, R., 158
misguided behaviors
　case example, 223–24
　parts of self with, 221–24
misguided behaviors script, 222–23

Monster in the Closet metaphor, 184
Monster in the Closet metaphor script, 184
movement
    ARD through, 119–22
Multidimensional Inventory of Dissociation (version for adolescents), 271
murder
    Therapeutic Story for girl whose parent was victim of, 179

National Institute for Health and Clinical Excellence (NICE)
    on EMDR therapy, 13
NCs. *see* negative cognitions (NCs)
negative beliefs
    stuck, 29–30
negative cognitions (NCs)
    in brain-based conditions, 242
    grief-related, 202
    in History-Taking Checklist, 263–64
    identifying, 277
    types of, 143
neglect
    CDC on, 12–13
neurodivergence
    described, 231
neurodivergent
    described, 231
neurodivergent conditions. *see also specific types, e.g.,* autism spectrum disorder (ASD)
    types of, 231–33
neurodiversity
    described, 231
neurofeedback therapy
    for ADHD, 235
NICE. *see* National Institute for Health and Clinical Excellence (NICE)
"nonattachment" disorder, 9
nonsecure/disorganized attachment patterns in children, 6–8

obstacle(s)
    cognitive interweaves in helping kids zero in on, 192
opiates
    prenatal exposure to, 231

orphanage care
    Therapeutic Story for, 175–76
others
    negative beliefs about, 29–30

parent(s)
    adoptive. *see* adoptive parents
    ARD activities in tapping into love preparation for, 103–4
    attachment patterns transmitted to child from, 267–69
    biological. *see* biological parents
    Bodywork script for, 63
    Breathwork script for, 63
    EMDR script for, 96
    EMDR therapy for most relevant targets of, 254–55
    in family therapy activities, 56–57
    with highly dissociative kids, 213–15
    invitation to do their own therapy script, 38–40
    involvement in EMDR trauma work, 183–85
    Messages of Love activity prompts for, 106–7
    murder by, 179
    participating in their own therapy, 38–40
    with preoccupied pattern, 37
    RDI self-help tool for, 104
    RDI with future rehearsals for, 250–51
    RF for, 245–57. *see also* Reflective Functioning (RF) for parents
    Safe Place for the Smaller Child on the Inside activity script for, 113–15, 114*f*
    S-RDI script for, 123
    suicide by, 178–79
    with unresolved/disorganized pattern, 37–38
    unwilling. *see* unwilling parents
parental attachment struggles
    attuning to, 35–38
    dismissive attachment pattern, 36
    preoccupied pattern, 37
    unresolved/disorganized pattern, 37–38

parental grief
  RF for, 256
Parent Narrative
  in Therapeutic Story, 170
parent psychoeducation
  for brain-based conditions, 235–38
parent psychoeducation and case conceptualization, 3–51
  described, 21
  in IATP-C, 18f, 21–22
parent psychoeducation sessions, 28–40
  addressing social and cultural trauma, 31–32
  attuning to parents' attachment struggles, 35–38
  couples in crisis, 40
  dismissive parent script, 36
  downstairs brain script, 30
  grief and loyalty script, 31
  IATP-C–related, 28–40
  integrative parenting strategies, 32–33
  integrative parenting strategies script, 32–33
  invitation to do their own therapy script, 38
  inviting parents to participated in their own therapy, 38–40
  mentalization script, 34
  modeling/encouraging mentalizing state, 33–34
  for parents with highly dissociative children, 34
  prefrontal brain script, 30–31
  preoccupied parent script, 37
  promoting accommodations in the home, 35
  stuck negative beliefs about self and others script, 29–30
  stuck traumatic memories script, 29
  talking about their child's grief, 31
  unwilling parents, 40
  "What's wrong with my child?," 29–32
past, present, and future activity
  case example, 166–68
  in Therapeutic Story, 166–68

past events
  in History-Taking Checklist, 263
the pause
  in widening the window of tolerance, 62
the pause script, 62
PCs. see positive cognitions (PCs)
peer consultation
  in IATP-C, 25–26
permanency
  children without. see children without permanency
  lack of. see lack of permanency
  teens without. see teen(s) without permanency
Perry, B., 30
personality
  ANP of, 213
photograph(s)
  coaching with, 127–28
picture(s)
  imagined. see imagined pictures
Playing Baby activity, 121–22
polysubstance exposure
  prenatal, 231
positive cognitions (PCs)
  in brain-based conditions, 242
  in History-Taking Checklist, 265
  identifying, 277
  validity of, 277
positive feelings
  maladaptive, 158–61. see also maladaptive positive feelings
Potter, A., 118, 134, 217, 219
power animal
  strengthening of, 100–1
prefrontal brain script
  in speaking to parents, 30–31
prenatal alcohol/drug exposure
  case example, 238
  types of, 229–31
preoccupied parent script, 37
preoccupied pattern
  parents with, 37
preverbal trauma, 200–1
  described, 200

Index

targeting imagined pictures related to, 201
targeting memory fragment related to, 200–1
Therapeutic Story for child with, 177–78
problematic dissociation
attachment lens in conceptualizing, 212–13
creating internal safety/nurturing for children with, 118–19
EMDR activities for, 216–21
EMDR therapy for, 225–26
enhanced Safe Places for the Smaller Child Parts on the Inside activity, 216–18
Magical Cord of Love activity, 218–19
misguided behaviors, 221–24
recognizing, 211–13
reinforcing dissociative patterns, 215–16
repeated future rehearsals for strengthening biggest kid self, 216
strategies for, 211–27. *see also* dissociation
Structural Dissociation model in conceptualizing, 213
symptoms of, 211–13
Therapeutic Story for, 224–25
time orientation through past/present activity, 221
Tucking in the Smaller Parts activity, 219–21
working with parents of kids with, 213–15
psychoeducation
parent. *see under* parent psychoeducation

RAD. *see* reactive attachment disorder (RAD)
RDI procedures. *see* resource development and installation (RDI) procedures
RDI self-help tool
parents' script, 104
reactive attachment disorder (RAD)
diagnosis of, 9
DSM-5 on, 9

reevaluation
in EMDR therapy, 280–81
reflection
expanding capacity for, 147–50
Reflective Functioning (RF)
described, 245–47
for parents, 245–57. *see also under* Reflective Functioning (RF) for parents
Reflective Functioning (RF) for parents, 245–57
BLS in, 251–52
carried beliefs/themes of childhood related to, 246–47
engaging parents in, 247–48
helping create safety on the inside, 252–54
history taking in, 249–50
individual work initiation, 248–50
for parental grief, 256
preparation/stabilization, 250–52
RDI procedures in, 250–51
through EMDR therapy, 245–57
treatment-planning sample cases, 249–50
relational games
in strengthening relationships, 82–83
relationship(s)
activities in strengthening, 82–91. *see also specific activities and* relationship strengthening activities
relationship strengthening activities, 82–91
Jobs of Mom and Dads activity, 83–85
relational games, 82–83
skills practice, 88–91
types of, 83
Who Has the Floor? activity, 85–88
reprocessing phases
for brain-based conditions, 242–43
research
IATP-C–related, 14–15
resistant children
Magical Cord of Love activity for, 110
Messages of Love activity for, 107–8
RDI self-help tool for, 104

resource development and installation (RDI) procedures
  with future rehearsals for parents, 250–51
  in RF for parents, 250–51
RF. *see* Reflective Functioning (RF)
rhythm
  ARD through, 119–22

sadness
  cognitive interweaves in helping kids with, 193
Safe Place for the Smaller Child on the Inside activity, 111–18, 114*f*
  for brain-based conditions, 240
  in building good feelings, 97–98
  case examples, 98, 114–19, 217–18
  doll in nurturing, 116
  enhanced, 216–18
  internal attachment repair, 112–15, 114*f*
  meeting needs of younger parts, 116
Safe Place for the Smaller Child on the Inside activity scripts, 112–15, 114*f*
Safety and Nurturing for the Parents' Younger Parts script, 253–54
second person parent narrative
  for child with preverbal trauma, 177–78
secure attachment patterns
  in children, 6
self
  biggest kid, 213
  front, 213
  misguided behaviors and, 221–24
  negative beliefs about, 29–30
self-help
  RDI, 104
self-regulation development and installation (S-RDI), 18*f*, 23, 122–30
  for brain-based conditions, 241
  coaching during, 124–30. *see also* coaching during S-RDI
  described, 122–23
  in foundational EMDR therapy activities, 122–30

parents' script, 123
  reinforcing positive experiences from, 127
Settle, C., 170
sexual abuse
  therapeutic story for sexual reactivity subsequent to, 174–75
sexual reactivity
  Therapeutic Story for, 174–75
shame
  stuck in. *see* stuck in shame
Shapiro, F., 11, 43, 282
Shapiro, R., 161
showing
  telling vs., 276–77
Silberg, J. L., 215
skills practice
  case example, 89–91
  in strengthening relationships, 88–91
slow BLS, 23
  coaching with, 124–27
Smaller Child on the Inside activity, 78–82
  case examples, 79–82
  coaching script for, 125
  doll in, 116
Smaller Child on the Inside activity script, 79
Small Wonders: Healing Childhood Trauma with EMDR, 169
social trauma
  talking to parents about child's, 31–32
song(s)
  ARD through, 119–22
  as healthy responses to triggers, 154–55
S-RDI. *see* self-regulation development and installation (S-RDI)
story(ies)
  therapeutic, 164–81. *see also under* Therapeutic Story
Strange Situation, 212–13
strengthening biggest kid self activity
  in building good feelings, 98–100
  case examples, 99–100
strengthening their power animal activity
  in building good feelings, 100–1

Index

strengthening their power animal activity script, 101
Structural Dissociation model
   conceptualizing dissociation through, 213
stuck in shame
   cognitive interweaves in helping with being, 196
stuck memories activity, 69–70
   case example, 69–70
stuck negative beliefs about self and others script
   in speaking to parents, 29–30
stuck point
   cognitive interweaves in helping kids zero in on, 192
stuck sadness
   cognitive interweaves in helping kids with, 193
stuck traumatic memories script
   in speaking to parents, 29
stuffed animal
   in Messages of Love activity, 107–8
subjective units of disturbance (SUD)
   identifying, 277–78
SUD. *see* subjective units of disturbance (SUD)
suicide
   Therapeutic Story for boy who lost parent to, 178–79
Swimm, L. L., 18–19

target assessment
   in EMDR therapy, 276–78
teen(s)
   who lack permanency, 107
teen(s) without permanency
   Magical Cord of Love activity for, 110
telling
   showing vs., 276–77
theme(s)
   childhood. *see* childhood themes
Therapeutic Story, 164–81. *see also under* Therapeutic Story method
   animal story, 176
   BLS in reading, 172–74
   for boy relinquished by adoptive parents, 178

   for boy who lost parent to suicide, 178–79
   for brain-based conditions, 224–25
   characters in, 169–70
   for child bullied due to gender identity, 179–80
   for child with no permanency, 177
   for child with preverbal trauma, 177–78
   continued readings, 173–74
   custody-related, 176
   for difficult events, 174–80
   for dissociation, 224–25
   for early orphanage care, 175–76
   for girl whose parent was murdered by other parent, 179
   introduction, 165
   known events in, 165–66
   outline, 171–72
   overview, 165–81
   Parent Narrative in, 170
   past, present, and future activity, 166–68
   persons in, 169–70
   second person parent narrative, 177–78
   sequencing of, 170–71
   for sexual reactivity subsequent to sexual abuse, 174–75
   stuffed animals in, 174
   The Tale of the Hamster and the Porcupine Coat, 180, 273–75
   Timeline activity, 168–72, 169*f*. *see also* Timeline activity
   writing during/outside of session, 172
Therapeutic Story method. *see* Therapeutic Story
therapist(s)
   IATP-C. *see* IATP-C therapist
The Tale of the Hamster and the Porcupine Coat, 180, 273–75
thought(s)
   cognitive interweaves in helping mentalize, 192–93
Timeline activity, 168–72, 169*f*
   for brain-based conditions, 243–44
   Candy Land, 169

Timeline activity (*continued*)
 creative, 169
 described, 168–69
 sample, 169*f*
 in Therapeutic Story, 168–72, 169*f*
tobacco
 prenatal exposure to, 231
tolerance
 level of. *see* level of tolerance
trauma(s)
 attachment. *see* attachment trauma
 cultural. *see* cultural trauma
 developmental. *see* developmental trauma
 EMDR therapy for, 18*f*, 24–25, 182–207. *see also specific types and* EMDR therapy
 explaining causes for, 77–78
 healing of, 131–207
 preverbal. *see* preverbal trauma
 social. *see* social trauma
Trauma Symptom Checklist for Children/Trauma Symptom Checklist for Young Children, 272
traumatic memories
 stuck. *see* stuck traumatic memories
traumatic past events
 in History-Taking Checklist, 263
trigger(s). *see also* Trigger Tolerance Protocol
 Detective Work activities in exploring, 138–40. *see also* Detective Work activities
 EMDR of, 18*f*, 24–25
 expanding tolerance for, 147–50
 family therapy activities in understanding, 134–40, 135*f*
 healing of, 131–207
 in History-Taking Checklist, 262–63
 reprocessing present-day, 150–52
 songs as healthy responses to, 154–55
 tricky things about, 143
Trigger Tolerance Protocol, 143–52. *see also under* trigger(s)
 assessment phase, 144–46
 case examples, 145–46
 cognitive interweaves in, 147–50. *see also* cognitive interweaves
 described, 143–44
 of EMDR, 143–52. *see also* Trigger Tolerance Protocol
 EMDR Continuum and, 152
 excerpts from sessions reprocessing present-day triggers, 150–52
 Phase 8 reevaluation, 154
 processing strategies, 147–52
trust
 building capacity for, 53–130
Tucking in the Smaller Parts activity, 219–21
 case example, 220–21
Tucking in the Smaller Parts activity script, 219–20
Tumbling Towers activities
 coaching with, 128–30
"two-hands method," 161–63
 case example, 162–63
"two-hands method" script, 161–62

UCLA PTSD Reaction Index for *DSM-5*, 272
unhealthy compulsive behaviors
 case example, 157–58
 DeTUR model, 156–58
 targeting of, 155–63
 targeting of maladaptive positive feelings, 158–61. *see also* maladaptive positive feelings
 "two-hands method," 161–63. *see also* "two-hands method"
unhealthy compulsive behaviors script, 156
unresolved/disorganized pattern
 parents with, 37–38
unstable environments
 creating internal safety/nurturing for children with, 118–19
unwilling parents
 therapy for, 40
upstairs brain
 downstairs brain vs., 138–40

Index

validity of the positive cognition (VOC), 277
van der Kolk, B. A., 11
video game metaphor script, 184–85
virtual therapy
  EMDR–related, 142–43
VOC. *see* validity of the positive cognition (VOC)

Wesselmann, D., 118, 217, 219, 273*n*
What Babies Need activity, 75–76
  case example, 75–76
What Do You Notice? activity, 65–66
  case example, 65–66
"What's wrong with my child?," 29–32
WHO. *see* World Health Organization (WHO)

Who Has the Floor? activity, 85–88
  case example, 86–88
Wide Range Achievement Test, fifth ed., 272
Williams, J., 72*n*
window of tolerance
  activities in widening of, 58–74, 60*f*, 61*f*, 67*f*. *see also specific activities*
World Health Organization (WHO)
  on EMDR therapy, 13

younger children
  ARD through movement, song, and rhythm for, 119–22
  Magical Cord of Love activity for, 109–10
  suggested books for, 284

Zeanah, C. H., 9

ABOUT THE AUTHOR

Debra Wesselmann, MS, LIMHP, has dedicated her career to transforming the lives of individuals affected by attachment trauma. In 1995, she discovered the profound healing power of EMDR therapy. This discovery reshaped her clinical approach, leading her to integrate EMDR into her work helping children, adults, and families on their path to recovery.

In 2008, Debra cofounded The Attachment and Trauma Center of Nebraska, where she continues her hands-on clinical practice while training the next generation of EMDR practitioners. As a faculty member of the EMDR Institute, founded by Francine Shapiro, PhD, she played a key role in developing a child-focused EMDR basic training curriculum.

Debra has published research and authored or coauthored several books, articles, and chapters—including two cowritten with EMDR pioneer Francine Shapiro. She serves on the board for the *Journal of EMDR Practice and Research* and presents keynotes and workshops for organizations both nationally and internationally.